MEGA
Professional Knowledge: Middle School (062)
SECRETS

Study Guide
Your Key to Exam Success

MEGA Test Review for the
Missouri Educator Gateway Assessments

Dear Future Exam Success Story:

Congratulations on your purchase of our study guide. Our goal in writing our study guide was to cover the content on the test, as well as provide insight into typical test taking mistakes and how to overcome them.

Standardized tests are a key component of being successful, which only increases the importance of doing well in the high-pressure high-stakes environment of test day. How well you do on this test will have a significant impact on your future, and we have the research and practical advice to help you execute on test day.

The product you're reading now is designed to exploit weaknesses in the test itself, and help you avoid the most common errors test takers frequently make.

How to use this study guide

We don't want to waste your time. Our study guide is fast-paced and fluff-free. We suggest going through it a number of times, as repetition is an important part of learning new information and concepts.

First, read through the study guide completely to get a feel for the content and organization. Read the general success strategies first, and then proceed to the content sections. Each tip has been carefully selected for its effectiveness.

Second, read through the study guide again, and take notes in the margins and highlight those sections where you may have a particular weakness.

Finally, bring the manual with you on test day and study it before the exam begins.

Your success is our success

We would be delighted to hear about your success. Send us an email and tell us your story. Thanks for your business and we wish you continued success.

Sincerely,

Mometrix Test Preparation Team

Need more help? Check out our flashcards at: http://MometrixFlashcards.com/MEGA

Copyright © 2016 by Mometrix Media LLC. All rights reserved.
Written and edited by the Mometrix Exam Secrets Test Prep Team
Printed in the United States of America

TABLE OF CONTENTS

Top 20 Test Taking Tips 1
Student Development and Learning 2
Assessment, Instruction, and the Learning Environment 34
The Professional Environment 97
Practice Test 116
   Practice Questions 116
   Constructed Response 139
   Answers and Explanations 141
Secret Key #1 - Time is Your Greatest Enemy 155
   Pace Yourself 155
Secret Key #2 - Guessing is not Guesswork 155
   Monkeys Take the Test 155
   $5 Challenge 156
Secret Key #3 - Practice Smarter, Not Harder 157
   Success Strategy 157
Secret Key #4 - Prepare, Don't Procrastinate 157
Secret Key #5 - Test Yourself 158
General Strategies 158
Special Report: How to Overcome Test Anxiety 164
   Lack of Preparation 164
   Physical Signals 165
   Nervousness 165
   Study Steps 167
   Helpful Techniques 168
Additional Bonus Material 172

Top 20 Test Taking Tips

1. Carefully follow all the test registration procedures
2. Know the test directions, duration, topics, question types, how many questions
3. Setup a flexible study schedule at least 3-4 weeks before test day
4. Study during the time of day you are most alert, relaxed, and stress free
5. Maximize your learning style; visual learner use visual study aids, auditory learner use auditory study aids
6. Focus on your weakest knowledge base
7. Find a study partner to review with and help clarify questions
8. Practice, practice, practice
9. Get a good night's sleep; don't try to cram the night before the test
10. Eat a well balanced meal
11. Know the exact physical location of the testing site; drive the route to the site prior to test day
12. Bring a set of ear plugs; the testing center could be noisy
13. Wear comfortable, loose fitting, layered clothing to the testing center; prepare for it to be either cold or hot during the test
14. Bring at least 2 current forms of ID to the testing center
15. Arrive to the test early; be prepared to wait and be patient
16. Eliminate the obviously wrong answer choices, then guess the first remaining choice
17. Pace yourself; don't rush, but keep working and move on if you get stuck
18. Maintain a positive attitude even if the test is going poorly
19. Keep your first answer unless you are positive it is wrong
20. Check your work, don't make a careless mistake

Student Development and Learning

Sigmund Freud's developmental theory relative to the adolescent years

After a latency period wherein school-age children suppress sexual id impulses to focus on developing social relationships and learning academic content, Freud termed his fifth and final stage of psychosexual development the genital stage, which begins with puberty and continues throughout life. Freud considered this stage as a kind of reprise of the phallic stage in early childhood, when children first discovered their genitals. Both stages are periods involving *exploration*. A physician by training and background, Freud accorded primary importance to the physical areas and processes of the body. Each of his stages is organized around an erogenous zone: oral in infancy, around nursing; anal in toddlerhood, around toilet-training; phallic and genital in preschool and teen years respectively, around sexual drives, with a calm latency period in between when such urges are buried in favor of the outward focus on friendships and school. The powerful physical changes and events of *puberty* are Freud's focus for the genital stage. Unlike his follower Erikson, Freud felt the personality was basically formed by adolescence and did not essentially change much thereafter; so this was his final stage, which he believed applied to adults as well.

Erik Erikson's developmental theory regarding the years of adolescence and early adulthood

Unlike his predecessor and strong influence, Sigmund Freud, Erikson believed people continue to develop throughout life. Hence he proposed stages for each life period until death. He identified the nuclear conflict characteristic of every stage as being identity vs. role confusion in adolescence (c. 12-18 years). Teenagers begin developing their individual personal identities. *Social relationships* are the focus of this stage. Teens that are successful in defining their personal roles and identities develop feelings of being *true to themselves*. Teens who fail in this endeavor develop *confusion about their roles* in life and *weak and/or poorly defined self-images*. Young adults (c. 19-40 years) are included in teenage years because Erikson's theory associates the final teen year as part of young adulthood. This is Erikson's stage of intimacy vs. isolation. Once adolescents have defined their personal identities, they progress forming intimate, loving relationships with other young adults. *Relationships* are the focus of this stage. Successful individuals develop *strong relationships*; those failing develop *isolation and loneliness*.

Albert Bandura's contributions to education

Albert Bandura's social learning theory emphasized the importance of social interaction in learning. Bandura accepted principles of behaviorist learning theories like antecedent stimuli, behaviors, and consequent stimuli that punished or rewarded (reinforced) behaviors. However, internal cognitive processes, and social contexts of learning, became more central in Bandura's theory. Also, he believes learning does not necessarily change behavior. Bandura discovered children learned indirectly by watching others—i.e., vicarious or observational learning: seeing others receiving rewards for certain behaviors, they imitated those actions to obtain similar rewards. This discovery contradicted the empiricist claim that learning requires direct experience. Bandura also discovered children witnessing violent actions by living persons (cf. his Bobo doll experiments) or by people they saw in video recordings would then display more aggressive behaviors imitating what they observed. This influenced education and parenting: adults, realizing children's behavior was influenced not just directly by experiencing violence, but also indirectly by observing it, became more concerned about controlling what children observed. Bandura identified attention, retention, reproduction, and motivation as conditions necessary to modeling and observational learning. Bandura's concept of reciprocal determinism states individuals and environments mutually influence each other. His concept of self-efficacy identifies belief in one's individual competence to perform specific tasks and skills.

Jerome Bruner's contributions to education

Bruner, like Piaget and many others, embraces constructivist philosopher, i.e., by interacting with their environments, children actively construct their learning, knowledge, and realities. His emphasis on discovery learning is based on constructivism. He defined learning as not only remembering existing, culturally imparted or acquired ideas and actions, but moreover inventing or creating these on one's own. Bruner feels "culturally invented technologies" amplify human abilities, rather than providing all knowledge. He influenced education by advising that its goal should be producing autonomous learners. Bruner posited three modes of representation in child cognitive development. 1) Enactive representation: action-based information based on motor responses, retained in muscle memory, emerging in infancy. 2) Iconic representation: visual image-based information, emerging around 1-6 years of age. 3) Symbolic representation: coded or symbolic storage of information, emerging c. 7 years and older. For example, the category "dogs" symbolically represents all dog breeds, types, and individuals. We remember information symbolically in words, numbers, etc. Bruner's concept of the spiral curriculum enabled teaching complex ideas to all ages by initially structuring them simply and increasing difficulty gradually. Bruner (with Wood and Ross) originated the concept *scaffolding*—temporary, gradually withdrawn support matching student needs.

John Dewey's contributions to education

Psychologist, philosopher, educator, and social activist John Dewey was a prominent member of the Progressive social reform movement, a president of the American Psychological Association, a functional psychology pioneer, a Pragmatist and Instrumentalist philosopher, and the foremost theorist in modern American education. Like Rousseau and Froebel, he believed in experiential "learning by doing." He shifted schools from authoritarian and teacher-centered, rote-learning methods to democratic classrooms, relevant curricula, and participatory activities. He emphasized the social, interactive nature of the learning and educational processes. Dewey believed education not only conferred knowledge, but moreover taught children how to live. His humanist psychology and instrumental philosophy informed his opinions that education should enable children to realize their full potential, and to apply those abilities toward the greater good. He also viewed education as an important force for social reform and change. He believed education should not concentrate exclusively on being either child-centered or curriculum content-centered, but balance the two. Like Bruner, he believed education should prepare autonomous learners—who were also ethical and reflective. He also professionalized the role of teachers as social service providers producing higher character and community intelligence standards, not merely vocational trainers preparing students for work with limited job skills and information.

Jean Piaget's theory of cognitive development

Piaget, like Bruner and others, believed in constructivism, i.e., children were not passive learners but actively constructed their own learning, knowledge, and worlds through interacting with their environments. He observed children as being "little scientists" from birth who experimented with and acted upon the environment to learn about it. Piaget formulated four stages of cognitive development. 1) Sensorimotor: infants respond to sensory input with motor responses. 2) Preoperational: wherein young children are *egocentric*, unable to see others' physical or mental perspectives. They think *intuitively*, not logically, unable to focus on more than one physical attribute of an object at a time (*centration*), categorize and classify, or follow structures and sequences of reasoning. They see things *animistically*, by attributing human qualities and behaviors to inanimate objects; and *magically*, by attributing events and others' actions to their own thoughts or words. 3) Concrete operations: school-age children can classify, perform other logical mental operations, and reverse them as long as they have concrete objects or events for reference. 4) Formal operations: preadolescents and adolescents develop the ability to perform abstract mental operations without concrete support, understanding and manipulating abstract concepts in math, philosophy, law, politics, etc. Piaget's theory influenced education, guiding educators not to present content to children who are not cognitively ready or able to understand; and introducing concepts and material appropriately to cognitive levels.

Lev Vygotsky's contributions on teaching practices today

Like theorists after him, e.g., Erikson, Bruner, Bandura, and others, Vygotsky, who lived during the Russian Revolution, stressed the importance of social interaction to learning. He differed from his contemporary Piaget's belief in invariant stages of cognitive development, believing instead that it varied among societies because culture heavily influenced it. Two of the most influential concepts in Vygotsky's theories were the more knowledgeable other (MKO), i.e., a person (or a computer, software program, etc. can be included) with a higher level of skill or understanding—whether peer, older child, or adult—than a given student; and the zone of proximal development (ZPD), which interact with one another. The ZPD is the distance between two levels of cognitive development: (1) the level of actual development, where a student can accomplish something independently; and (2) the level of potential development, where a student can accomplish something with guidance or assistance from an MKO. Vygotsky emphasized ability and potential above knowledge: what one could learn was more important than what one already knew. He also was first to prove that self-talk or inner speech (whose existence others agreed to, but not its cognitive value) was important to activity self-regulation, social competence, and learning.

Lawrence Kohlberg's theory of moral development

Kohlberg based his theory on Piaget's two stages of moral development, heteronomous (other-directed) morality and autonomous (self-directed) morality; but Kohlberg extended these to three distinct levels and six stages, with each level encompassing two stages. Similarly to Erikson's belief regarding psychosocial development, Kohlberg believed moral development continued throughout life. Kohlberg's level one is preconventional morality. In stage one, obedience and punishment, young children (and some adults) view rules as absolute and fixed; obedience averts punishment. In stage two, individualism and exchange, children judge actions by whether they meet one's own interests or needs. They can understand and appreciate *reciprocity,* but only if it also is in one's best interests. At level two, conventional morality, stage three involves interpersonal relationships, nicknamed *"good boy-good girl."* Conforming to meet social roles and expectations, concern for how choices affect relationships, and being "nice" predominate. Stage four, maintaining social order, focuses on respecting authority, doing one's duty, following rules, maintaining law and order, and considering overall society. Level three is postconventional morality. In stage five, social contract and individual rights, people still find laws and rules important, but only with individual members' agreement. By stage six, universal ethical principles, individuals apply internalized justice principles, regardless whether they conflict with rules and laws.

Bloom's taxonomy

Bloom organized learning into a hierarchy of six cognitive levels, from simplest to most challenging. Remembering involves retaining, recalling, retrieving, recognizing, reproducing, or repeating names, facts, lists, and other pieces of information. Understanding requires also being able to find, identify, select, describe, explain, discuss, review, restate, and/or translate information, rather than only remembering it. Applying requires learners to interpret information they understand; to use it appropriately, e.g., for solving problems; to illustrate, demonstrate, or dramatize it; write about it, etc. Analyzing means that learners must be able not only to remember, understand, and apply information, but moreover to break it down into component parts; assign information to different categories; make comparisons and contrasts between and among pieces or sets of information; use information to make calculations; differentiate and discriminate among different information; examine information; question its truth, accuracy, or credibility; experiment with it; test its veracity; and criticize information. Evaluating demands the learner assess and appraise information, make estimates and/or predictions based on it, rate it, judge it, and defend it. Creating, the highest level, involves proposing, developing, planning, designing, formulating, preparing, collecting, composing, organizing, and managing information, including both original ideas and/or original uses of existing information.

Physical and cognitive characteristics of typically developing children

Early Childhood
Physically, children gain c. 2.5 inches and 5-7 pounds, decreasing yearly. Preschoolers become taller and slimmer, losing baby fat. Preschooler heads are less oversized for bodies than top-heavier toddlers', but still somewhat large. *Cognitively*, continuing brain maturation plus wider life experiences enable significant progress in attention, planning, and language. Reasoning develops from 4-7 years, but is not logical. By 5 years, gross motor skills gain automaticity, and fine motor skills improve significantly.

Middle and late childhood
Physically, growth is slow and consistent—2-3 inches and 5-7 pounds annually. Heads and waists become smaller proportionately to height. Bones and muscle tissue strengthen. Motor skills gain coordination and smoothness. By 10-12 years, fine motor coordination and manipulative skills approximate adults'. *Cognitively*, brain circuitry continues developing, especially in the prefrontal cortex, improving cognitive control, attention, and reasoning. In Piaget's concrete operations stage, children can reason logically and reverse mental operations, but need physical objects, events, or examples for reference.

Adolescence
Physically, puberty combines physical and sexual maturation with hormonal changes. *Cognitively*, structural changes improve information-processing, reasoning, decision-making, and self-control. However, though the emotion-related amygdala matures earlier, the prefrontal cortex controlling emotions only matures by 18-25 years. Adolescents reach Piaget's formal operations, understanding abstract concepts and performing and manipulating entirely mental operations.

Linguistic, affective, and moral characteristics of children with typical development

Early Childhood
Linguistic: greater sensitivity to spoken phonological features; linguistic rule systems understanding; learning and applying syntactic rules to speech; dramatic vocabulary development; changing speech "registers" and styles based on situation, improving conversational skills.

Affective: by 4-5 years, self-awareness; self-conscious emotions like guilt and pride; understanding of and ability to discuss both personal and others' emotions, causes and results, increase.

Moral: most are at Kohlberg's level one of preconventional reasoning with external punishments and rewards until c. 9 years.

Middle and late Childhood
Linguistic: understanding the alphabetic principle; categorizing; whereas younger children respond sentence-sequentially, e.g., prompted "dog" and saying "barks"; or "eat" and "lunch"; older children respond with like parts of speech, saying "cat" or "horse" to "dog," and "drink" to "eat." From age 6-11, vocabulary grows from c. 14,000-40,000 words. Complex grammar comprehension develops, and metalinguistic awareness, knowing, and thinking about language.

Affective: more varied coping strategies. Self-regulation and self-efficacy influence achievement.

Moral: many are at Kohlberg's level two conventional reasoning, stage 3, "good boy-good girl", adopting parental morality.

Adolescence
Linguistic: skills advance, including complex spoken and written sentences; writing stories following story grammar rules; consistently accurate inferences from text; understanding figurative language, idioms, and metaphors.

Moral: Kohlberg's postconventional reasoning is possible—recognizing alternatives, social contracts, and developing universal moral standards transcending laws.

Developmental milestones for adolescents

Physically, most adolescents will have completed puberty by the time they are around 15-17 years old. While girls are more likely to be mature physically by these ages, boys may still be in the process of physical maturation: girls are typically about two years ahead of boys in physical growth spurts and sexual maturity. It is common for adolescents to be concerned about their bodies, e.g., their weight, size, or shape. Adults need to be vigilant for eating disorders during later adolescence, particularly in girls. Cognitively, older teenagers may begin to learn more clearly defined work habits, especially if they begin to work after or before school, on weekends, and/or during the summers. They typically become more concerned about their future plans for attending post-secondary school, getting jobs, and what kinds of work they will want to do. They develop the ability to provide reasons for the choices they make more competently, including being able to explain their moral decisions regarding what is right and wrong. Adults should encourage adolescents' adequate sleep, exercising, and nutritious diets; and be available to provide support and advice while creating opportunities for and encouraging teens to use their judgment, problem-solving, and conflict resolution skills.

Emotionally and socially, teenagers around 15-17 experience decreased conflict with parents, and display more independence from them. Socially, they spend more time with friends, less with parents. They demonstrate more interest in dating and relationships, developing emotional capacities for sharing and caring more deeply and more intimacy. While it should not be ignored, it is also typical for teenagers to feel considerable depression or sadness. These emotions can contribute to reduced school performance, unprotected sex, and substance use or abuse. Morally, older teens can think abstractly according to Piaget and hence are capable of the highest moral development levels according to Kohlberg, understanding the concept of the social contract and even developing universal moral principles of human rights beyond legalities. Adults can show affection; spend time in mutually enjoyed activities with teenagers; encourage teen volunteerism and extracurricular interests and pursuits; ask about their feelings, including suicidal ideations; observe any behavior changes; respect teen opinions; show interest in teen activities; compliment and celebrate efforts and achievements; encourage responsible decisions, including regarding Internet and social media use; help teens plan ahead for difficult situations, e.g., involving peer pressure and/or others' risk behaviors; discuss responsibilities, expectations, and respectful behavior in workplaces and public; and respect teen privacy needs.

Ways in which different types of student development can respectively interact

When a student's cognitive development is ahead of his/her physical development, the child is likely to become frustrated when s/he can conceive of many things mentally, but cannot execute them physically. This is especially of younger children still having more physical development to achieve. Conversely, when a student's physical development is ahead of his/her cognitive development, young children are apt inadvertently to damage property and/or harm peers, younger children, or pets. Linguistic development affects social development in that more advanced language levels often facilitate social communication—but not always: some children show advanced language skills development, yet lack commensurate social skills. In another way, some less linguistically advanced students are skilled at using nonverbal communication skills to support social interactions. Some young students also have superior emotional intelligence (EQ) without necessarily having equally high academic or linguistic skills. More advanced affective development in elementary-age children can influence their moral development: the more children are able to share, take others' perspectives, empathize, and engage in prosocial behaviors, the more able they are to understand and internalize less rigid, more mutual, and socially-oriented morality.

Linguistic development interacts with cognitive development: psychologists find very high positive correlations between vocabulary and intelligence test scores. Teachers can enhance adolescent linguistic mediation skills with exercises regarding literal vs. metaphorical word meanings, and enhance pragmatics (using language to meet needs) through question-asking skills instruction. Teens whose cognitive development precedes their physical development excel academically but not athletically may be stereotyped by peers as "nerds," and those with superior physical skills but lacking equal academic success as "dumb jocks." Teens whose physical development far precedes their cognitive development may inadvertently harm others, particularly when rapidly gaining adult strength. Similarly, adolescent affective development influences cognitive development because the amygdala matures sooner, generating intense teen emotions; yet the prefrontal cortex, which will eventually control those emotions, does not mature until young adulthood. Affective maturity influences moral levels in that the more emotionally mature the student, the more able s/he is to relate to others' needs, use prosocial behaviors, and understand universal human rights. Teen social interactions are increasingly influenced by emotional intelligence (EQ) development. Both affective and social developments interact with moral development when teens must make difficult ethical decisions involving others in social contexts.

Teacher considerations for students in early and later adolescence

Middle school teachers who find some 6th-graders acting out in class or not completing work may attribute these instances to behavior problems, but experienced teachers with developmental perspectives point out that they may actually be adjustment problems: transitions between schools can be difficult for students; teachers may not realize the extent of variation among schools. Distinguishing adjustment or developmental difficulties from more severe problems is easier for teachers who have worked with students of every age. Whereas elementary-age students have concrete operations, including reversibility, adolescents have formal operations, including application of abstract concepts to specific phenomena. For example, an 8-year-old understood objects that looked smaller underwater did not shrink because, with reversibility, s/he could see they were the same size when removed; but did not understand why they looked smaller underwater. By the student's teens, s/he understands water is denser than air, light waves travel at differing speeds through media of different density, and applies this to understand why objects look smaller underwater. Teachers can use deductive reasoning with teens that younger students could not follow. Hypothetico-deductive reasoning or "if-then" propositions enable adolescents to speculate about possibilities, e.g., going to college, moral dilemmas about justifying killing, etc.

Impacts of community, racial, and cultural differences

With American demographics rapidly changing, schools reflect societal racism. Racial and cultural differences cannot be overlooked anymore. It is not only necessary, but moreover healthy for minorities to express their racial and cultural identities. Teachers, administrators, school staff, parents—all school community members—must be involved in designing learning experiences founded on understanding and respect for racial and cultural diversity. While educational experts believe this requires the whole society to unite for success, they concede that as this has not occurred, the educational system must still strive for resolution of racial and cultural conflicts through collective efforts. While schools are desegregated, surrounding cities and suburbs are not. Neighborhoods, the foundations of American society, are subject to racial and economic limitations. Because children learn from each other, their education is strongly affected by community factors of housing costs, incomes, lending policies, and racial and institutional discrimination. While some Latino parents believe bilingual education can overcome discrimination and black parents believe desegregation promotes equality, some Latino parents see desegregation as impeding their objectives by dissipating Latin influence and destroying bilingual programs. Experts call for compromise, noting that both must coexist by law.

Stages in adolescent development from the perspective of developmental psychology

Despite age variances and overlaps, early adolescents develop new self-images based on physiological changes and apply emergent logical cognitive and rational judgment skills. Mid-adolescents endeavor to separate from parents; their cognitive and emotional abilities expand. They become adventurous, experimenting with various ideas while exploring their relationships to self, the opposite sex, and groups; and struggling to differentiate or reconcile their own values vs. those of parents and authority figures. They develop responsibility and self-reliance, assume greater control of educational and vocational opportunities and activities, and seek to establish their place in and contribute to society. Late adolescent identity and social role stabilizes; they gain integration and consistency in psychology and worldview. Balance among fantasy, reality, and aspirations; shifts from immature self-interest toward caring for and giving to others; and establishment and pursuit of realistic life goals are characteristics. Teachers must determine overall class functioning levels for planning lessons. For instance, lessons should help adolescents advance cognitively from Piaget's concrete operations to formal operations stage. To resolve Erikson's conflict of industry vs. inferiority, younger adolescents must experience school success; to resolve identity vs. role confusion, older adolescents must form satisfying future action plans. Hands-on activities like those Piaget offered can further these goals.

Early adolescent cognitive development

Individual differences in early adolescent cognitive development vary widely. Young teens develop metacognition, independent thought, high curiosity, and broad interests, though they typically do not maintain most. They prefer learning peer interactions, active experiences over passive ones, and learning about subjects useful and interesting to them. These teens develop abstract thought, analyze and synthesize information, formulate and test hypotheses, think reflectively, tackle complex ideas, understand metaphorical nuances and traditional wisdom's meanings, consider ideological issues, argue positions, question authority, and appreciate sophisticated humor. As Piaget stated, they make sense of the world building on their background knowledge and individual experiences. Young adolescents are more interested in authentic and real-life learning than traditional academic content. They frequently observe adult behavior keenly and are inquisitive about adults. Their abilities to anticipate needs, develop personal goals, and consider the future improve. Teachers must offer widely varied educational materials and approaches, from structured to challenging for concrete to abstract learners; plan curriculum around real-life concepts; provide experimentation and other authentic activities; enable peer and adult discourse; hands-on experience and direct environmental interaction; acknowledge changing interests by ensuring exploration opportunities; supplying forums for exploring reasons for home, school, and societal rules; and teach by example as role models.

Adolescent moral development

The ability to make principled choices increases with moral development. Young adolescents, developing abstract thinking, typically become idealistic, highly valuing fairness in human interaction. They start reconciling their understanding of others caring about them with their own adolescent egocentrism as they advance into Kohlberg's moral development stage of interpersonal conformity. They graduate from self-centeredness to more consideration for others' feelings and rights. They ask impossible, sweeping questions, and do not tolerate trivial adult answers. They typically embrace parental values while developing personal values. They cease seeing complex ethical or moral issues in black-and-white, realizing shades of gray but unready to address these—putting them at risk for unsound ethical or moral decisions. Teachers must acknowledge and utilize the connection between teen cognitive and moral development by planning lessons cultivating critical thought, higher-order thinking skills, and higher moral reasoning levels. For example, writing assignments articulating their feelings and thoughts; opportunities for examining behavior options and consequences; experiences requiring contemplating ethical or moral dilemmas and potential responses—helping students solve problems, develop values, and set their own behavioral standards. Teachers can provide scenarios whereby students explore concepts of justice, equity, and fairness. Schools should also offer curricula and programs addressing racism, sexism, discrimination, and similar social issues.

Adolescent emotional and psychological development

Seeking unique personal identities and independence characterize adolescent emotional and psychological development. While searching for adult identities, teens try to balance peer approval with adult acceptance, experiencing conflict from competing family and peer allegiances. Self-discovery and identity quests can increase vulnerable feelings as sensitivity to self-other differences grows. Young adolescence is typified by unpredictability and intensity. Teens tend to display restless, moody, inconsistent, or erratic behavior, including alternating inferiority and superiority and swings between anxiety and bravado. Self-esteem is fragile or low at these ages. Teens are notoriously self-conscious, and hypersensitive to criticism of their exaggerated perceived flaws. Emotional situations can provoke childish behaviors, unilateral arguments, and naïve opinions. Emotional volatility places teens at risk for poor decisions. As David Elkind noted, adolescents think their experiences are unique in the "personal fable." Teachers and schools can support identity formation with curricular and instructional exploration opportunities, organizational structures, advisory programs, and educational practices supporting positive adult and peer relationships, group cohesion, and caring atmospheres. Other positive outcomes include building student self-esteem, explaining its importance to development; explaining friendship's importance and the normalcy of changing allegiances; avoiding sarcasm, humiliation, or harsh criticism; providing self-expression and self-assessment opportunities, including reading, role-play, and drama; and helping teens realize their problems are not unique.

Elements of classroom instruction used to differentiate among students

Based on each student's learning profile, interests, readiness, and learning levels, teachers can differentiate classroom instruction. Four elements for differentiating instruction are: (1) content to learn; (2) the process students use to master content; (3) products students will produce, requiring practice, application, and extension and elaboration of what they learn in a unit; and (4) learning environment, i.e., how the classroom functions and how students experience it. Some examples of differentiating processes include: (1) set up interest centers where students can explore subcategories of class subjects they find most interesting. (2) Assign tiered activities with different levels of complexity, challenge, or support for acquiring the same skills and understanding. (3) Provide hands-on supports, like manipulatives, for students needing these. (4) Combine work commonly assigned to the entire class with individualized work for specific students into lists of tasks, making personal agendas to complete during designated and/or spare time. (5) Differentiate durations students take to finish tasks, allowing advanced students to examine topics in-depth and enable added support for struggling students.

Decision-making and goal-setting skills helping students develop self-direction

Young people are able to develop some independence and recognize they have some control over their lives by learning to set goals. First they must decide what they want to accomplish. This decision-making helps motivate children to achieve things, not for external rewards or to please other people, but for their own satisfaction. This helps them develop internal locus of control and intrinsic motivation. One step adults can help with is first defining what a goal is. They might use the analogy of a hockey or soccer goal. Explain that winning a goal is the end product of much hard work; setting a goal is describing what you want to get done or the place you want to get to, and that involves planning for something you want to understand or do better. Another step for adults to help children determine their priorities is by listening more than talking. Observing some strengths and needs is acceptable, but encourage children to talk about themselves. For example, observe a child has learned something, and ask what s/he next wants to do with this skill. Ask if a child is worried about anything in school that will be difficult.

Assignments for developing goal-setting, peer interaction, and decision-making skills

Grades 6-8: identify resources (e.g., research sources) furthering goal progress. Analyze influences of supports and obstacles in completing goal action steps, and better ways of overcoming barriers and using supports. Differentiate long- and short-term goals. Apply goal-setting skills to academic success development. Set a positive social interaction goal. Teachers: use interest or incentive inventories, planning sheets, discuss goal-setting steps, and lead self-regulation and self-monitoring games. Grades 8-10: set a goal in a sport, hobby, musical instrument, or interest to accomplish in a month or two. Plan goal timeframes and action steps. Monitor progress and adjust plans as necessary. Evaluate goal achievement levels, and identify contributing or detracting factors. Analyze what you learned and would do differently. Grades 9-11: identify who helped you achieve a goal and how. Analyze why you could or could not overcome goal obstacles, an unexpected opportunity's goal achievement impact, why schedule conflicts could require changing goal timeframes, how substance use could impede and academic achievement contribute to long-term goal achievement. Grades 10-12: set long-term academic or career goals with action steps and completion dates. Anticipate obstacles and make contingency plans. Analyze how current health behavior decisions might affect long-term educational or career goals. Evaluate summer job goal feasibility based on your ability to execute action steps timely. Self-evaluate goal achievement. Create a behavioral contract to enhance a coping strategy and document progress in a journal.

Impacts of student substance use and abuse on development and learning

Not only are the physical and neurological development of younger children incomplete, even adolescents have yet to undergo full brain development. Therefore, using alcohol and other drugs can cause damage to their central nervous systems and other body systems and organs. Damage can be temporary or permanent, reversible or irreversible. In addition to interfering with attention in school, substance use can interfere with myelination, whereby brain and nerve cells develop coating sheaths, both protecting them and facilitating impulse and signal transmission. This process continues into young adulthood. The heart, lungs, liver, kidneys, other organs and systems are still developing and can be damaged, sometimes irreparably, at early ages. Substance use also undermines motivation to learn and achieve. Under the influence, students attend to the effects they experience, not acquiring new information or getting anything done. When use becomes abuse, addiction causes focus only on getting more of the needed substance to relieve withdrawal symptoms and reproduce the original high—which latter is impossible and leads to ingesting increasing amounts. Students neglect hygiene and schoolwork, attendance and grades fall, and dropouts become more common. Substance use and abuse triggers or exacerbates anxiety, depression, paranoia, schizophrenia, bipolar disorder, and other mental disorders.

Conditions leading to gang involvement

The organizational structures and activities of gangs are extremely complex social phenomena. In low socioeconomic urban neighborhoods, gangs often develop in part to protect members against violence from adult criminals and other gangs. This positive motivation and protective benefit are still accompanied by undesirable effects. Gang involvement is more likely during adolescence, when students search to form personal identities. Many economically disadvantaged urban youth lack adult supervision, mentoring, and role models. Gang membership fills needs for group affiliation, belonging, identity, rules, and behavioral direction (even if behaviors are undesirable). Youth struggling to reconcile newly discovered abstractions and complexities find security in adversarial relationships among gangs, defining "us vs. them" mentalities that are less equivocal or contradictory. These enmities also provide concrete foes for youth feeling helpless to control or combat larger, seemingly unassailable foes of social ills like poverty, illiteracy, crime, discrimination, lack of opportunity, etc. Even in affluent communities, gangs may form to fulfill the same needs for social acceptance, allegiance, group identity, rules, etc.—sometimes particularly with inadequate parental or adult involvement, communication, and role modeling. Youth with unformed or unstable identities, vulnerable to peer pressure, are at higher risk for committing criminal acts as gang members. This can curtail their education, work, freedom, and life.

Peer-related issues

Before adolescence, very young children first developing autonomy find it very important to become their own persons and do things independently. These early assertions of self are reflected in the very individual, sometimes bizarre way young children may dress or eat when allowed to select their own clothing, unusual dietary choices, etc. However, social acceptance and peer pressure are extremely powerful forces. By the time they are in school, children begin showing concern for belonging to groups and fitting into social contexts. Student responses to social pressures reach greatest prominence during adolescence. Although adolescent quests for personal identities and defining social roles seem to recapitulate early childhood's assertion of autonomy in some respects, teenagers are additionally both hypersensitive to peers' perceptions and opinions and highly concerned with social acceptance. Teens struggling with identity issues can also feel threatened about defining their individuality, which informs their impending adult identities—which signal accompanying adult responsibilities. Conforming to group norms assuages adolescent self-consciousness and hypersensitivity to criticism by preventing teens from standing out; and reassures them that, as group members, they are not facing adulthood and its responsibilities alone.

Middle and high school teachers find many students very concerned with wearing certain clothes, eating and drinking certain foods or drinks, listening to certain music, and doing many things simply because "everybody" is doing them. "Everybody" can be everyone in a class, a school, a certain grade or age group, a circle of friends, etc. Adolescents develop exaggerated self-consciousness and hypersensitivity, leading to preoccupation with others' opinions and fear of standing out, seeming different, and not fitting into a group. As teens are also working to define their individual identities, teachers can appeal to adolescent investment in this process by reinforcing their independent choices, individual decisions, and affirming their uniqueness as persons. They can support teens in resisting peer pressure, whereby adolescents take advantage of others' social vulnerability by attempting to control them to conform by asking them what is right for them, not others; and expressing and demonstrating their approval and pride in students' asserting and being themselves. Teachers can also exploit peer-related issues by assigning cooperative learning projects; encouraging and rewarding academic club participation; and emphasizing other learning experiences involving positive social interactions, whereby group identification and interdependence promote collective and individual learning.

Contemporary model of the whole child approach

The Association for Supervision and Curriculum Development (ASCD) and US Centers for Disease Control and Prevention (CDC) have collaborated to produce the Whole School, Whole Community, Whole Child (WSCC) model to coordinate public health, school health, and educational processes, policies, and practices to improve health and learning, which are interrelated. They say a whole child approach to learning, teaching, and community involvement means each child deserves to be safe, healthy, supported, engaged, and challenged. Related to this model, ASCD's Whole Child Initiative aims to help educators, policymakers, families, and community members realize a vision of educating the whole child through collaborative, sustainable action. ASCD's School Improvement

Tool is a totally online needs assessment that educators in schools and districts worldwide can use to determine what practices to implement or improve to realize the whole-child education vision. The tool enables educators to survey, numerically score, and color-code schools regarding key criteria, e.g., all students enter school healthy, and learn about and practice healthy lifestyles; learn in physically and emotionally safe environments; are actively engaged in learning, connected to school and community, and supported by caring, qualified adults; have access to personalized learning; are challenged academically, prepared for college or employment success; and school whole-child approaches are sustainable.

Typical challenges encountered by middle and high school students

Students entering puberty are experiencing rapid physiological and psychological changes. For some, the magnitude and speed of these changes present major adjustment challenges. For example, a formerly small boy suddenly grows a foot within one school year. Understanding limb pain and becoming winded easily are normal with growth spurts will help; he may also need help adjusting to his change in appearance. Though increased height and muscle mass are gratifying and get girls' attention, he must modify his self-image accordingly. A girl practicing gymnastics since childhood, formerly compliant with coaches' rigorous demands, begins rebelling at these now while developing her individual young adult identity. She resents pressures for weight control because she cannot stop her body from growing larger and developing new curves. Educators can help her decide if she wants to continue, possibly with different coaches, in less competitive capacities or reduced hours. Another girl practicing ballet since childhood, responding to external and internal pressures, over-exercises, severely restricts her diet, and purges for weight control, developing anorexia and bulimia. In addition to referral to counseling, educators can encourage her to talk, give her permission not to be perfect, avoid pressure, offer choices, and provide things and activities she can control other than her body.

Helping students address educational and career issues

Most adolescents are aware of which things they find interesting, but may need some assistance in relating these interests to higher education and career paths. For example, several students share a love of animals. However, one of them excels in and enjoys all math subjects, biology, and chemistry. Another absolutely hates math and science, but loves bathing, drying, combing, brushing pets and making them look beautiful, and has a talent for handling animals gently. A third student is extremely nurturing, always rescuing lost and hurt animals and nursing them back to health. A fourth student loves animals but admires wildlife more than pets; is concerned about endangered species and extinction, already volunteering for conservation efforts; and wants to improve habitats for captive animals. The first student may consider a career as a veterinarian, the second as a professional pet groomer, the third as a veterinary technician or in an animal rescue organization, and the fourth as a wildlife biologist and/or zoo curator. Some students need higher education to qualify for careers they want, others to explore further or discover career preferences, and others for additional life experience and social maturity.

Processes whereby adolescent students acquire and integrate new knowledge

Younger children have had less time to generate a limited repertoire of schemata about the world and either fit new experiences into these or create new ones. However, older students, having had more time and life experiences, have accumulated more schemata and made more modifications in them to construct more extensive, detailed, and sophisticated knowledge. The first learning process they engage in when encountering new information or experiences is activating their existing knowledge, examining what they already know and believe. When new information or skills are congruent with prior knowledge and extend or supplement without significantly redefining it, older students integrate these into their present belief and value systems. This second process represents assimilation, i.e., acquiring additional knowledge without disequilibrium. When new information and experiences challenge adolescents' fundamental understandings, beliefs, or values, this creates cognitive dissonance, hence disequilibrium. Students then accept or reject the new input, reconstructing or repositioning existing beliefs if needed and resolving dissonance. This third process represents accommodation, i.e., acquiring new knowledge through encountering and resolving disequilibrium, and restoring a new equilibrium informed by new positions or beliefs. Teachers can facilitate ELL access to meaningful learning by relating new concepts taught in English to student L1s, activating their prior or existing knowledge. When teachers pair unfamiliar with familiar language and experience, this facilitates concept understanding and acquisition.

Sources of academic difficulty for ELL students

Some school difficulties for ELL students are directly attributable to teaching and learning environment deficits. These include lack of student access to effective ESL or bilingual instruction, mismatches between middle-class-oriented instruction and low socioeconomic student backgrounds, cultural and linguistic differences that create communication gaps between learners and teachers, etc. Other ELL students may additionally have specific learning disabilities, which require specialized instructional methods to enable successful learning. Experts believe many educators lack expertise to differentiate limited English-language proficiency from true learning disabilities as sources of school failure, evidenced by overrepresentation of ELL students in special education classes. Additional problems include shortages of both assessment instruments and trained assessors that are appropriate and linguistically and culturally relevant, and in special educators trained in concurrently addressing linguistically related as well as disability-related student needs. Factors necessary to ELL success include recognizing the importance of student L1s, collaborative community and school relationships, shared educator knowledge bases of effective instructional methods for ELLs, effective teaching, and academically rich programs that integrate instruction in basic and higher-order cognitive skills in both L1s and English.

Influence of teacher expectations on teacher behaviors with students and student performance

In an experiment, Harvard psychologist Robert Rosenthal (1964) told teachers a standardized IQ test was a "special" test predicting dramatic IQ growth, identifying randomly selected students as about to make significant intellectual gains. In the following two years, teacher expectations became self-fulfilling prophecies: those students' IQs actually did increase. Rosenthal's additional research identified myriad, nearly imperceptible ways teacher expectations influence interactions with students. They consistently smile, nod at, and touch; give more approval; offer more specific feedback; and allow more time for answering questions to students they expect to succeed. Exemplary teachers strive to motivate all of their students to achieve more than they thought they could through high expectations. Dean of University of Virginia's Curry School of Education and researcher Robert Pianta (c. 2012) compared two approaches to changing teacher expectations: talking to convince teachers via information that their beliefs are incorrect, vs. intensive training in new teacher behaviors. The latter shifted teacher beliefs more than the former. For example, a teacher believing boys are disruptive quashes a boy's loud, effusive response, emotionally disengaging and frustrating the student. Contrastingly, a teacher without that belief encourages the student to continue, but while sitting quietly. Different beliefs prompt different interpretations of the same behavior.

Interacting with students who display problematic behavior

Experts observe we must change our own behavior to change others' behavior. Educational researchers have found teacher expectations and resulting behaviors subtly yet powerfully influence student behavior. There are several suggestions for teacher behaviors to influence student behaviors. For instance, observe how every student engages, interacts, and what s/he likes doing to comprehend their capabilities. Listen to students, try to understand their goals and motivations, and note their perceptions of classmates, yourself, and assignments you give. Engage with students: ask about and listen to their individual interests without offering opinions or advice. Experiment with different responses to challenging behaviors. Instead of your first impulse, stop and consider the behavior's motivation or function, which could be to connect with you. If or when time permits, interact with students in nonacademic games or activities of their choice; observe student strengths and interests. Assign projects wherein students use preferred media to express, individually and in groups, their extracurricular interests. Consider school through students' eyes. Reflect on your own worst and best teachers, supervisors, and bosses. List five words describing how you felt when interacting with them, and what they did or said specifically to evoke those feelings. List how your students might describe you. Consider parallels between your beliefs and their responses, and how your expectations shape their perceptions of you.

Robert Marzano's strategies for improving teaching quality and student achievement

According to expert Robert Marzano, instructional strategies for effective teaching and learning include: (1) identifying similarities and differences. Students more easily understand, and frequently solve, complex problems through analyzing them more simply by breaking concepts into similar and different characteristics. Teachers may identify these directly and then guide student inquiry and discussion, or have students identify them independently. Research finds the former helps identify specific items, while the latter promotes broader understanding and variation. Venn diagrams and charts are useful visual graphics for showing similarities and dissimilarities. Teachers should also engage student classifications, comparisons, analogies, and metaphors. (2) Summarizing and note-taking. Students comprehend better through analyzing subjects, revealing essential content, and restating it in their own words. Studies find students must be aware of the information's basic structure and delete, retain, and replace some components. Teachers should give students summarizing rules; prepare notes; use consistent note formats, allowing student refinements as needed; have students question, clarify, and predict coming occurrences in texts; and provide time to review and revise notes, often the best test study guides. (3) Reinforcing effort, giving recognition. Connect effort and achievement through success stories and student log-keeping and analysis. Personalize or individualize symbolic, not tangible rewards.

Marzano's strategies include: (1) homework and practice. Students extend learning beyond classrooms. Studies find homework amounts should vary by grade levels, parents should be minimally involved, students should adapt skills as they learn them, and the primary indices of practice effectiveness are speed and accuracy. Teachers should explain homework purposes to students and parents; try to give students feedback on every assignment; vary feedback delivery to maximize effectiveness; inform students whether homework is practice or to prepare for coming units; establish homework policies, advising students to maintain consistent settings, time limits, and schedules; assign timed quiz homework, having students report speed and accuracy; allocate practice time, focusing on difficult concepts. (2) Visual or nonlinguistic representations: studies show knowledge is stored in linguistic and visual forms, and students achieve more using both. Visual representation both stimulates and increases brain activity. Represent information with physical models and movements, relationships with symbolic images and words. (3) Cooperative learning: applied consistently and systematically—not overused—with small groups, cooperative activities enhance learning. Group students by multiple criteria, e.g., common interests or experiences; vary objectives and group sizes; and design projects around core components of individual and group accountability, face-to-face interaction, group processing, appropriate social skills, and positive interdependence.

(1) Objectives and feedback: give student learning direction through setting goals—not overly specific, readily compatible with students' personal goals. Setting each unit's core goal, inviting student personalization identifying areas where they want to know more, helps students consider their own interests and engage actively in goal-setting processes. Define specific student goals and grades they will receive for achieving them through writing contracts. Feedback should be corrective (comparing student achievement to specific knowledge levels as with rubrics), specific, and timely. Invite students to lead feedback sessions. (2) Hypothesis formulation and testing: studies show deductive reasoning—from general principles to specific predictions—most effective. Students must explain hypotheses and conclusions, whether deductive or inductive (from specific observations to generalizations). Ask students to predict what might occur if some aspect of government, transportation, or some other familiar system changed. Have students build things using limited resources, generating inquiries and hypotheses about what might or might not work. (3) Help students apply pre-existing knowledge for additional learning using questions, cues, and advance organizers. Studies find these must focus on important content, be highly analytical, and presented before lessons or activities. Pausing briefly after questions increases students' answer depth. Vary advance organizer styles—graphic images, skimming text, telling stories, etc.—for pre-"learning" exposure.

Learning activities promoting critical thinking skills and ownership of learning

In *Democracy and Education* (1916), John Dewey wrote that true student involvement is stimulated by activities that "give pupils something to do, not something to learn; and the doing is of such a nature as to demand thinking, or the intentional noting of connections; learning naturally results." Thus the same learning activities that promote higher-order thinking, including critical thinking and organizational and time-management skills, also promote student ownership of learning. While interests in community issues fluctuate, students regularly find school-based issues important. Issues—curricular, extracurricular, or leadership-related—must also be relevant, reflecting student identities, interests, and passions; and student roles meaningful, enabling their design, implementation, and evaluative participation for improving student learning and schools. Schools can involve students as planners in designing new buildings, developing classroom behavior guidelines, selecting textbooks, researching careers and planning coursework accordingly, participating in principal or administrator hiring, etc. Students as teachers learn about all curriculum subjects in exchange for instructing teachers how to use technology, enhancing ownership and meaningful involvement. Students as professional development partners collect and analyze data and participate in team development as learning community members. Students as decision-makers in student government influence school climate, policy, and curriculum.

Age-appropriate study skills

Research finds when students must analyze information to identify its most important aspects and then express it in their own terms, they need to know how the information is basically organized, and be able to remove, replace, and preserve elements of it. Thereby they understand it better. These learning processes are included in note-taking and summarizing. Teachers can provide students with rules for summarizing; prepare their own notes for students; and adhere to regular note-taking formats, including necessary student refinements. When teachers prepare their lecture or lesson notes in outline form, students can more easily take notes in outline form. Having students question text, clarify as needed, and make predictions improves their summarizing skills. Allotting time and encouraging students to review and revise their notes frequently enables them to study for tests at their highest potential. Advance organizers help students activate and build on their prior knowledge to learn further. Teachers should introduce analytical advance organizers concentrating on essential subject matter before learning experiences and vary their style, e.g., skim text, tell stories, produce graphic images, etc.

Steps involved in writing research papers

(1) Topic: appeal to student curiosity; possible yet somewhat challenging for student skill and learning levels; support grade-level standards so library research matches classwork. Triangulate data, confirming topics in three kinds of available, readable sources; cross-check encyclopedias to broaden or narrow as needed. (2) Subtopics: informed by what students want to know; provide blueprints or outlines for examining topics. Brainstorm for general subtopics, e.g., physical characteristics, habitats, diets, enemies, offspring of specific animal species. "Pre-search" specific subtopics in topic-specific book tables of contents and encyclopedia subheadings. Research time management depends on controlling subtopic number (minimum three) and difficulty. (3) Sources: three kinds minimum, print or non-print; text, images, ideas. Consider student age, ability, topic for primary and secondary sources. Require MLA, APA, Turabian, or other accepted styles to prevent plagiarism and cite sources or use Creative Commons. Teach fair use and copyright regulations. Source evaluation offers lifelong skills. (4) Read, think, select: model, discuss, practice critical reading strategies—scanning, skimming, visual clues, chunking; asking what is important; identifying information supporting subtopics. (5) Note-taking: using subtopics as titles, pre-sort notes; beginners copy facts, phrases, and keywords, citing sources; experienced researchers summarize or paraphrase. (6) Sort notes by subtopic, then into paragraphs. Advanced is logical plan-based, e.g., concepts, timeline, etc. Rereading all notes per section, rearranging into logical order consolidates new information, cementing learning. Number notes consecutively. Write from notes, inserting previous knowledge.

Roles played by teachers and students in different instructional models

In traditional teacher-centered instructional models, the teacher plays the most active role, delivering instruction through lectures and lessons; assigning homework; and creating, administering and grading tests while the students play more passive roles of attending to, absorbing, retaining, and repeating information. In more progressive student-centered instructional models, if the model espouses inquiry and discovery learning, for example, students play more active roles as teachers encourage and guide them to ask their own questions, form their own hypotheses, investigate and test these, and draw their own conclusions. When teachers differentiate instruction for students with diverse needs, teachers may play varying roles of part-time individual tutor; part-time whole-class instructor; and, when teachers include small-group cooperative learning, part-time group facilitator and guide. Teachers providing one-on-one intensive training to students with profound disabilities play highly directive, active roles. At the other end of the spectrum, when students conduct independent projects, teachers may serve only as consultants or occasional advisors until they grade the projects. While some students need explicit instruction, research also finds that while rote memorization works with factual information, active student participation and teaching learning or thinking *skills*, not just information, produces more original thinkers and lifelong learners.

Affect of community, home, and school on teaching and learning

Community: socioeconomic factors affect learning. For example, students living in more affluent communities have more educational resources and supports like after-school activities, learning and tutoring centers, and educational product stores. Affluent neighborhoods are also populated with more highly educated residents: students are expected to pursue post-secondary educations. In low-income neighborhoods, economic survival often takes precedence over education, or high school diplomas are primarily for obtaining after-graduation employment. Home: parents with higher incomes can access more educational resources. Frequently more educated, they regard education more highly, have higher educational expectations and goals for children, serve as their role models, and either directly or indirectly educate them. Doctors, lawyers, educators, etc. are more likely have children pursuing similar educations and careers. Conversely, some children with less-educated parents have been motivated to become first in their families to attend college. School: urban schools where riots occur make school unsafe. Students cannot concentrate, so they stop attending. Less dramatic but equally important is classroom environment. Consider true stories of a speech language pathologist (SLP) required to conduct therapy between library shelf "stacks," and a teacher's aide instructing ELL students in school hallways. Such uncomfortable, distracting, and/or noisy settings interfere with teaching and learning.

Characteristics shared by effective learning groups

Experts find all kinds of effective learning groups share certain common characteristics. For example, their teachers are always involved actively as guides, coaches, questioners, evaluators, and resource people in student group learning processes. Groups are given work to do that is meaningful to students and challenges them. Teachers ensure students clearly understand learning objectives and schedules, and teachers monitor these. Cooperating is more important than competing. All students in each group are actively involved; groups are heterogeneous. Learning group processes enable students to feel comfortable with asking questions and discussing topics and issues. Students in learning groups experience the sense that they are able to achieve more by learning with each other than they could by learning individually. Although learning groups demand adequate social skills and interpersonal interactions, grouping is not primarily for social purposes. Group time is not considered "free time" for either students or teachers. With effective learning groups, teachers can evaluate individual student members, whole groups, or a combination of both. Teachers are able to assess group work through multiple instruments, e.g., presentations, interviews, portfolios, rubrics, quizzes, etc.

Incorporating different learning modalities to optimize individual student learning

Students need not have sensory or cognitive processing disabilities to learn better through one sensory modality than another. All students have learning styles. Teachers can optimize classroom learning by including multiple and alternative modalities in lessons. For example, some students are auditory learners: they have greater sensitivity, attention, comprehension, and retention for what they hear than what they see or touch. Teachers can provide audiobooks and earphones along with books during reading times. This strategy also benefits students who do have visual impairments. Other students are visual learners: they attend, understand, and remember what they see better than what they hear or touch. Pairing visuals with sounds enhances their learning and other experiences. For example, Walt Disney's classic film *Fantasia* provides visually rich animated sequences accompanying classical music by Tchaikovsky, Grieg, Mussorgsky, etc. Students with haptic learning styles respond to tactile stimuli. Teachers can give younger students materials with varied textures to accompany story reading, assigning older students projects to interpret literature, science lessons, etc. by constructing collages, models, or displays with different textures. Students with kinesthetic styles learn through physical movement. Teachers can let them dance to music and apply exercise and sports movements to physics, mathematical, and other principles, etc.

Benefits of learning theory to education

Behaviorism, or learning theory, has given educators a wealth of tools because it is practical, not only theoretical; applies to all organisms including humans, regardless of cognitive or intellectual level; gives clear procedures and steps to follow; deals only with observable, measurable behaviors, eliminating much ambiguity; follows logical sequences; can change behaviors much faster than other methods; and has undergone much research, yielding specific information about reinforcement schedules and corresponding response rates, effective and ineffective techniques, etc. For example, for students with cognitive or intellectual disabilities (ID) who have difficulty understanding or remembering complex tasks with multiple steps, task analysis derives from behaviorism in its principle of breaking tasks down into smaller, more manageable steps, teaching them separately until mastered, and then connecting them one more at a time. Students with autistic spectrum disorders (ASD) as well as IDs can have horrible trouble making transitions between activities. Behaviorist shaping, via reinforcing successive approximations toward an ultimate target behavior; and chaining, similar to the step-connecting portion of task analysis; are both highly valuable. Students with communication deficits might scream in class to get teacher attention; differential reinforcement of another behavior (DRO) or differential reinforcement of an incompatible behavior (DRI), e.g., raising a hand, waving, touching the teacher's arm, or operating a signal button or switch teaches more acceptable replacement behaviors.

Howard Gardner's theory of multiple intelligences

Gardner outlines eight distinct intelligences that people use in problem solving: namely, linguistic, musical, logical-mathematical, spatial, bodily-kinesthetic, naturalistic, interpersonal and intrapersonal, with a possible ninth: existential. Schools traditionally emphasize linguistic and logical-mathematical. Gardner placed emphasis upon learning skills in context, such as apprenticeships, rather than solely by textbooks. Traditional subjects, like English and math, should be taught in ways that appeal to all the multiple intelligences. History, for example, could be taught through dramatic reenactments, biographies, and architecture. He also thought that assessments should be tailored to different abilities and that student choice with assessments would ensure that the students were completing the task to the best of their abilities and utilizing the intelligence in which they were most skilled.

Constructing knowledge

Knowledge is constructed via a dynamic process wherein learners assimilate new information into existing mental schemes or concepts; modify existing schemes to accommodate radically different or new ideas; reorganize ideas to connect them into coherent patterns; and draw on existing knowledge to make sense of new information, actively interpreting it based on established insights, attitudes, and beliefs. Four iterative learning processes (Timperley et al, 2007), one or more of which are involved in cycles for developing new skills and understandings, are: (1) cueing or retrieving previous knowledge; the outcome is an examination and/or consolidation of existing knowledge. (2) Integrating new skills and information into current belief and value systems; the outcome is an adoption or adaptation of new knowledge. (3) Creating cognitive dissonance with an existing belief, value, or position; the outcome is the rejection or acceptance resolving dissonance;

reconstruction or repositioning of current belief and value system. (4) Developing self-regulated learning related to testing instructional effectiveness; the outcome is the monitoring of student proficiency; adjustment of teaching practices to maximize efficacy. Cycle (1) prepares the way for cycles (2) and (3).

Acquiring skills

In early childhood, children acquire motor, cognitive, language, emotional, social and other skills through playing. Learners of all ages acquire skills through direct instruction from educators. Students in public schools learn academic content in required courses, and may also enroll in elective or outside courses to learn other desired specific skills. Students also learn by doing. Many skills, e.g., riding a bicycle, driving a car, dancing, all PE skills, art skills, etc. require hands-on learning and practice. Students may read books about a specific skill or skill set—not only required class textbooks, but on their own; not only to learn in more depth, breadth, and specificity about a school subject, but also learn other subjects. For example, a high school student interested in becoming a photographer might find his/her school offers art classes in drawing, painting, and sculpture but nothing in photography; and then enrolls in an outside course, and/or reads books on photography. Today, students have access to a plethora of YouTube video tutorials covering a diverse range of subjects. They can search a topic to find videos teaching specific skills. Internet searches also yield more information to read about skills. Apprenticeships and internships combine instruction, observation, imitation, and hands-on experience and practice.

Metacognition, schema, transfer, self-efficacy, self-regulation, and ZPD

Metacognition: thinking about thinking and understanding one's thought processes. Example: a student observes, "I learn better from a picture of something than words about it." Schema: coined by Piaget; a mental construct or representation of a concept. Example: a toddler has a schema for cows. Seeing a large, brown dog, she says "moo"—it fits her cow schema. Told this is a dog, she forms a new "dog" schema. Transfer: applying a learned skill to another activity or setting. Example: a child learns to make a clay pot in art class, then makes clay pots at home. Self-efficacy: coined by Bandura; a sense of competence for specific tasks. Example: based on experience, a student has high self-efficacy for getting an A grade in AP English, but low self-efficacy for passing calculus. Self-regulation: the ability to monitor, control, and adjust one's behaviors. Example: a high school student's grades are not high enough for his preferred college admissions; he watches less TV nightly and studies more. ZPD: coined by Vygotsky; the difference between what one can do unassisted vs. with what s/he can do with help or guidance. Example: a 4-year-old who can read a few words acquires more phonics rules and vocabulary from reading with her 6-year-old brother.

Classical conditioning and operant conditioning

Ivan Pavlov discovered and described classical conditioning. Experimenting with dogs, he placed meat powder on their tongues, causing them to salivate. At the same time he rang a bell. After repeatedly pairing the bell and meat powder, Pavlov found he could ring the bell alone without meat powder and the dogs still salivated by association. Classical conditioning involves evoking a reflexive response to a stimulus that did not originally evoke it through associating it with another stimulus that does trigger the response. Applying this to humans, if someone shines a bright light in your eyes, your pupils will reflexively contract. If someone says the word "contract" along with the light, after enough repetitions the person can say "contract" without shining the light and your pupils will contract. Based on Thorndike's Law of Effect, B. F. Skinner coined the term operant conditioning, differentiating it as "operant behaviors" from classical conditioning, which he called "respondent behaviors" (i.e., reflexive). Operant conditioning involves choice. Thorndike's law says actions followed by desirable consequences are likely to be repeated, while those followed by undesirable consequences are less likely to be repeated. Skinner found behaviors could be increased, decreased, or otherwise shaped through manipulating rewards and punishments.

Developing skills and making sense of the world through play

Children and all humans learn through adaptation to the environment, as Piaget described it. Humans and other beings or organisms naturally seek to establish and maintain equilibrium, or balance. Adaptation seeks equilibrium, encompassing processes of assimilation and accommodation. If a young child can fit a new concept or experience into an existing schema—e.g., things I can eat, throw, or stack; people I know and trust, etc.—s/he assimilates it. If new information is radically different from any existing schema, the child accommodates to it by either altering the existing scheme or creating a new one—e.g., gum is something I chew but do not eat or swallow. Piaget also said children learn by interacting with and acting upon their environments. In play, children interact with the world at much earlier ages than academic activities. They learn physical concepts through their visual, auditory, tactile, olfactory, and gustatory senses. They learn and develop concepts—spatial, like under, over, through, etc.; temporal, like before and after, etc.; numerical and serial; sharing, taking turns, compromising, negotiating, and leading others, developing social skills; gross and fine motor skills through movement; language and literacy skills, including phonological awareness and conversation skills; self-esteem through demonstrating skills, accomplishments, and peer comparisons; and thinking, decision-making, independence, and cooperation and collaboration, including with diverse others, to prepare for adulthood and master life.

Human development vis-à-vis behaviorist and social learning theories

Because psychoanalytic theories of human development, e.g., Freud's psychosexual and Erikson's psychosocial theories, made claims about internal processes that could not always be substantiated by empirical evidence, behaviorist learning theorists sought in response to restrict their examinations to outwardly demonstrated behaviors they could observe, quantify, and measure. As an example, a child who falls and feels some pain will initially cry as a natural reaction. However, when adults respond to the fall by rushing to help the child and expressing concern, this attention reinforces the crying behavior—not the fall, because the child associates the consequence immediately following with the most recent preceding event. The reinforcement of attention increases the probability the child will cry again next time s/he falls, whether it hurts or not, to reduplicate the attention. This is an example of what Skinner termed operant conditioning. In a related example illustrating Bandura's social learning theory, we have all witnessed a child falling, not feeling significant pain, and looking around at adults to gauge whether to cry or not. Bandura found children can learn by observing others' actions and their consequences (rewards and punishments), and can imitate others' behaviors that they observe.

The behaviorist approach to learning theory is justified in limiting its principles and practices to observable, measurable behaviors in that change cannot be proven nor accurately quantified unless existing behaviors can first be observed and measured to establish baseline rates; and subsequent behaviors following intervention can be measured again for comparison to assess changes from baselines. However, a primary limitation of this approach is that it fails to account for or explain maturational, hormonal, and other changes occurring throughout the human lifespan. For example, puberty, the major experience during adolescence, typically has many outward physical, social, and behavioral manifestations as well as many inward physical, cognitive, and emotional changes.

These changes are primarily driven by hormones (though of course societal roles and expectations interact). This internal biological mechanism is not addressed by theories that behaviors are responses to external environmental stimuli. Hence human development has impact on learning theory: finding this theory incomplete, development demands explanation informed by additional biological, psychological, and sociological knowledge about how hormonal maturation, emotions, thinking, and social interactions are interrelated and interdependent, and how they ultimately combine to affect human behavior.

Student transitions from elementary to middle school

Middle school students contend not only with pubertal changes in their bodies and feelings, but also changes from elementary to middle school, e.g., differences in location, learning environments, scheduling, activities, classmates, etc. While early teens become preoccupied and anxious about their appearances, behaviors, and peers' perceptions, they also become more independent, expressing more of their own personalities and interests and making more autonomous choices in friends, school, studying, sports, appearance, etc. Adults must realize this independence prompts greater privacy needs, as well as withdrawing from parents, seeking friends and other adults as role models, identifying their own peer groups, finding groups and friends more important, and experiencing peer pressure. Students' emotional and social development changes their self-perceptions, and educators should adjust instruction accordingly. The adolescent's "imaginary audience" causes self-centered hypersensitivity to others' perceptions; the "personal fable" is the belief their experiences and feelings are unique, and that nobody understands (Elkind). Educators should avoid overreactive discipline interfering with student self-regulation, overwhelming teens; establish safe classroom environments, discussing issues and emotions. Teachers can issue each student a (counterfeit-detecting designed) "leave me alone" pass—not applicable on test or quiz days—to excuse active participation or interaction during class on some days, promoting student empowerment, control, and stress management.

Student growth model

A number of states use student growth models to track student progress. These models are statistical methods to gauge student progress on standardized tests, typically from the end of one school year to the end of the next school year. Statistical models allow students to be evaluated more appropriately, based on a dynamic growth measure instead of a static placement measure. A number of background factors (e.g., ELL status, learning differences, or student exceptionalities) may have contributed to low-achieving scores. Growth models incentivize BOTH progress toward proficiency in underachieving students and continued improvement in proficient students. Teachers and schools can be graded based, in part, upon success in facilitating student improvement and are not penalized for having students who begin an assessment cycle with low-achieving scores.

Response to Intervention (RtI) model

The RtI model is a framework for providing high-quality instruction for all K-12 learners. RtI's three tiers are: 1) research-based **core** classroom instruction, 2) **targeted** instruction for students in need of additional challenge or support, and 3) **intensive** instruction for students whose needs are not accommodated by the first two tiers. The needs of all learners are addressed through the RtI framework with research-based instructional practices, curriculum adaptations responsive to students' individual backgrounds, and appropriate interventions including the extension of the standard curriculum toward greater rigor. The RtI model is data driven. Analysis of student data guides instructional decisions. RtI instructional decisions are made via collaborations of teachers and administrators. No one individual teacher or administrator is capable of implementing RtI. The best interests of the students are served by teachers and administrators teaming to interpret data and decide whether students are in need of additional tiers of (targeted or intensive) instruction.

Universal Design for Learning (UDL)

The Universal Design for Learning is a curriculum implementation/development framework for guiding educational practice that specifically addresses the "what," "how," and "why" of learning. The framework moves away from the "one-size-fits-all" nature of traditional curricula that teaches to the "average" student while overlooking exceptional students. The three principles of UDL are: 1) provide multiple means of representation ("what"), 2) provide multiple means of action and expression ("how"), and 3) provide multiple means of engagement ("why"). UDL embraces learner variability through flexibility in its methods and goals. Learners do not have to start from some predefined point. Rather, teachers are able to differentiate their curriculum implementations, maximize learning opportunities for each student, and empower all students to aim for the most appropriate levels of success.

Cognitive theory

In cognitive theories, e.g., Piaget's theory of cognitive development, the individual seeks to establish and maintain equilibrium or balance to keep things the same, i.e., homeostasis. When unexpected events occur and/or the individual encounters novel environmental stimuli, these disrupt equilibrium. To restore balance, the individual must adapt. The process of adaptation consists of assimilation and accommodation. In learning to understand the world, Piaget said children form schemata. A scheme is a mental construct about some aspect of the environment—people, things, events, and/or categories of these. A baby might form schemata for "things I can suck on," "things I can shake that make noise," and "people I know," for example. When a child encounters a new stimulus, s/he either assimilates it—fitting it into his/her existing schema for similar things; or accommodates to it—modifying an existing schema to accommodate some different characteristics of the new stimulus; or forming a new schema for it. Thus the process of learning, especially for children, involves frequently forming new schemata and changing existing schemata by adding to, subtracting from, or modifying the characteristics they include as experience and interaction with the environment progress.

Cognitive information processing theory

As computers were developed to function analogously to the human brain in many aspects of receiving, encoding, storing, and retrieving information, so in turn computers were used as concrete models for information processing theory to describe how humans execute and sequence cognitive activities. Information processing theories characterize how people attend to environmental events, encode new information and relate it to existing knowledge, store new information in memory, and retrieve information as needed from storage. According to the computer metaphor, people receive sensory input in the sensory register or sensory memory; attend to it through the process of attention; "chunk" and rehearse it temporarily via working memory in short-term memory; encode it for transferring to long-term memory, where it may be stored indefinitely; and then retrieve it as needed, transferring selected data via working memory from long-term to short-term memory. Encoding includes grouping data into categories, outlining, establishing hierarchies, and developing concept trees as organizational mechanisms. It also uses imagery and mnemonics. Retrieval includes recalling information from memory independently, and recognizing provided information matching remembered information. Cognitive mapping (Tolman, 1948) mentally represents the literal physical and metaphorical environment according to relative importance of features for the individual, enhancing navigation, learning, and recall.

Social learning theory

According to Albert Bandura, who originated social learning theory, students need not experience everything directly and personally to learn. Bandura found that children could observe other children engaging in certain behaviors and receiving desirable rewards (reinforcers) for doing so; they would then imitate the other children's behaviors in the hope of receiving similar rewards. Children not only imitate the actions of peers, but also the actions of adults, as all parents have observed. Bandura referred to these examples of behaviors provided by adults as modeling. He thus extended the behaviorist concept that an individual will emit a behavior to get a reward; once it is rewarded, the individual will repeat the behavior to obtain repeated rewards, by showing that because learners also emit behaviors they have observed others emitting, they can learn to produce behaviors based on their observation of others being rewarded for those behaviors. Bandura refers to this process as observational learning or vicarious learning.

Reciprocal determinism

Albert Bandura concurred with many concepts found in behaviorist learning theory, e.g., that individuals emit responses to environmental stimuli; that desirable consequences immediately following a behavior reinforce or strengthen the probability that an individual will repeat the behavior; and the deterministic nature of behaviorism in its attribution of behaviors to environmental causes. However, whereas behaviorism is sometimes called "learning theory," Bandura calls his theory "*social* learning theory." This name emphasizes a key difference in his theory: his orientation to the social contexts wherein learning occurs. Unlike behaviorists, Bandura finds social interactions vital to learning. This relates to Bandura's concept of reciprocal determinism. By this he means learning is a process involving the individual, the environment, and the behavior. The environment includes other people as well as physical surroundings and stimuli. The individual includes personality; cognitive factors; past experiences with reinforced behaviors; and psychological processes like beliefs, thoughts, expectations, etc. The environment and behavior mutually influence one another. Individual, personal characteristics and social factors reciprocally influence and are influenced by individual behaviors. Bandura identified the conditions of attention (observation), retention (remembering), reproduction (imitating or copying), and motivation (a good reason—past, promised, and/or vicarious rewards) for an individual to learn from a model's behavior.

Constructivism

Constructivist philosophy and psychology view learning as a process whereby the learner actively constructs or builds his/her own knowledge and understanding of the world. Cognitive developmental theorist Jean Piaget was a constructivist. He proposed that children learned by interacting with and acting upon their environments. He likened them to "little scientists" who gathered information about the world, experimented with aspects of the environment by interacting with it, and drew progressively more informed conclusions about the world from observing their results. On the basis of this approach, children need experiences interacting with the environment to learn. Consistently with Piaget's characterization of young learners as scientists, problem-based learning is important to constructivist approaches: like scientists who conduct experiments to answer questions and solve problems, children develop higher cognitive capacities and learn more when they experiment with the environment and learn better trying to solve problems than only for obtaining external rewards or avoiding external punishments. Inquiry and discovery learning involves such active student questioning and inquiry and discovering answers or solutions. Vygotsky's zone of proximal development is the area between where a learner can accomplish something independently vs. with assistance, guidance, or encouragement, illustrating how more knowledgeable others (MKOs) enhance learning. Scaffolding is temporary needed support, gradually withdrawn as learners gain proficiency.

Classical and operant conditioning

Pavlov discovered and described classical conditioning when he found he could condition dogs to respond reflexively to a secondary, previously unrelated stimulus by repeatedly pairing it with the stimulus originally producing the reflex. Ringing a bell every time he gave them meat powder, causing them to salivate, eventually enabled the bell alone to stimulate salivation without the meat. Skinner later described what he named operant conditioning. Based on Thorndike's law of effect that a desirable consequence increased the probability of repeating a behavior while an undesirable one decreased that probability, Skinner found through experiments that new behaviors could be established, existing behaviors made much more frequent, and other behaviors made less frequent or extinguished through controlling the antecedents (events or stimuli immediately before) and consequences (events or stimuli immediately after) each behavior. The key difference between classical and operant conditioning is that classical conditioning manipulates reflexive or involuntary behaviors, whereas operant conditioning manipulates conscious or voluntary behaviors. Both contribute to the behaviorist proposition that behaviors can be established, increased, decreased, eliminated, connected, and shaped through manipulating related environmental stimuli. Skinner called classical conditioning "respondent" to differentiate it from operant conditioning, which involves choice.

Internal and external rewards

According to behaviorist theories of learning, rewarding specific behaviors reinforces or strengthens the probability of their repetition. Rewards can be internal or external. Internal or intrinsic rewards originate within the individual, e.g., feeling gratification at learning or knowing something for the sake of additional knowledge, feeling self-efficacy for being able perform a given task successfully, feeling general competence or self-esteem for acquiring more knowledge or skills, engaging in behaviors congruent with one's self-image, etc. Both traditional and radical behaviorism ignored internal states as not outwardly observable or measurable, but many related theories, e.g., social learning theory, cognitive-behavioral theory, etc. incorporate sources of motivation and loci of control. External or extrinsic rewards are provided by other people or the environment. Research finds internal rewards more powerful for increasing and especially maintaining behaviors than external rewards. Behaviorism defines reinforcement as any consequence strengthening the probability of repeating a behavior. This can be positive reinforcement, i.e., introducing something desirable; or negative reinforcement, i.e. removing something undesirable. Positive punishment, conversely, is introducing something undesirable or aversive consequently to a behavior, making that behavior less likely to recur. Negative punishment is removing something desirable or removing a reinforcer, also decreasing the probability of behavior repetition.

Student diversity

Many people think of visible racial differences—African-American, Caucasian, Asian, Asian Indian, Hispanic, Native American, Pacific Islander, etc.—when they think of diversity. However, diversity also includes socioeconomic, from the highest wealthy tiers to the impoverished and everything in between; homelessness; living in transitional housing; all manners of disabilities, both obvious and "hidden"; intellectual and creative giftedness; urban, suburban, exurban, and rural living; different home cultures; learning English as a new language; illiterate families, parents with advanced degrees, and everything in between; younger and older ages than classmates; and many more. General principles include: treat students as individuals with unique, complex identities; ask open-ended questions, inviting reports of experiences and observations. Do not ask students to speak for their minority group. Pronounce every student's name correctly. Be aware of influences on student responses by making eye contact with everybody. Extend wait time to include more reflective and less assertive students. Ask questions challenging dominant students by drawing out quieter students in small groups; talk with and encourage students outside class. Vary teaching methods to address various learning styles and expand student strategy repertoires. Establish egalitarian norms and rules, promoting respect. Be cognizant of potential student performance anxiety in competitive settings, but not overprotective. Empathetically and tactfully give clear, straightforward standards, assessment criteria, and early feedback.

Native English speakers, including teachers, may take for granted the many idiomatic expressions we use, e.g., "between a rock and a hard place," "once in a blue moon," etc. But because they do not convey literal meanings, these sayings confuse students whose first language is not English, causing them to miss important concepts. Teachers should avoid using idioms. If they do, they should translate and/or explain them. All students benefit from linguistic redundancy, e.g., seeing print or writing while hearing speech; ELLs especially benefit. Teachers reinforce information by presenting it in multiple forms. They should also examine whether the examples they give assume or favor certain experiences or backgrounds, e.g., hobbies or activities preferred by one gender; examples based on regional, cultural, historical, or political knowledge unfamiliar to students from other countries, regions, or cultures. Teachers should provide diverse examples. They can learn some of these from their students. Teachers should not assume students who do not speak up do not know class material: Asian and other cultures find silence respectful and frown on attracting attention, while some students have learned responses to aversive consequences for participating. Teachers should also examine classroom humor to ensure jokes do not disparage any groups or differences, which occurs surprisingly often.

Cognitive disabilities

(1) Intellectual disability (ID): students function intellectually two standard deviations or more lower than average age peers. Adaptive functioning may be equal, higher, or lower than intellectual functioning depending on strengths, background experience, and training. Students often learn the same ways as others, but at slower rates. Developmental milestones occur at later ages; learning accomplishments take longer periods to acquire. Emotional and social maturity often correspond to mental age, but also frequently advance beyond it with experience. Students have difficulty understanding abstract concepts, interpreting things literally and concretely. (2) Autism spectrum disorders (ASD): considered an emotional as well as cognitive disability, the spectrum ranges from profound to negligible impairment in activities of daily living and behavior. Intelligence ranges from profound ID to gifted. ASDs often impair social understanding and interaction, e.g., observing, interpreting, and producing nonverbal signals indicating emotions, attitudes, etc. Students have difficulty recognizing sarcasm, figurative language, humor; starting conversations; and

conversational give-and-take. Behavioral characteristics include repetitive actions, restricted interests, rigid routines or schedules, focusing on one activity for long times, and difficulty transitioning among activities. (3) Specific learning disabilities: students are not intellectually impaired, but have deficits processing linguistic and/or numeric information. Typically their school achievement is far behind their intellectual ability.

Auditory disabilities

(1) One auditory disability not involving the hearing mechanism is central auditory processing disorder, a neurological deficit in interpreting the structure and meanings of speech sounds. Other auditory disabilities involve hearing loss. (2) Totally deaf students cannot hear any sound, often not even with hearing aids. (3) Hard of hearing students have hearing loss but some residual hearing. Hearing loss can be sensorineural, i.e., the cochlea, cochlear hair cells, and acoustic or auditory nerves do not function; or conductive, i.e., something in the outer or middle ear prevents conduction of sound waves, e.g., outer-ear wax buildup, middle-ear pus, fluid from otitis media infection, fused or immobilized middle-ear ossicles from otosclerosis, etc. Sensorineural hearing loss is irreversible, but cochlear implants enable hearing for some. Conductive hearing loss is most often treatable with surgery, medication, hearing aids, etc. Slight hearing loss, i.e., inability to hear whispering, is measured at 25-40 dB; mild hearing loss, i.e., understanding conversation with normal loudness up to 3-5 feet, 41-54 dB; moderate hearing loss, i.e., only understanding loud speech nearby, 55-69 dB; severe hearing loss, i.e., hearing only loud voices a foot away, 70-89 dB; profound hearing loss, i.e., feeling vibrations but not hearing tones, 90 dB or more. Noise-induced hearing loss is only at middle frequency (c. 4000 Hz).

Visual impairments

The definition of 20/20 vision is reading at 20 feet from a Snellen eye chart what one normally should see. Comparably, 20/200 vision is reading at 20 feet what one should see at 200 feet. Legal blindness is defined as 20/200 after correction in the better eye. Low vision is described as anywhere from 20/200 to 20/70 after correction in the better eye and a visual field of 30 degrees or less. A visual field of 20 degrees or less is tunnel vision. Travel vision ranges from 5/200 to 10/200. Motion perception is 3/200 to 5/200, typically for moving objects. Seeing bright light from 3 feet away but not movement, i.e., below 3/200 vision, is light perception. Not seeing strong light directly in the eyes is total blindness. Students may be born blind or become blind adventitiously. Some children are born with congenital cataracts, causing opacity clouding the lenses and blindness unless surgically removed with a replacement lens implanted. Students with diabetes can develop diabetic retinopathy, i.e., vascular changes causing retinal hemorrhaging and blindness. Some students inherit glaucoma, wherein inner-eye fluid buildup creates pressure which causes visual impairment and blindness when untreated. Genetically, students may inherit total or red-green color-blindness; lack of pigment in albinism causes photosensitivity and vision problems. Accidents or injuries include retinopathy of prematurity from insufficiently regulated incubator oxygen, eyeball punctures, and retinal dislocation or detachment.

Motor or physical disabilities

Physical or motor disabilities impair mobility and may also affect coordination, balance, strength, and/or flexibility. Some students are missing one or more limbs, congenitally or through accident, injury, or amputation. They may use prostheses and/or wheelchairs, walkers, canes, crutches or other mobility aids. Students with cerebral palsy have neurological deficits in control and coordination of muscular movements. Impairments range from a slight limp to being in a wheelchair or bed-bound. Cerebral palsy (CP) patients often have dyspraxia or apraxia, i.e., impaired development of their motor coordination. This can affect any body parts, e.g., speech muscles, hand grasp, fine motor skills, walking, etc. with varying degrees of severity. CP also causes spasticity, i.e., excessive muscle tension or rigidity; athetosis, i.e., excessive involuntary body movements; or both combined. Students born with spina bifida may have foot, ankle, or lower-limb weakness to below-waist paralysis, depending on the spinal level of incomplete neural tube closure. Students with severe type 1 diabetes may require amputations when the disease impairs blood circulation, especially in their lower extremities. In addition to assistive and adaptive devices and prostheses, treatments include physical therapy for large muscles, occupational therapy for small muscles, recreational therapy for adapted activities, etc.

Speech or language disorders

Speech or language disorders may involve speech only, language only, or both. Speech-only disorders include articulation disorders, the most common of which makes children distort, substitute, or omit certain speech sounds—typically consonants—at ages above typical norms for correct pronunciation. Typical remediation is speech therapy, which can include exercising articulatory muscles, audio feedback, targeting correct articulatory positions, tools (tongue depressors and bite plates), etc. Voice disorders include hypernasality, often secondary to cleft palate; hoarseness secondary to vocal polyps, nodules, or dysarthria (a neurological muscular control disorder); too-high, too-low, or unstable pitch; volume control problems, etc. Treatment depends on causes: nodules and polyps are surgically removed, clefts are repaired, and therapeutic techniques address other problems. Another speech disorder is stuttering, or rate and rhythm disorders. A variety of therapies exists, such as breathing methods, delayed auditory feedback, etc. Some stutterers actually outgrow the condition regardless of therapy. Some become "fluent stutterers." Some benefit greatly from some therapies, some little or none. Language disorders include delayed language development, secondary to intellectual disability or environmental deprivation; aphasia, secondary to neurological damage or deficits, e.g., traumatic brain injury or cerebral palsy, impairing expressive and/or receptive language processing; and language-related learning disabilities, like dyslexia (reading) or dysgraphia (writing). Language disorder therapies include stimulation and practice.

Impacts sensory impairments have on learning

Students with visual impairments miss a lot of input in our highly visually-oriented society. Orientation and mobility specialists can help them navigate school and other public environments more independently. Blind students may have canes or service dogs to aid mobility; teachers must plan for these and classmate interactions with them. In classrooms, blind and visually impaired students benefit from magnifiers, large-print texts, seating close to the board and teacher, audiobooks, and text-to-speech computer software for adapting texts; speech-to-text software for dictating written compositions; Braille materials or OptaCons for reading; and modified lighting, brighter and/or with less glare depending on the type and degree of impairment. Teachers can also provide materials with bright, solid colors and bold black outlines. Students with hearing impairments are safer in environments that accompany sound-based fire alarms with strobe lights. Teachers and classmates must remember to face or touch them to get their attention; speak face-to-face with students who read lips; include American Sign Language (ASL) interpreters in conversations or lessons for students who have them; and accompany spoken instruction and discussion with supplementary visual information. Speech-to-text software enables deaf and hearing-impaired students to read spoken language. Educators must also respect and teach classmates the importance and strength of deaf culture for students identifying with it.

Behavioral disorders

Attention deficit hyperactivity disorder (ADHD) is familiar to many: student attention spans are deficiently short; students are too easily distracted; self-regulation deficits cause impulsive behaviors; students display excessive physical activity and have difficulty sitting still, focusing attention, and persisting in the same activity for extended durations. Medication like Ritalin, Cylert, other stimulants—even caffeine—enable better focusing, but must be accompanied by behavioral therapy. Some students are identified with oppositional defiant disorder (ODD), symptomatized by irritability, aggression, hostility, negativity, and defiance. They frequently lose their tempers, argue with adults, purposely irritate others, blame others for their behaviors and mistakes, express or demonstrate anger and resentment, and act vindictively and spitefully. Roughly half of preschoolers with ODD outgrow it by age 8, a few develop ADHD instead, and some develop comorbid disorders (anxiety, depression). Some develop conduct disorder (CD) in a few years. ODD students tend to have better school performance but worse social skills than CD patients. CD is the severest childhood psychiatric disorder, involving physical aggression to people and animals, bullying, cruelty, property destruction, lying, theft, and serious rule or legal violations. Nearly 20 percent of teens with ODD or CD have antisocial personality disorder (APD)—an extension of CD—in adulthood. Multisystem therapy is most effective; many improve, but few completely recover.

Different disorders can cause similar classroom behaviors. For example, students with intellectual disabilities (ID), autism spectrum disorders (ASD), communication disorders, attention deficit hyperactivity disorder (ADHD), and others can all display disruptive behaviors. The reasons may differ, but the net results are the same. Some inappropriate behaviors are caused by lack of maturity or understanding, as with IDs. Students with ASDs, communication disorders, or ADHD may explode out of frustration over not having their needs met. Students with communication deficits may scream, hit, or throw things in lieu of having the language or speech skills to express what they feel, need, or want. ADHD students unable to sit still or concentrate often disrupt classes with out-of-seat behavior, excessive movements, vocal interruptions, etc. ASD students can have "meltdowns" or tantrums at sensory overload, having to switch activities, etc. Students with IDs or emotional or behavioral disorders often have immature or deficient self-regulation abilities. Attention-seeking behaviors are frequently inadvertently reinforced by the attention of adults trying to address them. While it requires planning and consistent, systematic implementation, behavior modification techniques can successfully resolve many behavioral dilemmas by teaching more acceptable replacement behaviors for communicating, meeting needs, making adjustments, and establishing and reinforcing self-control and social interaction skills.

Learning style, gender, culture, socioeconomic status, and prior knowledge and experience

Learning style: student A is nonplused by verbal teacher explanation of a new physics concept, but lights up immediately when shown a drawing of it (visual learning style). Student B does not understand the drawing, but "gets" it exactly when guided by the teacher to act it out physically (kinesthetic learning style). Gender: boys are physically aggressive; girls engage in relational aggression (hurting feelings, undermining self-esteem and reputations). Boys respond positively when educators redirect their aggression to athletic competition; girls when educators redirect their energy to performing services helping others. Culture: students from Asian, Latin, and Native American cultures prefer cooperative over competitive activities; helping others and being part of the group is more important to them than standing out individually. They volunteer to speak in class less not for lack of preparation but to show respect. Socioeconomic status: students in poverty miss school from lacking proper clothing and shoes. Malnutrition impairs ability to concentrate, remember, and perform. Affluent parents can afford private tutoring if their children struggle with academic subjects; poor ones cannot. Prior knowledge and experience: students with marginal literacy cannot write stories but excel at oral storytelling, a strong and familiar tradition in their cultures and families.

Motivation, self-confidence, self-esteem, cognitive development, maturity, and language

Motivation: the best-designed and implemented instruction will fail if students are not first motivated. Research finds internal locus of control, wherein students attribute their success or failure to causes within themselves (ability, effort, interest, or ambition, for instance), more motivating for achievement than external locus of control, wherein students attribute their success or failure to outside causes (unfair tests, poor teachers, distracting classmates, classroom conditions). Teachers engage student interest by selecting subjects students want to know about, and offering choices of learning activities and specific subtopics to investigate. Self-confidence: students lacking overall self-confidence hesitate to try anything, anticipating failure. They need encouragement and approval of themselves as persons, plus ample reinforcement of every initial small success. Others only lack self-confidence for specific tasks or subjects; Bandura calls this self-efficacy. Providing alternative learning methods and enabling successful experiences improve self-efficacy. Self-esteem: largely determines self-confidence. Teachers can raise self-esteem by showing and communicating that they value and care about students, entrusting them with responsibilities, and recognizing their accomplishments. Cognitive development: students cognitively ahead of or behind classmates need differentiated instruction appropriate to their cognitive levels for engagement and achievement. Maturity: teachers must consider whether emotional or social maturity differs from physical and/or cognitive maturity and interact appropriately. Language: many teachers mistake ELL deficits for learning disabilities, causing overrepresentation in special education.

Americans with Disabilities Act (ADA)

Signed into law in 1990, the ADA granted the same civil rights protections based on disabilities as previously accorded by the 1964 Civil Rights Act based on race, color, religion, gender, or national origin. The ADA was thus modeled on the Civil Rights Act, and also on the 1973 Rehabilitation Act requiring federally funded programs and activities to provide equal access to persons having disabilities. The terms of the ADA include public buildings, facilities, programs, and activities, which include all public school buildings, facilities, programs, and activities. Hence this law makes it illegal for public schools to prevent students with disabilities from accessing them because of architectural and other barriers. Titles II and III of the ADA include enforceable standards for accessible design and construction of buildings and facilities, barrier removal, alterations, and accessibility. Predating the Individuals with Disabilities Education Act (IDEA), which would more extensively address the rights of children with disabilities to education, the ADA also requires equal opportunities, participation, and benefits from public facilities for individuals with disabilities, "in the most integrated setting appropriate to the needs of the individual." This foreshadowed the IDEA's later emphasis on inclusion. The ADA prohibits discrimination based on disability.

Individuals with Disabilities Education Act (IDEA)

Passed in 1975 and reauthorized a number of times since, IDEA guarantees the right of children with disabilities to a free, appropriate, public education (FAPE) in the least restrictive environment (LRE) possible that meets their educational needs. The right to education of school-aged children is covered in IDEA Part B; Part C, added subsequently, addresses the right to early intervention and early childhood education of babies and toddlers with disabilities. The LRE clause has dual purposes: (1) to prevent segregation of children with disabilities to special schools or classes, and (2) to be interpreted differently according to the needs of every individual student. An important provision of IDEA is that every student to receive special education and related services for an identified, eligible disability must have an Individual Education Plan (IEP). An IEP team including students, teachers, parents, special educators, therapists, and others involved develops the student's IEP, identifying goals the student needs and is able to achieve; related, specific learning objectives; timeframes; and numerical criteria for determining success. The IEP includes any assistive and adaptive devices and equipment and other supports the student requires to achieve identified educational goals.

Section 504 of the Rehabilitation Act of 1973

Section 504 protects the rights of people with disabilities in activities and programs receiving federal funds by prohibiting discrimination against them based on disability. When the US Department of Education (ED) provides financial assistance to public school districts and other local or state education agencies, activities, or programs, it enforces Section 504. ED also has an Office for Civil Rights (OCR), headquartered in Washington, D.C. with 12 enforcement offices, to ensure civil rights laws including Section 504 are followed. Section 504 requires school districts to provide "free, appropriate public education" (FAPE) to each of their qualifying students with disabilities. This law defines an appropriate education as designed to meet disabled students' individual educational needs as well as ensuring that non-disabled students' needs are met; provided together with non-disabled students as much as meets the needs of the student with disabilities; having established evaluation and placement procedures to prevent inappropriate placement or misclassification, and periodic reevaluations; affording due process for parents to receive mandated notices, review their children's records, and challenge identification, evaluation, and placement choices.

Elementary and Secondary Education Act's (ESEA)

According to President Barack Obama and the US Department of Education, the new Elementary and Secondary Education Act (ESEA, aka No Child Left Behind or NCLB) demands fair, rigorous accountability for all school performance levels; meeting diverse learner needs; and more equitable provision of fair opportunities for student success; to ensure opportunity and equity for every student. The ESEA reauthorization requires its programs to offer a wide range of supports and resources enabling students to graduate, attend college, and establish careers. ESEA includes programs for meeting the special educational needs of ELL students, students with disabilities, homeless students, Native American students, migrant workers' children, and delinquent and neglected students. It states the federal government's responsibility for giving assistance to rural school districts, districts sustaining impacts of federal activities and properties, and other high-need areas and regions. The 2010 ESEA reauthorization also proposed to increase support for inclusion and better outcomes for students with disabilities as a supplement to funding for the Individuals with Disabilities Education Act (IDEA). This support includes more appropriate, accurate assessment measures of students with disabilities; better teacher and administrator preparation for meeting diverse learner needs; and better locally and state-determined curricula, incorporating universal design principles, implemented by more districts and schools.

The ESEA's 2010 reauthorization continues formula grants to states and school districts for ELL programs, allowing a variety of program types and ELL teacher professional development. The 2010 reauthorization requires new state criteria for consistent eligibility determination, placement, and program or service duration based on valid, reliable state ELP assessments; and system implementation for evaluating ELL program effectiveness and garnering data on ELL subgroup achievement for driving better district program improvement decisions and effective program selection. This reauthorization also proposed new, competitive grants to states, districts, and nonprofits for innovative program development; best-practice knowledge base building; ELL instructional practice improvement; and funding research, leadership, and partnerships for effective teacher development. Another provision requires states to adopt and implement statewide ELP standards by grade, aligned with state academic content standards for college and career readiness. Strengthening formula grants for meeting migrant student educational needs included updating the funding formula for timelier, accurate data incorporation; and facilitating and reinforcing interstate endeavors for supporting migrant student transitions into local communities and schools. Funds for homeless students were changed from Title I allocation shares to allocations based on student numbers. The administration proposed to remove service obstacles, clarify statutory ambiguities causing service delays, and require grantees to report academic outcomes.

Characteristics of ELL students as a population

The ELL student population is widely heterogeneous. Some families speak no English at home, only English, or several languages. They may identify only with American culture, strongly with several cultures, or deeply with one non-American culture. They have been stigmatized for not speaking English, speaking English, or how they speak English. They live in communities sharing common culture, without other ELLs, or have lived in America for generations. They struggle or excel in school—some in specific subjects. They may feel competent or disaffected in school. ELL immigration status, birthplace, socioeconomic status, academic knowledge, language proficiency levels, and expectations of school all vary. ELL student prevalence has extended from a few to all US states. This diversity within and among ELLs requires multiple responses for meeting educational needs. Disabilities are not more prevalent among ELLs: research shows assessments not distinguishing ELL status from disability cause misdiagnoses. Educators should not assume ELL students learn English easily or readily. Also, English oral fluency does not equal mastery: systematic academic assessments are necessary. Differing L1s, previous education, socioeconomic and immigration status mean not all ELLs learn English the same way. Accommodations benefit not only ELLs, but others. Vocabulary is not the sole focus of ELL instruction: structures and meanings are equally important, even with limited ELP.

Instructing ELL students effectively

Teachers should give ELLs challenging, meaningful curriculum content, text choices, and authentic reading and writing activities. Placement by academic achievement, not ELP, with high-quality instruction in challenging classes enables greater learning and performance. Technology supports ELL motivation, writing and editing skills development, and class blog and website collaboration. Teacher awareness of ELLs' previous literacy experiences, backgrounds, and L2 learning benefits and challenges enables more effective instruction. ELLs are challenged to understand implicit cultural norms and knowledge; learn to translate and code-switch; develop metalinguistic awareness; negotiate differences between school literacy practices and home or community; and address the social, cultural, and political dimensions of linguistic status issues. Studies show ELL reading comprehension, writer identity development, and peer collaboration are developed through extracurricular composition. Teachers can use these methods to promote ELL investment in school learning, decrease home-school distance, and help students view their home languages and cultures not as obstacles or discards, but educational resources and contributors. Teachers should teach K-12 ELLs academic literacy basics and help them connect school content to their own knowledge.

Assessment, Instruction, and the Learning Environment

Classrooms where all students participate and have their educational needs met

Establish a classroom climate where students feel safe, secure, and engaged in learning rather than unchallenged or threatened. Discuss how students want the classroom to work and how to maintain the best climate. Promote cooperation, involvement, and a stimulating, inviting, productive, learner-friendly environment with functional, appealing arrangements and displays through a classroom plan, including students in decision-making processes. Organize the classroom to allow movement, stations for long-term involvement and learning, and easy technology and information access. Engage students in the processes of developing, comprehending, and maintaining procedures and routines, with a limited number of positively stated, specific, clear rules; practice and reinforce these throughout the school year. Assign and manage meaningful assignments with purposes, in real-life settings with audiences. Prepare for teaching: active student involvement in planning, preparing, implementing, and assessing learning units reduces behavior and discipline issues. Consider having students create and submit actual proposals to organizations, corporations, or city councils needing new ideas. Consistently communicate and reinforce class procedures and routines. Discuss behavior in class. Discuss adding, removing, or changing procedures. Have students enforce rules. Students' having a voice enables superior classroom functioning. Consistently celebrate success. Evaluate and reflect daily or weekly throughout the year.

Inclusive practices in regular education classrooms with special education students

According to expert Peter Westwood (2003), research into effective instruction finds that effective teachers keep the focus on academics; give students maximal opportunities for learning; demonstrate good classroom management; use work-oriented, business-like styles; express enthusiasm; communicate high expectations to students of what they can achieve; apply strategies for keeping students motivated, on-task, and productive; introduce new material step-by-step; use explicit and direct instruction techniques; structure all content; give clear explanations and instructions; closely monitor student activities; demonstrate appropriate strategies for approaching tasks; utilize varied resources; adjust instruction to individual student needs; reteach as needed; give students frequent feedback; and spend considerable amounts of time doing whole-class, interactive teaching. In classes including special education students, teachers include: descriptive praise and encouragement, ample guided practice, fast-paced lessons, high engagement and participation levels of all students, careful curriculum content sequencing and control, positive peer assistance and interactions, many practice and application opportunities, modeling of effective school task completion methods, interactive group teaching, and teaching students how best to attempt new learning tasks.

Creating supportive, positive classroom environments for student diversity

(1) Teachers can intentionally teach responsible behaviors. To afford a multidimensional approach for every student, particularly those requiring more intensive intervention, teachers can collaborate with parents, school psychologists, and counselors. General behaviors to teach include communication skills, social skills, character development, anger management, self-control skills, conflict resolution, decision-making skills, taking responsibility for one's actions, and developing

emotional intelligence (EQ). (2) Teachers can establish classroom harmony through creating warm, supportive atmospheres wherein every student feels s/he is an important class member. Class meetings, class-building and team-building activities engender senses of a learning community and class ownership. Experts use the acronym "VIABLE": students develop self-respect and respect for authority figures when they feel they are *valued* by teachers and classmates, *included* in classroom activities, *accepted* in their classrooms and schools, have senses of *belonging* to cooperative learning groups, and adults who *listen* to and *encourage* them. (3) Teachers can empower students and promote their sense of class ownership by involving them actively in disciplinary processes. Instead of being part of the problem, students become part of the solution. Activities include arranging study and homework buddies; peer tutors, mediators, and counselors; peer recognition; assigning classroom responsibilities; and student-led conferences.

Invite or involve parents to meet student needs together. The "crucial Cs of parental support" are parent-teacher Communication, Connection, and Collaboration. Invite other teachers and staff—administrators; school psychologists, counselors, social workers, nurses; speech language pathologists (SLPs), occupational therapists (OTs), physical education (PE) teachers, special education teachers, music teachers; ELL or bilingual teachers, etc.—to collaborate in solving learning and discipline problems. Encourage and praise students' positive steps, efforts, strengths, progress, and improvement, not just finished products. Encouragement helps students self-validate and reflect on their own responses to their strengths and accomplishments. Effective praise is informative and appreciative, not evaluative or controlling. Build senses of accomplishment and capability in all students, and particularly in those lacking the following: focus on improvement, not perfection; turn mistakes into learning opportunities; let students struggle and succeed within ability levels; build upon student strengths; analyze past successes, then focus on the present; acknowledge task difficulty; use task analysis; teach positive self-talk; celebrate all students' successes and achievements. Develop positive teacher-student relationships to receive and give respect. Listen to students. Communicate positive expectations. Involve students in class decision-making: use a suggestion box; provide "voice and choice." Show enthusiasm for teaching and learning. Show interest in student interests. Keep communication open. Accept and value diversity and individual differences. Model positive, helpful, and kind behaviors.

Statistical reliability and validity

Reliability: whether a test gets consistent results over repeated administrations. Test-retest reliability retests the same respondents with the same test, e.g., two weeks or a month later. Difficulties include having to write different questions on the same material, etc., to control for memory and practice effects. Internal consistency reliability compares two versions of a test concurrently, evaluating whether they correlate or measure the same construct. Validity: whether a test measures what it purports or intends to measure. Criterion validity: whether a test reflects certain abilities. One type is concurrent validity: whether a test correlates with benchmark or criterion tests. Another type is predictive validity: how well a test predicts abilities by testing respondents for a given construct, then comparing future results. Content validity: whether a test represents all of a given construct. Construct validity: whether a test measures its identified construct and not others—e.g., depression, not stress or anxiety. Convergent validity: whether constructs we believe are related are actually related. Divergent or discriminant validity: whether constructs we believe unrelated are unrelated. Bias: subjective slant toward expected results. Example: IQ test item "cup and (a.) saucer, (b.) fork, (c.) table," presumed student familiarity with cup-and-saucer sets; but low-income students chose "table," having experience only with cups on tables, not cups in saucers.

Formal and informal assessments

Standardized tests are a primary example of formal assessments. They have been used to test large numbers of students; data from results are mathematically calculated and summarized; standard scores, percentiles, or stanines are provided. Statistical analyses support conclusions based on test results, e.g., a certain score range is the average for representative samples of the student population in a given grade, hence other scores can be defined as above or below average and by how much. These are typically norm-referenced tests. Informal assessments are performance- and content-driven, not data-driven. For example, a running record of how well a student is reading a particular book is an informal assessment. Typical scores are most rubric scores; percentage of words read correctly; 15 correct answers out of 20 questions, etc. These are typically criterion-referenced or performance-based tests. To compare students to peers their own age, compare student strengths and weaknesses with those of peers, or assess overall achievement, formal assessments suit these purposes. To inform and improve ongoing instruction, as in formative assessment, informal assessments meet those purposes. Formal tests, statistically proven, are good for summative, not formative assessment and generalized data, not individualized data. Informal tests, more individualized, are good for ongoing assessment but less objective or statistically supported.

Formal assessments all include standardized methods for their administration, scoring, and interpretation of the scores. Some examples of formal assessments include all standardized achievement tests, which are often national or statewide; so-called high-stakes examinations; standardized intelligence or IQ tests; many standardized screening tests; and many standardized diagnostic measures. Standardized testing instruments have been statistically proven valid, i.e., they test what they are meant to test; and reliable, i.e., they yield consistent results across repeated administrations. Their manuals include statistical methods for scoring and interpreting the scores, and tables or charts showing the average scores of samples of students that represent the test-taking population, plus other scores and how many standard deviations these are from the average. Quizzes and exercises at the ends of educational textbook chapters, sections, and units are also examples of formal assessments. Informal assessments do not typically include standardized instruments, though some exist, e.g., standardized reading fluency measures. Teacher observations, class or student question-and-answer sessions, running reports, student projects, presentations, and experiments, student portfolios, and performance assessments are examples of informal assessment measures. Some find peer teaching and debates informal assessments as well.

Formal assessments provide quantitative data because they are standardized and report standard scores. Informal assessments provide qualitative data because they are not standardized, so the results reported by teachers using them are more subjective. Formal assessments enable comparison of individual students with peer groups, but typically not specific details about individual students. Informal assessments can give more detail about an individual student's strengths, needs, and performance; but less objective comparison of individual student performance with age, grade, or peer performance. Formal assessments are norm-referenced tests comparing student performance to norms for their developmental level, age, or grade. Informal assessments are typically criterion-referenced tests comparing student performance to pre-established criteria students are expected or intended to achieve and teachers are expected or intended to teach. Some students experience significant test anxiety when standardized formal tests are administered in whole-class or group settings. Some students also experience significant anxiety, even panic, when teachers single them out to answer questions in class as informal assessment. Hence it is important that teachers obtain sufficient results from both formal and informal assessment, and multiple forms of each, to develop more comprehensive pictures of student abilities and achievements.

Student scores from standardized intelligence scales and standardized scales of adaptive functioning are often used to inform student placements into specific schools, grades, and types of classes most compatible with their educational strengths and needs. While tracking is generally unpopular these days, educators seek to place students into groups where ability levels are similar and teachers can offer material (even if via differentiated instruction) that is sufficiently challenging, neither impossibly, inappropriately, or overwhelmingly difficult nor overly easy or boring. For students with certain disabilities, e.g., autism spectrum disorders (ASDs), many formal assessments exist to inform educators where a student is on the spectrum; intellectual and adaptive functioning levels; individual interests, difficulty areas, and specific behaviors, which can be both typical of the disorder and vary widely individually. Formal assessments are given at ends of school years to measure student achievement. These results are used for purposes of individual student grade promotions; to compare year-end student performance to baseline scores to assess student progress toward instructional objectives; and school accountability, to compare school effectiveness by comparing rates and percentages of student achievement to those of other schools, inform school improvement plans, and secure or continue government school funding.

One of the most valuable and prevalent uses of informal assessment findings is to inform ongoing instruction. While teachers plan instruction based on initial student assessments, during implementation they may find some students are not responding to their methods or having difficulty learning new material. With new students and large classes, teachers can discover new individual student characteristics throughout the school year. For example, by using informal measures regularly as formative assessments, teachers may find early on a student(s) not progressing at the rate(s) projected. They can then either (1) change the timeframe when the student is expected to achieve certain objectives; (2) change objectives to represent smaller increments, amounts, or lower levels to achieve within the timeframe; or (3) change the instructional approach, techniques, or strategies to be more compatible or effective with particular students. Conversely, when students progress much faster than anticipated, teachers can adjust instruction to provide higher difficulty, enriched content, etc. Formative assessments also monitor and document on-target student progress. In addition to formative assessment, informal measures afford alternative ways of evaluating student performance that formal standardized tests cannot measure, e.g., performances, portfolios, creative projects, etc. Some students cannot respond to objective examinations but demonstrate their competencies in different formats.

Essay questions vs. selected response questions and written tests vs. performance measures

Essay questions have one obvious advantage of testing composition and writing skills as well as subject content knowledge when testing subjects other than English composition. They also enable students to go into depth and detail about topics, showing the extent of their knowledge. Essays afford students choices of subtopics, points they make, examples they use, how much they emphasize certain subtopics and points, how they organize their essays; allow them to persuade or convince readers through argumentation; require recall, not recognition; and showcase student higher-order thinking skills. Disadvantages include being more time-consuming to administer and write; requiring writing skills, which if deficient can obscure a student's other subject knowledge; and requiring far more time and subjective judgment to grade. Selected-choice questions are much faster to administer; can cover larger numbers of smaller points; allow teachers and testers more control of subject matter; are easier for students, requiring recognition, not recall; have more clear-cut right and wrong answers; are graded more objectively, and far faster, even electronically or automatically. Disadvantages include less information about individual students' overall knowledge; lacking elaboration or depth; and enabling some correct answers from sheer guesswork through probability. Written tests can be more objective; performance measures enable students to show what they can actually do, an advantage for those who do not write well.

Portfolio assessments

Portfolio assessments involve reviewing a collection of student work products gathered cumulatively over a period of time, e.g., a semester or school year. One of their advantages is that they can provide clear evidence of student progress, growth, and other longitudinal changes that a written test or single term paper will not show as clearly. Another is that products may be artworks, models, and other concrete objects, not just test answers, written essays, or papers. These are more individualized, demonstrating more student skills than tests or papers, including nonverbal skills like artistic ability, creativity, divergent thinking, spatial awareness, mechanical ability, nonlinguistic organization, etc. Students with different learning styles, who may not use the linear thinking needed for objective tests and/or lack organizational, language processing, and/or verbal skills for writing, but excel in other areas, can produce evidence of those strengths in portfolios. Another advantage is avoiding test anxiety for many students. Students also have less time pressure and can devote more total time to creating things more gradually. Portfolios can be used for both formative and summative assessment. Some disadvantages include more subjective teacher grading, time required to accumulate portfolio products, teacher time and effort to match products with learning objectives, and lack of standardization.

Considerations for selecting assessment formats and instruments

When choosing assessment instruments, educators and testers should first always remember that any comprehensive assessment must include multiple and varied methods, instruments, tools, and (when feasible) formats. They should never rely on a single test. One test might be most indicated for assessing a very specific skill, but even for single domains, e.g., language or adaptive functioning, multiple tests are better, as responses and scores can differ and some reveal abilities others overlooked. Age-appropriateness is important. For example, to use Wechsler's IQ scales with a young child, one would administer the Wechsler Preschool and Primary Scales of Intelligence (WPPSI), not the Wechsler Intelligence Scales for Children (WISC) or Wechsler Adult Intelligence Scales (WAIS). (If a gifted child exceeded WPPSI's top levels, administering the WISC would be interesting, though other giftedness instruments would also be indicated.) Students who are nonverbal—e.g., some with autism spectrum disorder (ASD), cerebral palsy (CP), intellectual disability (ID), or other disorders—can be evaluated using the Leiter, Raven's Progressive Matrices, UNIT, etc. Young and/or disabled students with receptive language understanding but absent or limited expression can respond to the Peabody Picture Vocabulary and other receptive tests.

A student's age or grade level are not the only factors to consider for selecting assessments. The educational context is also a key to format and instrument choice. For example, while intelligence scales give an idea of a child's intellectual capacity for purposes of educational placement, curricular and instructional design, individualized or differentiated instructional planning, etc., intelligence testing is not necessarily relevant or even significant to define adaptive functioning levels. Some children, due to innate characteristics, life experience, and training, function significantly higher in daily living and social skills than intellectually. Other children function adaptively much lower than their intellectual capacities would suggest due to behavior disorders like attention deficit hyperactivity disorder (ADHD), autism spectrum disorders (ASDs), learning disabilities (LDs), major mental disorders, etc. To ascertain daily living activities a child can perform compared to age peers and inform instructional design for developing adaptive skills, tests like the Vineland Adaptive Behavior Scales are indicated. When developmental delay is suspected in young children, tests like the Bayley Scales of Infant and Toddler Development help evaluate developmental levels. Because many school districts model their goals on their state education department's standards, the best way to align assessment with campus and district goals is often to administer standardized tests provided by statewide assessment systems.

Aligning instructional design and goals with statewide assessments

Teachers need not view the process of aligning their instruction with assessment as "teaching to the test." Instead, they first need to read the standards on which the statewide assessments are based. As an example, many states are now basing their statewide assessments on the Common Core State Standards (CCSS). This means that what students in the state are expected to learn to know and do via the instruction they receive is encapsulated within the CCSS. A teacher whose students will be taking a test based on the CCSS would need to first review the standards and align their teaching to ensure that everything included in those standards is also included in their planned curriculum for the year. Because the state tests are written to align exactly with the standards on which they are based, teachers can be assured that students who are adequately instructed in the knowledge and skills outlined in the standards will be measured appropriately by the exam, without the need for focusing on the test itself.

Monitoring student understanding and guide instruction

Rather than teach an entire unit and administer an end-of-unit test, only to discover most or all students did not understand key or major points the teacher wanted to convey, it is more useful to monitor student understanding early and often. For example, at any grade level, after a teacher makes introductory statements in a lesson, s/he can stop and ask the class questions whose answers should reflect whether they heard and remember the few main points, whether they can repeat one or a few key definitions the teacher gave, whether they understood the concepts communicated, etc. Seeing few or no volunteers or many students looking perplexed indicates a need to reteach and/or explain or demonstrate concepts differently. Quizzes at ends of lessons within units also monitor student understanding of shorter segments. When teachers assign small-group projects, they may have a member of each group orally report current group or project status and progress to the teacher or class periodically. Teachers can offer time-management strategies if they are falling behind schedule or advise reducing project scope, information amounts, etc. Teachers who find the majority of students not understanding or learning need to revisit and revise their instructional levels, approaches, methods, and/or techniques.

Formative and summative assessment

Formative assessments are conducted during instruction. Teachers use them to obtain feedback that they and their students can both utilize for improving the teaching and learning that will occur as it continues. For example, after giving a lecture, a teacher might ask middle or high school students to write down a sentence or two that identify the lecture's main point(s). Similarly, kindergarten and first-grade teachers can review an orally taught lesson by asking students to repeat one or two key vocabulary terms included, and/or one or two main points. When a teacher has told older students they will be assigned a paper as part of a unit, once the class has completed enough reading, teacher lessons, lectures, classwork, discussions, etc., the teacher can have students write and turn in outlines for the papers they will write. Summative assessments are conducted after instruction. They may evaluate learning from a unit, semester, or school year.

Teachers use these to determine course grades, student grade promotion, and evaluate class, grade, and school achievement compared to those of other schools for accountability purposes. For example, grading final exams, critiquing senior music recitals or art projects, etc. help determine final course grades.

Research finds that formative assessment reduces learning gaps. It also helps teachers design instruction targeting specific learning goals; supporting student learning; monitoring student progress; identifying strengths, needs, learning gains; differentiating instruction; evaluating instructional effectiveness; informing and adjusting ongoing instruction; promoting effective teaching practices; enhancing learning for struggling students, ELLs, and students with disabilities; improving all student learning outcomes; augmenting coherence through alignment or connection with state comprehensive assessment systems; and reforming curricula. Hence federal legislation like the Elementary and Secondary Education Act (ESEA, aka No Child Left Behind, or NCLB), the Individuals with Disabilities Education Act (IDEA), and state policies promote using formative assessment to narrow learning gaps. Researchers find: (1) to identify learning gaps, educators must understand differences between what students know and need to know to design instructional support enabling student progress toward learning goals. (2) Teachers must give clear, detailed feedback designed to close instructional gaps. Reciprocal teacher-student feedback informs student learning status and next instructional steps. (3) Active student involvement in learning and assessments, and student-teacher collaboration to develop shared knowledge regarding current learning status and actions needed for progress develop student skills for self-monitoring and knowing when they need help. (4) Teachers must break down major learning goals into smaller learning progression components to locate students on the skill set continuum required for mastering learning standards.

Diagnostic assessment

Whereas formative assessment is conducted during instruction and summative assessment is conducted after instruction, diagnostic assessment is conducted before instruction. Also called pre-assessments, these frequently focus upon one domain or area. Administering diagnostic assessments can give educators information about previous knowledge each student has about a subject. This informs teachers where to begin their instruction for all students in the same class to access it without experiencing either significant knowledge gaps or significant repetition of things they already know. Pre-assessments also inform teachers of existing student misconceptions to correct during instruction. And they establish student knowledge baselines to compare knowledge following instruction to assess learning and instructional effectiveness. Teachers can use diagnostic assessment results to inform their development of lesson plans, and also differentiated instruction for individual students within classes to meet their specific needs best. Pre-assessments also gauge student preparation during sequential learning, e.g., after teaching the Coriolis effect, teachers might determine student concept retention through diagnostic pre-assessment; and refresh or reteach as needed, before they proceed to begin teaching a unit about ocean currents.

Multiple-choice tests and oral questioning

Multiple-choice tests have stems—usually questions, sometimes statements—and several answer choices. One answer is correct, others incorrect; in some formats, there is more than one correct answer. These are efficiently, easily administered to large classes. They can be scored by teaching assistants, machines, or computer programs. These are effective to measure memory, knowledge, convergent thinking, and problem-solving in convergent subjects; but not when "correct" answers are equivocal, ambiguous, or disputable. Writing wrong answers reflecting common misconceptions or errors enables diagnostic value from wrong-answer pattern analyses. However, students cannot elaborate on topics. High-quality tests are harder to write than some teachers realize. Overuse can lead students to memorize separate pieces of information instead of developing overall subject understanding. Oral questioning is the most common classroom assessment. Teachers can use hypotheticals ("What would you have done if...?"), get explanations and reasons for specific student practices, challenge practices, and check understanding of underlying concepts or principles not directly observed. Not requiring reading and writing is often more inclusive and less discriminatory. It applies highly to assessing spoken, not written language. It is more valid than reliable, and time-intensive, indicating standard questions for summative assessments or multiple assessors. Recording is required for permanent documentation, which has its own considerations. Experts advise asking students' opinions of lessons and activities before questioning, for highest information quantity and quality.

Different assessment formats

For making preschool and kindergarten placement decisions, developmental scales are useful for assessing their developmental levels in various domains. These tests are also helpful in comparing developmental levels to age norms for diagnosing developmental delays. Developmental scale results then also become useful for designing instructional objectives whereby teachers can help children with developmental delays to reach or approximate normal development. When assessing students with significant disabilities, it is important to assess their adaptive well as intellectual functioning, as these sometimes differ widely. This also informs the levels, types, and weights of instruction for each. When older students are new to a school, diagnostic pre-assessments help educators evaluate their prior knowledge to determine classroom placement and where to begin instruction. When educational records are incomplete or unavailable, new assessments help determine intelligence, literacy levels, strengths and difficulties in specific academic subjects, etc. Standardized tests like ACT and SAT differentiate student verbal vs. quantitative abilities. For example, when a student more verbally than numerically gifted used a 166-point gap between verbal and quantitative SAT scores to justify her math struggles, her guidance counselor responded that her quantitative score nevertheless indicated she should be performing better in math.

Student self-assessment

Self-assessment promotes student reflective and metacognitive skills development, critical thinking in analyzing and judging effectiveness of teacher instructional practices and student learning strategies, and helps teachers identify and understand individual student differences to make their instruction more responsive to student needs. Having students create or contribute to rubrics defining success in group discussions, multimodal presentations, reading response tasks, etc. augments learning levels. Having students create and agree to learning contracts when beginning units engages students in defining learning goals, agreed activities, and products as evidence of learning. Teachers have students revisit contracts frequently during units to document new learning, identify points needing clarification, and obtain teacher or classmate feedback. Teachers can designate a classroom area for "muddy points," questions, or topics that students want the class to revisit. Teachers can build student learning ownership by periodically asking students to choose an item from this board. In the "nameless voice" method, teachers have students submit work samples anonymously for class sharing and discussion of similarities and differences with their understandings. Having students write end-of-unit letters to future students explaining what they learned, tips for learning, working with difficult texts, etc. This promotes both reflection and feedback on student thinking and learning.

Because student needs vary widely, educators must differentiate content, processes, and products of learning for individual student readiness, learning styles, and interests. Also, because of this student diversity, more than one record and voice are needed to recognize and report student growth, development, and learning needs. Moreover, research finds both conducting ongoing assessment and engaging students as partners in their learning and assessment vital. When students must analyze their own thinking and learning critically, they become more motivated to learn; they develop metacognitive skills, enhancing their engagement across subject areas and supporting lifelong learning motivation. When ongoing assessment is used to inform and adjust ongoing instruction, both students and teachers reap benefits of additional knowledge about what students do and do not understand from student feedback. However, students commonly lack the experience, training, and expertise to conduct assessments as teachers can. They obviously are less objective than others when assessing themselves. Individual student differences cause corresponding self-assessment differences, whereas one teacher's assessments of all students may be more uniform. Teacher assessments must accompany self-assessments, to standardize evaluation across students and mitigate self-interested, self-destructive, or overly subjective results.

Peer assessment

Constructivist and active learning theories provide foundations and support for peer assessment. By assigning peer assessment, teachers can empower students to take responsibility for and manage their own learning. They can help students learn assessment techniques and develop lifelong assessment skills. Peer assessment leads to exchanges of ideas and diffusion of knowledge among students, enhancing all individual students' learning. Teachers can also motivate students to engage in more depth with course materials by having them assess one another's learning. Teachers can incorporate peer assessment by identifying activities and assignments wherein peer feedback could benefit students. They can include peer assessment opportunities at different stages of larger assignments, e.g., an outline, first draft, second draft, etc. of a paper. Teachers should create rubrics or guidelines defining tasks clearly for students conducting peer reviews; and use learning exercises to introduce rubrics to assure student abilities for effective rubric applications. Peer reviews can be in-class, homework, online, etc.; teachers should determine these. Teachers must also model constructive criticism, appropriateness, and descriptive feedback in their own responses to inform peer assessment. Including small-group feedback sessions enables recipients to question, and peer reviewers to explain, written comments to recipients.

Before assigning peer assessment, teachers should explain to students the benefits and expectations of the peer review process. One disadvantage is that student relationships and interactions can influence peer review to be personal or subjective. Teachers can keep student work anonymous for peer review, making feedback more objective. Students inexperienced with peer assessment may not know what kinds of feedback are or are not useful and why or why not. Teachers can address this by giving students feedback on their feedback to classmates. They can also give examples to students of feedback with different levels of quality, and discuss with students which are more or less useful and the reasons why. To impart structure, norms, and appropriateness, teachers should provide time limits and clear direction for in-class peer review, and define deadlines for homework peer review assignments. Peer assessments are more valid when students are more familiar with and take more ownership of criteria, so teachers should engage students in discussing designated criteria. Teachers should offer necessary input and guidance during group feedback discussions. Peer assessment is better assigned for academic tasks that students have experience with, not professional tasks. To encourage more individual responsibility, avoid letting multiple students assess identical tasks.

Interpreting student assessment scores

In general, a student's raw score on a statewide assessment equals the number of items that a student answered correctly. Raw scores can only be meaningfully interpreted relative to both the total number of items on the assessment and the raw scores of other students in the same grade. Raw scores must not be compared among different test administrations since minor variations in the test can result in widely varying average performances. With the limitations of the raw score, many assessments use a horizontal scale score allowing score comparison by adjusting for varying test form difficulty in different administrations. Using the horizontal scale score, educators can compare student cohorts (age and grade groups) taking the same subject or grade assessment in different years, compare individual students taking the same subject or grade assessment, and identify satisfactory or advanced performance. A vertical scale score, meanwhile, allows educators to measure student progress across subjects or grades.

Communicating assessment results to students and parents

Experts recommend two steps in reporting assessment results to students: an initial briefing for the whole class or group tested; and then follow-up meetings with individual students, focusing on how teachers will meet their needs. Briefings should include an overview of the assessment program and instruments; how teachers, school, and districts use test results; the process for reviewing results with individual students; which results students receive; and any plans for recognizing outstanding assessment performance. Follow-up meetings should include assessed student strengths and needs, how these relate to other student information from other tests and/or teacher observations, and the plan of action recommended for addressing individual student needs. Teachers and school administrators should jointly report results to parents to build active partnerships for student learning. Individual parent-teacher conferences are ideal for explaining individual student results, reporting school-wide performance, answering parent questions, and explaining instructional improvement initiatives. If these are impossible, teachers can provide written reports carefully describing assessment processes and procedures, explaining how to interpret results, and including contact information for questions. Parent group meetings are alternatives if individual meetings are impossible. Parent newsletter articles describing assessment, scoring, overall school placement, improvement initiatives, FAQs, etc. are additional communication options.

Getting students engaged in class activities and increasing their on-task times

Seating arrangements appropriate to the specific activity enhance engagement and on-task time. Choosing course materials relevant to students, and emphasizing how they can apply the learning in real life, enables students to connect activities with prior knowledge and their lives. Students view schoolwork meaningful to them as more valuable, important, and worth the effort. Giving students some control and choice in learning, e.g., self-monitoring and self-evaluating progress or choice of paired or individual work, increases sense of autonomy, hence engagement. Assigning achievable yet challenging tasks for all students, including those with disabilities, at-risk, remedial, etc. enable students to feel successful, and to believe that they earned their success. Repetitive, rote tasks and seemingly impossible ones both discourage engagement. "Mystery" approaches give students partial or contradictory information and require they develop hypotheses based on available evidence, piquing their curiosity. This also fulfills needs for autonomy, competence, self-directed inquiry, and independent discovery. Assignments only teachers will read are unilateral: teachers typically do not need the information that students submit. Contrastingly, designing cooperative learning and other projects enabling students to share new knowledge with peers promotes reciprocal relationships, making learning activities more engaging.

Unanticipated learning opportunities

According to some experts, effective early childhood development programs combine adult-guided and child-guided educational activities. Adult-guided activities include active, significant roles for children; child-guided activities include intentional adult roles in which adults take advantage of both learning experiences they planned, and unexpected opportunities for learning. For example, consider the preschool teacher whose class collected acorns outdoors and brought them back into the classroom. The teacher observes two children playing with the acorns. One child divides the acorns into two halves. She spreads her half out into a long row and clusters the other child's half into a pile. The second child becomes upset that she has more acorns than he has. The teacher asks the children how they could find out whether they each have the same number of acorns. Prompted by this intentional question, the second child gets the idea of counting both groups of acorns. The teacher observes, gives supportive comments, and asks thoughtful questions. The children discover they have the same number of acorns despite their arrangements and appearances. This teacher used an unexpected opportunity, helping two children normally in Piaget's preoperational stage of cognitive development to achieve an insight associated with Piaget's later concrete operations stage.

Progress maps

When teachers find traditional test results do not give students the feedback they need to understand and correct their errors, they can design classroom assessments to help students organize their learning goals. This involves establishing benchmarks to use as criteria in rubrics; identifying transfer levels as referents for rubric expertise levels; making individual student progress maps, plotting their scores over time, and giving them feedback customized according to their developmental or expertise levels; plotting collective student scores on aggregate progress maps, and planning future learning opportunities in response to score clusters and deviations; and informing student self-reflection and personal goal-setting by embedding these progress maps into students' electronic portfolios. Progress maps describe knowledge, skills, and understandings in their typical developmental sequence, depicting longitudinal improvement in specific subjects and domains by organizing longitudinal assessment data according to subject knowledge and skill continua. They include initial baseline assessment data, e.g., at the beginning of a school year, relative to associated standards; and subsequent formative assessments throughout the year according to developmental benchmark criteria. Their visual nature enables quick, easy appraisal of student progress toward subject content standards. Technology makes data collection, organization, and storage most efficient.

Integrating technology

Examining patterns of teacher and student use of technology can show whether and/or to what degree technology is integrated into their teaching and learning environment. For example, an indication related to teacher activity is use patterns, e.g., the percentage of teachers using computer technologies for a variety of instructional and instruction-related tasks, including locating instructional resources; accessing resources and libraries online; downloading curriculum materials; communicating and networking with colleagues and other professionals; using computers to create instructional tasks, visuals, and/or materials; collaborating with remote teachers and classrooms on projects; communicating with parents; and publishing instructional materials online. Student use patterns, e.g., the percentage of students using computer technologies for various learning and instruction-related tasks, is another indicator of technology integration in the learning environment. Student instruction-related tasks include performing calculations; gathering information from varied sources; information organization and storage; collecting experimental or investigational data; making measurements; analyzing, interpreting, or manipulating data and information to draw conclusions, generate questions, discover relationships; reporting or communicating results, information, or conclusions; creating visual information or data displays; interacting or communicating with classmates, schoolmates, and others outside school; producing audiovisual presentations; composing, editing, and publishing text; creating original art, music, or graphics; publishing materials or projects remotely; and developing understanding of abstract or complex concepts and materials.

Rubrics and analytical checklists

A rubric defines in advance a specific behavior(s), skill(s), or task(s) to perform. It supplies basic guidelines for performing task components and criteria for successful performance of each component. Rubrics also typically define general performance ranges and levels, e.g., unsatisfactory, satisfactory, or excellent, briefly describing each level's characteristics. Teachers and/or students can create rubrics or select from existing ones. The teacher should first go over the rubric with students, explaining what each part means, demonstrating when necessary. Then the teacher directs students to follow the rubric as a guide in performing the task. Finally, the teacher uses the rubric's criteria to assess student work. Advantages include combining learning objectives, associated tasks, performance guidance, and task evaluation criteria; and brevity, conciseness, and clarity. Disadvantages include assigning performance levels, not more precise grades or percentages; and perhaps not lending themselves to more detailed assignments. Analytical checklists pre-define certain behaviors, skills, and tasks; teachers check observation of their presence or absence. Advantages include saving time and effort by pre-listing tasks, behaviors, and skills, enabling quick and easy assessment; and making assessment uniform across students in terms of tasks and components. Disadvantages include not identifying additional valuable accomplishments observed (without additional notes); and sometimes limiting assessment to Yes/No formats, though some checklists do incorporate performance levels like rubrics.

Scoring guides, anecdotal notes, and continua

Scoring guides are typically issued by authors of specific standardized assessment instruments to help teachers and testers score their tests. An obvious advantage of such a scoring guide is that it instructs scorers to follow procedures and interpretations designed by the authors, minimizing chances that scoring will be inaccurate, inappropriate, or interpreted incorrectly. Also, scoring guides do not force assigning specific responses specific scores, but allow some flexibility to use judgment according to individual student responses and test conditions within a reasonable range. Disadvantages include guideline misinterpretation or misapplication by users lacking experience or good judgment. Anecdotal notes have advantages of recording teacher observations of individual student behaviors often not included in standard checklists or test instruments; and collecting information outside of as well as during assessment, which can contribute to valuable insights. Disadvantages include lack of standardization, norms, or criteria for comparison unless a recording teacher includes these; and often, lack of supporting context. Continua offer the advantages of avoiding the limitations of discrete grades, percentages, and numbers, enabling more precise and individualized evaluative description; and more realistic, accurate performance ranges than exact numbers or cutoff scores. Disadvantages include difficulty comparing scores within or among students, classes, and schools without exact numbers, making continua more applicable to individualized than standardized assessment.

Standardized tests of ability and of achievement

Some standardized tests measure abilities, such as intelligence quotient (IQ) tests, which are the most prominent examples; tests of creativity, of divergent thinking (considered a key element of creativity); and more domain-specific abilities, e.g., verbal, numerical, quantitative, spatial abilities, memory, etc., which are often included as subscales on standardized IQ tests. Ability tests do not indicate or necessarily even predict student school grades. They only indicate what a student is capable of, i.e., they gauge competence, not performance. In addition to abilities, some tests measure levels of mental health constructs, e.g., Beck's Depression Inventory and Anxiety Inventory. In contrast to ability and competence or mental and emotional states, standardized achievement tests measure what students actually achieve rather than what they are capable of achieving. Standardized achievement tests are summative evaluations typically given at the ends of school years, not formative evaluations made during instruction. They test what students have learned and can demonstrate knowing and doing. This allows educators to compare individual student progress across years, compare students to peers, and compare their school to others.

Standardized aptitude tests

One thing that most standardized aptitude tests share in common with most standardized ability tests is that both types of instruments measure potential rather than accomplishment. For example, IQ tests measure intellectual ability in various cognitive domains, but not how students perform academically—i.e., what grades they actually get in school. Similarly, aptitude tests measure student interest and ability for certain subject areas and domains—not specifically IQ or cognitive levels, but how inclined a student is toward certain activities or areas of interest. Some tests evaluate broader domain aptitudes, e.g., for numerical or mathematical thinking and activities, verbal or literary thinking and activities, etc. Others evaluate interest and ability for more specific activities, e.g., preference tests often used in career counseling with high school students. While these identify discrete interest areas, when some tests combine responses, they may produce strange results not accurately reflecting the whole person or even applicable career directions, e.g., a student whose responses indicated liking books and nature received results recommending careers of librarian or forest ranger—neither was appropriate. Aptitude and preference tests, like IQ tests, differ from achievement tests by testing competence, ability, and interests; achievement tests evaluate learning a student has achieved and can demonstrate.

Norm-referenced tests

Norm-referenced tests are standardized tests that provide pre-established norms for student scores on given tests. Before publishing or marketing standardized tests, e.g., national or statewide achievement tests, test authors typically administer their test to groups of students they have selected as samples representative of the larger intended test-taking student population. They then conduct and publish statistical analyses of the scores received by students in the sample groups. These show what the average score or range of scores is, the proportion of students receiving this average, and the distribution of all other scores on the test. Once a test is statistically proven valid and reliable and is published, educators who administer it can compare their students' scores to the established norms supplied with the instrument. This enables school administrators and teachers to compare their students' average and individual performance on the achievement test to the performance of the students in the norm samples. Because the sample students were selected as representative of the national or statewide student population, their scores provide norms against which educators can compare their students' performance. Such comparisons are typically used to satisfy federal and state legal accountability requirements for all schools receiving federal funds to educate their students adequately.

Criterion-referenced tests

Whereas norm-referenced tests provide established norms in the form of average scores, all scores, and score distribution of students selected as samples representative of the larger student population, to which educators can compare their own students' scores, criterion-referenced tests do not compare student results to norms or other students. Instead, they compare student results to some pre-established criterion or criteria. Test authors have selected criteria to indicate successful student performance on each item tested. Criteria can include minimum percentage or number out of a total of correct items; minimum number of attributes included in responses; descriptions of required detail, clarity, and/or other features which responses must match or approximate; in some tests, rates of speed, e.g., assessments of oral reading or speaking fluency; or other criteria specific to the skills or learning being evaluated. Student result data from criterion-referenced tests can be used for formative assessment to monitor student progress, evaluate instructional effectiveness and adjust instruction; and/or as parts of summative assessment to demonstrate students have achieved pre-defined learning objectives, in addition to norm-referenced measures.

Validity, reliability, raw scores, and scaled scores

Validity in testing means that a test instrument measures what it intends and/or claims to measure. For example, a test validated for educational diagnosis and/or placement could be completely invalid for determining high school graduation. However, the same test might be used for both purposes on the condition that the test has been validated for both. Reliability is consistency, i.e., whether a test yields similar results over repeated administrations. Internal consistency is reliability determined by administering two forms of the same test concurrently and finding they correlate. If one such form is given to students and the other form to the same students a month later—eliminating practice and memory effects from giving the same form both times—and they achieve similar scores in both administrations, this establishes test-retest reliability. Tests can be valid but not reliable, or reliable but not valid. Raw scores are students' actual scores on test scales, e.g., number or percentage correct. Scaled scores convert raw scores to common scales permitting numerical comparison, of individual student progress across semesters and years, among students in subject areas, etc. Scaled scores typically vary within tests among different content-area subscales.

Standard deviation, mean, median, mode, grade-equivalent scores, and age-equivalent score

Percentile is a statistical ranking method indicating a score or value below which a specified percentage of scores falls within a group. For example, if a student's test score is in the 90th percentile, this means s/he scored higher than 90 percent of other students in the group tested. Standard deviation (SD or σ) is the "mean of the mean," measuring score, data dispersion, variance, or spread. Numerically, SD equals the square root of variance. SDs nearer to 0 indicate all data points clustered close to the average; higher SDs indicate wider distribution. The mean is the average of a data set or score distribution. The median is the middle score in a distribution. The mode is the value or number occurring most frequently in a distribution. Grade-equivalent (GE) scores indicate where on a continuum a student's test score falls. For example, if a 9th-grade student scores a 10.5 GE, this represents the raw score typical of a student in the fifth month of 10th grade. Age-equivalent (AE) scores are based on student age, not grade. For example, for a student aged 7.5 years, a 6 AE score indicates performance typical of a 6-year-old. GE and AE scores should only be used as comparative or relative, not absolute assessment measures.

Analytic scoring

Analytic scoring separately evaluates and scores discrete writing features, e.g., concise concept expression, creativity, grammar, punctuation, etc. Teachers may average these scores, but more often weigh them by relative importance. Analytic scoring helps teachers consider all writing elements, preventing them from, for example, giving too low a grade because of poor mechanics to an essay with excellent concept expression or problem analysis. By enabling final score breakdowns and teacher comments, it diagnoses areas needing improvement to guide further student efforts. Disadvantages include being time-intensive for teachers, not all students reading their teacher comments, and not using those teacher comments to benefit future assignments. Also, negative feedback, particularly combined with unclear or confrontational comments, can be counterproductive to student development. Written analytic scales define grading criteria and expectations for students. Teachers should weigh criteria by importance, e.g., if an assignment's goal is learning course information, then ideas, organization, and/or logic outweigh grammar and mechanics. Comments should balance challenge with support. Teachers should avoid confrontational practices like sarcastic comments; crossing, scribbling, or blocking out student work; etc.

Holistic scoring

When teachers have many essays to grade, holistic scoring is less time-consuming than analytic scoring, which divides writing into various components to score separately, deriving the composite score by weighing components according to assignment goals and purposes. Holistic scoring also enables multi-grader scoring. The original teacher chooses at least three student essays which, according to the teacher's criteria based on the learning objectives for the assignment, represent average, high, or low achievement. Using these as models, the teacher and other graders assess many essays written by a class (or classes) of students. Holistic scoring is found highly reliable and consistent as a method of scoring student writing. Because it takes so much less time than analytic scoring, holistic scoring is more efficient. Disadvantages include that, although scores are reliable, individual students are not necessarily informed of specific reasons for their grades. Most teachers write some final comment to give students some idea why their essays were worse, better, or similar to model essays. However, detailed comments throughout as formative feedback for student improvement are not provided as with analytic scoring. Holistic scoring is also most useful for two or more graders and can be impracticable for single instructors.

Explaining tests and results to parents and students

A common parental question is why their children were tested. Educators can explain to parents that standardized tests can identify their child's school strengths as well as areas where their child may need to improve. They can also evaluate and improve their child's school and the entire school district to provide better education. Educators should also tell parents their children are never evaluated based on a single test, and any assessment program is one among multiple tools evaluating student performance. Some parents are bewildered by scores like percentiles, stanines, grade-equivalent scores, etc. Teachers can help clarify these. For example, "stanine" refers to "standard nine," meaning that on a scale from 1-9, a score of 1-3 is below average, 4-6 is average, and 7-9 is above average. Percentiles tell what percentage of students scored below that percentile. Teachers should explain to parents that a score in the 75th percentile does not mean their child got 75 percent of test items correct; rather, it means their child scored higher than 75 percent of other students in the test group. If a student gets an 8th-grade-equivalent score on a 5th-grade reading achievement test, parents may think their child is ready for 8th-grade material; however, teachers should explain this means their child reads 5th-grade material as well as a typical 8th-grader.

When educators explain the meanings of scores like stanines, percentiles, and grade-level equivalents to parents, they should also explain that these are derived by comparing their child's scores with those of a comparison group, which may be a sample of students representative of the national population or the other students in the school district who took the test at the same time. Discussing a student's test scores relative to other students' scores makes test results most meaningful for parents: teachers can tell them how their child is different and/or similar to others in the group. Parents most often want to know what test scores mean. Teachers should compare student test scores with daily classwork before parent conferences to ensure scores match. Differences can be attributable to subscale scores. For example, a student's overall reading test score may seem adequate in the 75th percentile; but the student's subscale score in comprehension might be in the 85th percentile but in the 65th percentile for vocabulary, indicating need for vocabulary improvement. To track progress, teachers should compare students' present to past scores with parents whenever possible.

When explaining test results to younger students, teachers should avoid technical terms that the students will not understand. They can simplify while preserving general accuracy. For example, rather than telling a young child s/he scored in the 95th percentile, a teacher can say s/he did better than most of the other students. Even among parents, audiences vary, influencing how teachers should communicate test results. For example, if a parent is an educator and/or psychometrist, the teacher can likely give percentiles, stanines, grade-level and age-level equivalents without having to explain them. Such knowledgeable parents may only want to know which comparison group was used; or how their child's score compares to a larger, national comparison group, etc. However, for parents with completely unrelated backgrounds, occupations, or little formal schooling, teachers may omit technical terms entirely or give parents concise, clear definitions of them; either way, be prepared to offer a common-sense equivalent, e.g., their child is doing similarly, better, much better, or worse than most other students in the class, group, or school.

Some parents' cultures and/or countries view education as more unilateral and authoritarian than in America. They may punish children for low test scores; and/or avoid helping children with homework, studying, or getting involved in school, viewing these as inappropriately challenging school and teacher authority. In some cultures, students typically receive few years of formal education; parents from these cultures may have lower expectations for children's educational achievement. Regarding English language proficiency test results, some immigrant families want to abandon their native languages as soon as possible to acquire English, discouraging children from using L1s. When these children are still too young for verbal fluency, this can hinder their proficiency in either language. Educators can explain how L1 proficiency contributes to L2 acquisition. Some parental attitudes positively influence English learning. Parents in communities lacking opportunities for independent English learning have positive attitudes toward English acquisition. Most immigrants, viewing literacy positively as key to succeeding in America, want to learn how to help their children in school. While preserving native cultures and languages, many parents also want to participate in mainstream US culture. Many cultural family structures are stronger and more involved than in America; collective commitment to family exceeds individual motivations.

Curriculum scope and sequence

In curriculum design, curriculum scope is the breadth and depth in which it covers content in each subject; clearly identified learning objectives reflecting local, state, and national standards; or how coherent curriculum is made through instructing basic concepts across several years of content coverage. Scope includes both how much material teachers must cover on any specified topic, and how much teachers should expect students to accomplish resulting from instruction. Sequence is the order in which scope is taught. If educators fail to structure curriculum scope and sequence deliberately, they risk having students miss significant learning when instruction is delivered without adequate planning. As examples, elementary school teachers might use a curriculum organizer table or chart where they enter titles and descriptions of each learning unit by time period, and the subject focus of each unit (e.g., arranged horizontally in columns). In the first column, before the series of units per time period, they can label cells vertically to enter main ideas, i.e., core student understandings; key concepts and questions to focus learning; teacher focus, i.e., unit goals like language development, group work, a culminating activity, etc.; fundamental content; subject foci, e.g., literacy, math, and respective programs, tasks, texts, and resources to use.

Whereas scope represents breadth and depth of content coverage and learning objectives, sequence represents presenting material in logical order. Sequencing reflects the philosophy that students should be instructed starting with concrete concepts, becoming progressively more abstract throughout successive grade levels. After establishing scope, educators must determine when to teach it. This is important when certain learning is often dependent on previous other knowledge, e.g., understanding certain science or geography concepts requires certain numeracy skills. Even when some learning experiences are not reliant on mastering prerequisite knowledge, curricula may be sequenced instead according to increasing complexity, e.g., in science subjects; logical progression, e.g., from the local environment to the global environment in social studies; or psychological valence, e.g., from immediate to more distant interests in vocational education. Teachers must carefully sequence instruction, both within and across key learning areas (KLAs). For example, "reading effectively" would precede "writing effectively" in a curriculum sequence represented by a curriculum map showing English Language Arts (ELAs) taught by KLA because receptive language like listening and reading develops before expressive language like speaking and writing. Critical text interpretation follows reading and writing. Similarly, understanding and applying numbers precedes selecting and utilizing measures.

The scope of a curriculum refers to all of the content it will include within a specified length of time. The curriculum sequence refers to at which points during the time range specific parts of the scope of learning will occur. In other words, educators must decide which content should be taught during certain grade levels, or to certain classes or student groups. Teachers must also determine sequencing within work units, courses, and school years. Hence scope and sequence support maximal student learning, as well as providing continual opportunities for students to learn. By coordinating the scope of curriculum content and the sequence of curriculum instruction, educators give order to their delivery of curricular content. For teaching and learning to be effective, the important parts of all subjects must be included in scope, and must be delivered in the right order for students to benefit. By mapping curriculum scope, teachers can ensure they integrate the state and district learning standards guiding their curriculum. By mapping sequence, they can ensure they address curricular principles as well as matching knowledge prerequisites, increasing complexity, logical progression, psychological preferences, or other factors influencing temporal order.

Curriculum scope and sequence work together to furnish instruction with an organized structure which enables students to receive the maximum numbers of opportunities to learn and to take advantage of these to learn the most that they can. For educators to overlook important parts of subject content instruction is entirely too easy without the organizing structure of curriculum scope and sequence. It is also much more difficult to deliver instruction depending on previous learning, and avoid repeating material over grade levels, without planning sequence in advance. Most states develop scope and sequence directly from state-level standards. Some school districts design curriculum frameworks, which provide the scope of content and sequence in which to teach it. It is also popular for state education departments and district curriculum departments to divide learning sequences into developmental strands or bands. A common method of organizing a curriculum scope is to divide it into key learning areas (KLAs) or integrated themes used as curriculum organizers. Depending on their size, structure, and sector, different schools approach curriculum scope and sequence development through different processes. Some states define scope and sequence in certain subjects, but leave this to individual districts in others.

Standards-based learning

In standards-based education, all grade levels and subjects have clear learning goals; all instruction and assessment are aligned to these because the strongest school-level influence on student achievement is opportunity to learn: students are unlikely to learn specific content without opportunity. Students are given multiple opportunities to demonstrate achievement because reading, math, social studies, and science should be treated like PE and music: poor initial performances do not receive low grades, but rather require repeated practice until students master the skills. Formative assessments, giving feedback and promoting growth, are emphasized because research shows effective feedback is the strongest single classroom instructional change increasing learning and achievement. Rubrics and scoring guides are consistently employed because they enable teachers to give students better, criterion-referenced feedback about specific skill and knowledge levels, not merely norm-referenced feedback via percentage scores. This helps teachers evaluate their learning objectives as well as advance student achievement. Teachers regularly report student progress toward learning goals because specific, formative, more frequent feedback than annual standardized tests critically affects teacher conscientiousness and effectiveness with initiatives developing new reporting practices and forms; with instructing, assessing, and encouraging students; and student success. Instructional activities represent the "how," standards the "what" and "why" of school programs.

The US Department of Education (ED) funds and supports high curriculum standards in public schools, but does not itself develop them; individual state education departments do. ED has given over $350 million in funds to a consortium of the Council of Chief State School Officers and National Governors Association for developing the Common Core State Standards (CCSS). Most US states have voluntarily chosen to adopt these standards. The CCSS has a website with information. Additional sites with information on federal support of other state educational initiatives include a site on the Elementary and Secondary Education Act (ESEA, also known as No Child Left Behind, or NCLB) flexibility, whereby ED enables states to develop their own accountability systems; sites about the federal Race to the Top initiative and its assessment; and a webpage with US Secretary of Education Arne Duncan's speech about high standards. CCSS are concepts students should know and understand; school districts develop specific curricula, and teachers plan specific lessons, to help students master standards. Districts and schools have traditionally had printed copies of their state standards; today, these are typically also published online, the easiest way for teachers to access them—including any updates, which can be posted electronically more easily and frequently than printed.

While the abundance of federal-level and state-level curriculum standards might seem to facilitate teachers' preparing relevant classroom curricula, it can overwhelm educators trying to design standards-based learning units. However, teachers discover that standards enable more curricular focus, refinement of their previous work, clearer communication of expectations to students, and enhanced learning—provided some model and processes for classroom standards application, many of which are available today. Standards articulate clear expectations for what all students should know and be able to do—regardless of gender, minority status, socioeconomic status, history of academic success (or failure), and previous access or lack thereof to any kinds of educational opportunities—while addressing school constituencies' varying needs. Standards give states common referents for assuring coordinated functioning of educational system components across schools and districts; offer parents, businesses, and community stakeholders a common language for discussing educational processes and communicate shared learning expectations, enabling more effective partnering in education; provide impetus and focus for new school programs and innovations in organizing content, delivering instruction, and planning assessment; make teachers design more intentional, purposeful learning of important content; and for all students, clearly identify performance expectations and means for meeting them; promote more equitable, challenging, and rewarding experiences; and improve performance.

Cognitive, affective, and psychomotor domains

The cognitive domain represents mental skills, i.e., facts, information, ideas, and concepts that one can learn, understand, and apply. Among knowledge, skills, and attitudes that a learner can acquire, the cognitive domain corresponds most to *knowledge*. The affective domain represents emotional *attitudes* that one can develop and apply, with respect to the self and others. The psychomotor domain represents physical *skills* that one can learn and apply. For example, when a student reads some information about physical exercise, understands it, analyzes it, compares it with other information sources, judges it according to established criteria, and writes a paper about it, these activities are in the cognitive domain. When this student finds value in exercise knowledge, demonstrates this by voluntarily participating in athletic events, and becomes an accomplished athlete in a certain sport, these activities are in the affective domain. When this student watches, copies, practices, and perfects the specific physical skills required for his or her preferred sport, these activities are in the psychomotor domain.

Bloom's taxonomy

Bloom's 1950s taxonomy originally included levels or categories of knowledge, i.e., recalling learned information; comprehension, i.e., grasping, restating, and explaining meaning; application of knowledge to new and different situations; analysis, i.e., separating components of material and showing relationships among components; synthesis, i.e., bringing separate concepts and ideas together to create new wholes and relationships; and evaluation, i.e., judging the value or worth of information according to established criteria. Anderson and Krathwohl's 2001 revision changed these nouns to verbs: remember, understand, apply, analyze, evaluate, and create—also switching the order of evaluate from after synthesis to before create. Instructional objectives should include learning activities that address each of these categories, sequenced correspondingly from remembering to creating to reflect the hierarchy's progressively increasing difficulty. Krathwohl and Bloom's taxonomy in the affective domain covers receiving, or attending to something; responding, or showing new behaviors influenced by experience; valuing, or showing definitive commitment or involvement; organization, or integrating new values into priorities; characterization by value, or behaving consistently with new values. Dave (1970), Simpson (1972), and Harrow (1972)'s psychomotor taxonomies include observing a physical action or event; imitating another's action; practicing repeatedly; and adapting, i.e., fine-tuning performance. In all three domains, these taxonomies progress sequentially from basic to higher levels, as corresponding instructional objectives should.

Observable behavior

Educational interest in observable behaviors was influenced by behaviorist learning theory, which proposed that because internal mental or emotional states could not be externally observed or measured, the study and modification of behavior should be confined to observable behaviors, i.e., actions or states of being that others could outwardly observe an individual producing. However, because only observable behaviors could be accurately measured, these were the only kind that could be changed through behavior modification techniques based on operant conditioning principles. In applying Bloom's taxonomy to cognitive learning objectives, the same proposition is embraced in that only action verbs are appropriate. For example, under the second category of Understanding, the verb *understand* itself is not found because it is internal, hence impossible to quantify; action verbs under Understand include *describe, differentiate, discuss, cite examples of, demonstrate use of, identify, select, tell*, etc. Thus a good instructional objective would not require a student simply to know or remember something, which requires assuming the student knows or remembers, but rather to *recall, name, list,* or *repeat* it because these demonstrate the student's knowledge and memory in ways that others can observe.

Measurable outcomes

Learning objectives must be not only observable, meaning teachers and others can see, hear, or otherwise observe evidence a student has learned something; but also measurable, meaning there is some way to quantify the behavior demonstrating learning. Behaviorist learning theory pointed out only observable behaviors can be measured, therefore changed. As a corollary, it has demonstrated that by nature, observable behaviors can nearly always be measured because if people can observe another's behavior, they can also find a way of measuring it. To be measurable, outcomes or results must be specific. For example, "The student will use correct grammar" is not measurable because it is too vague, not specifying what or whether all or some percentage of grammar must be correct, etc. But the objective "The student, given a sentence written in the present or past tense, will be able to rewrite it in future tense with no contradictions (e.g., 'I will see them yesterday') or errors in tense" is a measurable objective, specifying the condition (given a sentence written in present or past tense) and behavior (rewrite it in future tense). These are elements of the ABCD method—*audience, behavior, conditions, degree of mastery* required (e.g. 100 percent, 95 percent, 90 percent, etc.).

Evaluating technological and other instructional resources

State education departments typically publish guidelines for their districts to evaluate instructional materials according to state criteria, aligned with state content standards and curriculum frameworks for each subject. In some instances, educators tasked with evaluating new instructional materials for certain subject domains (e.g., mathematics or science) and/or grade levels (e.g., preschool, elementary, middle, or high school), after studying various sets of evaluation criteria, found them all inadequate and decided to develop their own criteria instead. Some examples of elements found important to address and overlooked by existing criteria include: need for more authentic assessment practices within the materials evaluated; evaluation criteria focusing on technology's overall role in a specific instructional unit, rather than only criteria for evaluating individual pieces of technology; and criteria for evaluating whether an instructional unit is practical, e.g., whether teachers in schools with typical insufficient funding, overloaded classrooms, long hours, etc. can effectively implement the materials. Educators have consulted resources like standards published by national organizations for their discipline, e.g., the National Council of Teachers of Mathematics, National Council of Teachers of English; research articles and books on subject-specific assessment; local districts; and teacher and researcher experiences.

Learning resources vs. learning materials

Teaching resources include locations and means for finding teaching materials, e.g., websites, libraries, stores, etc.; intangibles, e.g., theories of learning or education, published research articles and books, or support from colleagues; and materials. Teaching materials most often mean concrete objects, e.g., worksheets, workbooks, or manipulatives including tools and games that students can physically handle and interact with to learn new concepts and skills. For example, younger students can use blocks to learn counting. Teaching materials should ideally be customized to the subject content, students in the class, and teacher using them. Students achieve more when their learning is supported by materials. For example, students learning a new skill in class have significant opportunities to practice it using a worksheet. This not only affords necessary repetition, but also enables independent student exploration of knowledge. Learning materials help structure lesson planning and delivery, especially in earlier grades, by guiding teachers and students through regular routines, e.g., having a weekly vocabulary game relieves teachers of pressure while giving students needed practice with new words taught weekly, as well as fun. Materials also facilitate differentiating instruction for individual students. Some teachers make their own; many more are available online, most free

Thematic instruction

Thematic instruction reflects a holistic belief that learning is best in the context of a coherent whole, and connected to real life. Teaching thematically organizes curriculum around overarching themes—teaching around experiences, not isolated disciplines. For example, a teacher might design a unit wherein students explore a broad environmental theme including river basins, rain forests, communities, energy use, etc., simultaneously integrating reading, math, science, and social studies into each lesson. Thematic instruction's goal is teaching these cognitive skills within the context of real-world topics, combining both enough broadness to enable creative exploration and enough specificity for practical application. Teachers and students first choose a theme, typically around a broad concept—weather, democracy, etc.; or a large, integrated system such as an ecosystem, city, etc. They then organize their core curriculum's content knowledge and process skills learning objectives around the theme, e.g., with river basins, literature could include Mark Twain or other authors' books involving rivers; science could include floods, weather, etc.; social studies, the characteristics of river communities; math, calculating water volume and flow. Designing instruction includes combining subject hours, adjusting class schedules, inviting outside experts, planning field trips, team-teaching, etc. Teachers also encourage and assign student projects, which are naturally compatible with thematic units.

Interdisciplinary instruction

Interdisciplinary or cross-curricular instruction applies knowledge, principles, and values to multiple school disciplines and subjects concurrently. Disciplines and subjects are often related through central themes—thematic units have been identified as interdisciplinary teaching's organizational structure—or experiences, processes, topics, problems, and issues. Schools first integrated listening, speaking, reading, writing, and thinking as language arts components, thereafter trending to more widely integrating all curriculum subjects through unifying themes. Cross-curricular instruction is often a remedy to recurring educational problems like instruction in isolated skills and fragmentary learning; and a means of supporting goals like giving students more relevant curricula, teaching reasoning and thinking, and facilitating skills transfer to other contexts. It enables students to apply and integrate knowledge across subjects, which isolated skills instruction does not; raises student motivation and engagement when, through participation, students realize the value of the knowledge; and supplies conditions for effective learning. Subject teachers collaborate, for example, a PE and math teacher may combine math skills of counting and graphing with PE skills of throwing, catching, hitting, and kicking balls, including student practice and teacher assessment of both physical and numerical techniques. Elementary classroom teachers may combine multiple subjects in one thematic unit, e.g., using a bean-growing project to teach science via botany, the life cycle, research questions, and observation; mathematics via counting and measuring; and English-writing reports.

Teachers of different subjects collaborate to plan interdisciplinary instructional units, generating topics, and developing instruction and assessment. For example, math and PE teachers have students count the number of times they can hit paddleballs consecutively, practice graphing them, and practice paddleball skills. Teachers might assess counting skills observationally, assess paddleball skills by observing student demonstrations, and assess graphing skills by reviewing handmade or computer graphing assignments. Elementary-grade teachers integrate English, math, and science, connecting classroom plant study to forest field trips, having students write about these connections. Vocational or technical high school students restored a historic landmark, integrating what they learned in math, journalism, and shop classes—applying learning to a real-life experience. Students also transferred learning, using creative, original thinking: after successfully completing the restoration project, they generated ideas for additional school and community service projects integrating various school subjects, presenting their ideas to teachers. A social sciences and math teacher co-taught students using ancient Egyptian computation techniques, comparing them to modern-day math. Students discussed ancient math in historical context, reflecting on past and present and what "modern" meant. Teachers find students gain more complex understandings of disciplines and their relationships through interdisciplinary instruction.

Lesson plan that builds on prior student knowledge

One model (Cunningham, ASCD, 2009) contains eight steps. (1) Introduction: state overall lesson reason or purpose. Introduce main idea, topic, and key concepts. "Hook" student attention with a challenge or a quirky or amazing fact, etc. Explain lesson relevance for extending prior knowledge and promoting future learning. (2) Foundation: confirm prior student knowledge, either by clarifying or double-checking. Connect the lesson to standards. Tell students precisely what they will know and be able to do from the lesson. Include additional information, preparing the main lesson. Introduce essential vocabulary visually, aloud, in reading, and in writing. (3) Brain activation: clarify concepts; add information through probing questions, engaging students and building background. Brainstorm concepts, ideas, and possibilities, enabling students to clarify and expand thinking. Plan activities revealing misconceptions; correct or clarify these. (4) Body of new information: present the main lesson via whole-class lecture, teacher-supervised small-group, or partner activity, including teacher input of new and key points, reading, problem-solving, and active student participation with specific goals. (5) Clarification: check for understanding with sample questions, problems, or situations; guide learning; give practice. (6) Practice and review: supervise practice; work with students. (7) Independent practice: supervise, selecting further strategies for small groups needing them; others work independently. (8) Closure: connect lesson steps and information; summarize; discuss lesson in larger learning context; have students write or explain learning, ideas, questions, and problems.

Eight step lesson plan

Introduction – 5 minutes: teacher writes Lincoln's quotation of the Declaration of Independence's "All men are created equal"; students discuss potential 1860s meaning. Foundation - 5-10 minutes: brief discussion about slavery, men and women, educated and uneducated white men; the goal is explaining the significance of the Gettysburg Address to American history and today's voting rights. Key vocabulary words and phrases include *conceived in liberty; dedicated; proposition; equal.* Brain activation – 5 minutes: ask what the words mean, why Lincoln phrased it thus, what would happen today with this speech, what the speech informs us about 1860s America, how the phrase connects to the American history then and now, and how the first paragraph leads to the ideas in the second and third paragraphs. Body of new information - 10-15 minutes: referring to specified textbook pages and illustrations, discuss the Battle of Gettysburg. Teacher writes key ideas or notes on overhead; students add to history notes. Clarification - 5-10 minutes: students write reflections on text. Practice and review - 5-10 minutes: small-group discussions of the battle's and speech's significance, Lincoln's speaking on the battlefield, and its turning point in the Civil War. Independent practice - 10 minutes: students select and write brief summaries of two or three other key phrases from the speech. Closure - 5 minutes: students share phrases with partners, write favorites with short explanations on "exit passes," and the teacher collects these to assess understanding and inform tomorrow's lesson.

Technology applications whereby teachers can more efficiently complete tasks

Today, mobile applications abound to save teachers time, effort, and space on administrative tasks, freeing more of their attention for teaching and helping students learn. One example is an app for the iPad called Paperless Teacher (Evon Technologies). It automates and customizes processes of taking attendance, planning lessons, creating rubrics, and entering grades in grade books. It weighs each gradable element, e.g., attendance, participation, assignments, tests, and homework, according to teacher specifications, and then automatically calculates grades. It enables teachers to email these results directly to students and parents. This eliminates the repetition of entering names, calculating numbers, and entering them manually one at a time. Users can easily share common data using this app; hence teachers can exchange student profiles or lesson plans anytime, remotely and effortlessly. The app features an integrated Dropbox framework, preventing data loss and enabling users with various other devices to access data. Its Message User Interface enables exporting and emailing data sharing in format allowing other users to open data directly in their apps. This facilitates notifying students of tests, assignments, schedules, etc. Semester planning and grade setting are customizable for multiple semester plans or grading systems. A protection feature keeps data safe for separate users.

Roles that special education teachers can contribute to collaborative teaching activities

Special education teachers have great expertise in how to adapt curriculum and instruction and provide classroom modifications and accommodations for students with various disabilities who receive special education and related services. They can share knowledge with classroom teachers about instructional considerations for each category of disability, individual special education students, and their needs. Since the Individuals with Disabilities Education Act (IDEA) legislation first mandated education in the least restrictive environment possible for students with disabilities, inclusive education has increased and mainstreaming is more prevalent today. This presents challenges to regular classroom teachers, and advantages to collaborating with special education teachers, who can help integrate Individualized Education Program (IEP) goals into daily classroom instruction. In addition to knowing more techniques and strategies for teaching students with special needs, they also are likely familiar with individual special education students at their school to inform classroom teachers from experience about particularly effective and ineffective specific techniques. They can show new teachers how task analysis, chaining, and shaping enable intellectually disabled students to learn complex behaviors; advise newly mainstreaming teachers on practical matters like classroom logistics with wheelchairs and assistive devices, teaching other students device and disability etiquette; and help teachers coordinate varied adaptations, modifications, or accommodations to prevent their interference with each other.

Collaboration between library media specialists and classroom teachers

Library media specialists are experts at locating information and resources, among other things. As information specialists, they contribute skills for accessing and evaluating information resources in different formats for both students and teachers. They function as models for students, showing them strategies for finding, accessing, and evaluating information that is available in their school library media centers and outside them. Due to the impact of technology development on library media center environments, library media specialists also keep up with mastering the newest, continually evolving electronic resources, and pay ongoing attention to the quality, character, and ethical use of information in traditional and electronic formats. They are instructional partners collaborating with teachers, other educators, and administrators. They identify connections among school expectations for student learning, student achievement, school curriculum content, student information needs, and available information resources. They work closely and cooperatively with teachers in designing authentic learning activities and assessments. Collaborating with teachers, they help integrate information and communication skills to meet content standards. They have knowledge of current research literature in teaching and learning, and expertise for its application. They help students find information from multiple sources, evaluate it critically, and use it to support learning, problem-solving, and critical thinking.

Collaboration between library media specialists and classroom teachers

Teachers of the gifted and talented have specialized training in instructing this population. Considering mainstreaming requirements, increasing demographic diversity, school underfunding, staff shortages, and oversized classes, classroom teachers are challenged to meet all student needs in one class. They may have to spend large portions of time on differentiated instruction to students with disabilities, in addition to satisfying whole-class accountability requirements to cover enough required curriculum content and enable every student to perform to standards on high-stakes, large-scale tests to meet Adequate Yearly Progress (AYP). Some teachers having limited or no experience with gifted students may assume they can work more independently and need less teacher attention due to their high IQs and/or special talents. However, advanced students are frequently bored or impatient with the pace of instruction for average student abilities. They can demand more material to learn, at faster rates; more in-depth, extended, or enriched content; answers to their pressing questions; and advice, guidance, and feedback even as they work independently on projects. Teachers specializing in giftedness and creativity can help take some pressure off classroom teachers, by both working directly with these students, and giving teachers ideas for enrichment activities and coordinating these with classroom units and lessons.

Collaboration between paraprofessionals and classroom teachers

Teachers today not only must differentiate instruction for individual students with a diverse range of needs, they frequently must also do this with excessive class sizes. Teachers' aides and other paraprofessionals provide vital help with these demands. Their collaboration with teachers includes not only concrete assistance like taking attendance; physically setting up activities; helping with adaptive devices, distributing materials, snacks, etc.; but also scoring tests, grading papers; participating in training they receive from teachers, specialists, therapists, etc.; and then working one-on-one with individual students to deliver differentiated instruction and help students needing individual supervision for classroom tasks. They may be trained by school psychologists to observe students and collect behavioral data, relieving teachers of these additional duties. In mainstreamed classes, teachers cannot always work with all individual students enough. Paraprofessionals are invaluable in making it possible for more students to receive more individualized attention, supervision, and instruction more regularly, for longer time periods, and more often. They can enable more students to achieve their individual educational goals.

Individualized Education Program (IEP) team members

Student IEP team members can include any or all the following and more: parents; special education teachers; classroom teachers; audiologists; occupational, physical, speech-language, activity, and/or other therapists; American Sign Language (ASL) interpreters; orientation and mobility specialists; school social workers; school nurses; school psychologists; counselors; advocates, etc. Parents collaborate with teachers, sharing their experience with their children, children's histories, personal preferences, effective behavioral and learning techniques; and may volunteer to help in the classroom and/or at school functions. By advocating, they help teachers meet children's special needs. Special education teachers help address IEP goals by incorporating related instruction and activities into daily classroom lessons and routines; and offer expertise in differentiated instruction, teaching, and behavior management strategies. Audiologists contribute knowledge of hearing loss, hearing aids, classroom accommodations, and modifications. Therapists add expertise in their respective disciplines—physical therapists (PTs) make or adapt devices, provide targeted postural and large-muscle exercises; occupational therapists (OTs), fine-motor, ADL development; speech language pathologists (SLPs) incorporate language development into instruction; ASL interpreters translate between hearing and deaf or hearing-impaired students and families; orientation and mobility (O&M) specialists help blind and visually impaired students navigate classrooms, schools, and communities. Social workers provide student and family histories, coordinate special services, and help families locate and access resources. School nurses help with medications, monitoring diabetic diets and blood checks; school seizures, accidents, and emergencies, etc. Psychologists administer, score, and interpret IQ tests; provide behavior management plans and training; data collection and analysis, etc.

Resources whereby teachers and schools can provide enrichment for students

The Stanford Mobile Inquiry Learning Environment (SMILE) uses technology innovatively for educational enrichment. This interactive learning model includes mobile software for learning management, plus its own server, which can run on a battery and functions as a Wi-Fi connection, router, and storage device. At schools adopting SMILE, students can exchange questions and ideas with other students worldwide; and teachers can instantaneously collect summaries of learning data analytics. Another American enrichment resource is Students for the Advancement of Global Entrepreneurship (SAGE), a program emphasizing civic responsibility and duty for high school students, who form teams and develop social enterprise businesses (SEBs) or socially responsible businesses (SRBs), which compete in the annual SAGE World Cup. An American remediation resource is Teach for All, a model teaching lifetime educational advocacy and leadership foundations at both local and policy levels, training and developing effective leaders to change education for the most disadvantaged students; and promoting innovation by encouraging best practice sharing. PenPal Schools teach six-week courses about world issues, giving students global partners to share multicultural understandings. Its Pay-What-You-Want policy enables low-income student participation. Many other resources are available in other countries or are shared among the US and other nations.

Vertical alignment and horizontal alignment

Vertical alignment is the process through which courses are sequenced across a curriculum. What a student learns in a 4th grade math course will prepare him or her for what he or she will learn in a vertically aligned 5th grade math course. Horizontal alignment is the process through which different sections of the same course are standardized such that what one student learns in a section of Biology with Ms. Smith is similar (though not exactly the same) as the material learned by a student in a section of Biology with Mr. Johnson. Typically horizontal alignment is addressed locally, perhaps through professional learning communities in coordination with district guidelines for course content. Vertical alignment is often developed on a state or even national level. School districts develop their course outlines in coordination with standards adopted from either the state or national level. Educators at the state level decide the general scope of the schools' curricula and choose yearly statewide assessments for students. Educators at the district level adapt the state course guidelines to fit local communities and teachers implement those curricula in their classrooms. The success of the entire system is dependent on educators at all levels working collaboratively in the best interests of the students.

Critical thinking and creative thinking

Critical thinking includes the abilities to question, evaluate, and judge information or material. For example, students should learn to distinguish opinions from facts in what they read and hear; look for evidence supporting author or speaker arguments, or lack thereof; evaluate supporting evidence, e.g., consider whether its source is reputable, proven, accepted by experts in its field, etc.; judge the quality of information or material through comparison, experience, and intuition. Creative thinking includes generating original ideas, coming up with problem-solving alternatives that differ from usual solutions, applying knowledge in novel ways and contexts, and divergent thinking. Traditional academics tend to emphasize and require convergent thinking, wherein multiple concepts, ideas, facts, and information come together or converge to yield the same answer or conclusion. Divergent thinking, by contrast, involves generating concepts, ideas, facts, and information that differ or diverge to yield varying answers or conclusions. For example, some informal assessments of divergent thinking include thinking of as many *different* categories of use for paper clips, or bricks, etc. (Bricks as projectiles represent *one* category, despite different targets and/or projection methods; bricks as building materials, also *one* category despite construction types or methods; using paper clips as fasteners is *one* category regardless of things fastened.)

Questioning, inductive and deductive reasoning, and problem-solving

Questioning promotes inquiry learning; gives students purposes for reading; focuses attention on learning targets; fosters active thinking, metacognition, and self-monitoring; augments comprehension; and helps students review new material and connect it to their previous knowledge. Student question generation can help them identify important ideas in learning materials and synthesize information. Teacher and student questions help students clarify meaning, find new information; analyze information by wondering about author intentions, meanings, and choices of content, genres, and formats; and pursue personally interesting topics related to learning material. Inductive reasoning is a bottom-up, specific-to-general process, beginning from accumulating specific observations or information; identifying regularities or patterns; and ultimately drawing general conclusions or principles. Conversely, deductive reasoning is a top-down, general-to-specific process; beginning from a general theory, principle, or field of information; narrowing this down to more specific hypotheses; testing these by collecting observations, information, and data to confirm or refute the theory; and draw a specific conclusion. Problem-solving involves identifying a problem, generating alternative solutions, testing these through implementation, and evaluating their effectiveness. This requires focus for problem identification, divergent thinking to generate alternatives, and critical thinking to evaluate results.

Planning, memory, and recall

Planning is an essential cognitive process which many students fail to do before plunging into activities. It requires abstract thinking and imagination to envision the processes of a task before actually performing them. While many higher-order cognitive abilities seem located in the frontal lobe of the cerebral cortex, planning appears to be in the prefrontal lobe. It is high among the higher-order thinking skills. By planning before writing, for example, students are able to organize their compositions in advance, preventing many major problems, failures, and starting over from scratch. Students must plan projects before beginning them to give them organized structures, devote equal or appropriately weighted durations to different parts, stay on schedule, complete them within prescribed timeframes, etc. Moreover, planning academic tasks provides essential practice for planning in everyday life, which facilitates many activities in similar ways on a larger, even more practical scale. Students use working memory to rehearse information in short-term memory and move it into long-term memory for retention. They retrieve information from long-term memory by recalling it directly or recognizing it among provided alternatives. Without memory retention and retrieval, students could not demonstrate, apply, or build upon what they learn.

Direct instruction vs. indirect instruction

Teacher-centered, direct instruction is the oldest, most widely used teaching model. Teachers give explicit, structured instruction using uniform lesson plans. Exploration, discussions, etc. are excluded. Most contemporary K-12 schools use updated versions. Examples include DISTAR, Hooked on Phonics, etc. Some longitudinal research shows Montessori, Waldorf, and other more flexible methods more effective. However, direct instruction is among the few scientifically confirmed ways of improving curriculum. Siegfried Engelmann originated a more specific direct instruction (DI), comparing it with 21 other methods during the federally funded Project Follow Through (1968-1995), meant to extend preschooler education following Head Start programs. Although funding was discontinued when data showed little or no benefit for this purpose, empirical evidence proved DI most effective of 22 methods for teaching reading, language, spelling, arithmetic, and positive self-image—the only one producing positive results consistently. Indirect instruction is student-centered and interactive; teachers facilitate small-group and cooperative learning. Students construct or transform material into new or different, meaningful responses. Encompassing all Bloom's taxonomy levels, it includes reading for meaning, cloze, concept mapping, case studies, inductive and deductive reasoning, content organization, examples and non-examples, questions, student experiences, self-evaluation, and discussion. DI aids learning facts, rules, and sequences; breaking down textbook or workbook material; lower Bloom's taxonomy levels; piquing student interest. Indirect instruction aids learning abstractions, concepts, patterns, inquiry, problem-solving, and discovery learning.

Independent study

Independent study is not a single instructional method per se, but rather a type of instructional strategy that encompasses a range of different instructional methods. Teachers intentionally provide independent study types of methods for the purposes of developing initiative, self-determination, self-reliance, self-direction, and self-improvement in individual students. In addition to individual students working alone, the definition of independent study can also include paired, partnered, or small-group learning. In each case, the teacher functions as a facilitator and guide rather than directing or controlling the entire activity. Some advantages of independent study include giving students more choices of learning materials, topics, approaches, practices, and more autonomy in completing assignments. These increase student motivation. Another advantage is flexibility: teachers can use it with one, two, or several students and another strategy with the rest of the class; combine it with other strategies; or make it the main whole-class instructional strategy. An additional advantage is freeing teacher time. However, teachers must ensure students have developed skills required for it. Some examples of independent study activities and methods include doing homework, writing reports or essays, learning contracts, correspondence courses and lessons, computer-assisted instruction, research projects, learning activity packages, assigned questions, and learning centers.

Experiential learning

Experiential learning is a student-centered, activity-oriented instructional strategy whereby students use inductive reasoning to discover information and insights. Process takes precedence over product. Activities involve "hands-on" learning. Rather than passively listening to teachers, only reading text, or viewing video or other visuals, students actively participate in direct experiences. This participation increases student motivation, as does communicating their activities to classmates so that, in effect, they teach one another. Critical components of effective experiential learning include formulating plans to apply learning to other contexts, and reflecting personally about learning experiences. Studies find student comprehension and retention are much higher through experiential learning activities than passive or receptive activities. Examples include administering surveys, building models, taking field trips, making field observations, conducting simulations, playing games, role-playing, synectics, focused imaging, and conducting experiments. Experimental learning involves the scientific method: asking research questions; formulating hypotheses regarding answers; testing hypotheses by experimenting, e.g., qualitative research like surveys and observations, or quantitative like randomly selecting participants, not treating a control group and manipulating independent variables with a treatment group to see if dependent variables are affected or unaffected to support or refute the hypothesis; reporting results; drawing conclusions and communicating these.

Interactive instruction

Interactive instruction is a teaching strategy that enables a range of different interactive methods and ways of grouping students. It is interactive because it places a major emphasis on having students share and exchange ideas, questions, activities, and tasks, and engage in discussions of their work and learning with classmates. Students in pairs, threes, small groups, or whole classes may participate in interactive discussions, projects, or assignments. Some examples of activities involving interactive instruction include holding debates; participating in student panels; engaging in role-playing exercises, which are also used in experiential learning; discussion, which is also a feature of indirect instruction; group brainstorming to generate ideas; practicing academic skills and tasks with peers; cooperative learning groups, which are always interactive and sometimes also involve independent study; laboratory groups, which can also involve experimental and experiential learning; problem-solving activities; circle of knowledge group activity sessions; tutorial groups, including peer tutoring; and conducting interviews with peers and/or others.

Organizing and implementing effective instruction

First review national and state standards, their course textbooks, supplementary materials, and any test preparation materials required, to ascertain which concepts they must teach. Create a plan of study based on this information. To visualize and organize instruction, make a personal lesson plan calendar. Using the plan of study and calendar, plan instructional units and timelines. Next, write detailed lesson plans for each unit. Effective lesson plans should include learning objectives; student activities; estimates of time needed; materials required; alternative plans for any students absent during lesson activities; and assessment methods, including tests, homework, and classwork. Transfer the general unit plan to a planning book, assembling all unit plans to get an overall picture of the school year, supporting organization, focus, and implementation. Write daily lesson outlines and agendas. Some teachers write detailed information and notes, while others make simple outlines including times. Being organized and making smooth transitions are important to maintain student attention. Collect or create required materials, e.g., lecture notes, overheads, handouts, manipulatives, any planned daily warmups, etc. Request media in advance. Create emergency lesson plans for substitutes and mini-lessons to fill extra or leftover time to plan for the unexpected.

Continuous monitoring and charting of student performance

Continuous monitoring and charting (1) gives teachers information on student progress with short-term, discrete objectives. They can respond flexibly to student understanding, engagement, lacks thereof, and feedback, adjusting instruction by re-teaching or reviewing skills and concepts immediately instead of only finding students did not learn certain things after having covered several topics; and (2) gives students visual depictions of their learning. Having students chart and graph their own performance can enhance their engagement in learning. Continuous monitoring functions as ongoing evaluation, visual representation, immediate feedback; a diagnostic tool; instructional planning guide; communication mechanism with students, parents, other teachers, and administrators; and an evaluation practice that can motivate and engage students. However, it is not an independent student practice activity. Critical elements are frequently assessing student understanding and performance of discrete skills and concepts; ability to replicate assessment procedures over several days; tally, graph, or chart student responses; and involve students in tracking that progress and setting goals. To implement, select a specific instructional objective; design an assessment sheet students can complete in a few minutes with items reflecting the target skill, and where indicated, concrete, representational, or abstract understanding level; administer and score; have students plot correct or incorrect responses on graphs; discuss; draw goal lines on graphs; repeat.

Scaffolding

Scaffolding, in a metaphorical iteration of literal building construction scaffolding, is temporary support enabling students to complete tasks they cannot accomplish on their own at the time. As students master these tasks, the scaffolding can be gradually withdrawn until students perform the tasks independently without support. During this process, the role of the teacher is shifted from being the dominant expert on academic content to becoming more of a facilitator of learning and a mentor. As students learn how to perform tasks with support and gain increasing proficiency and independence, the responsibility for learning shifts from the teacher to the student. Scaffolded instruction establishes a supportive learning environment wherein students are able to give feedback, ask questions, and support one another in learning new material. Using scaffolding in teaching gives students motivation for adopting more active roles in their learning. Because teachers provide scaffolds for tasks students cannot initially achieve independently, scaffolding requires students to advance past their current knowledge and skill levels, sharing responsibility and taking ownership for teaching and learning.

Scaffolding can be implemented with individual students, small groups, or whole classes. It is useful whenever students cannot understand a certain concept or are not progressing in some aspects of tasks. Step 1: the teacher models how to perform a difficult or unfamiliar task, for example, how to use a graphic organizer when students have never done so. The teacher might prepare an incomplete graphic organizer with some parts completed for handouts and a projection. The teacher describes how the graphic organizer illustrates relationships, asking students to "think aloud" about this. Step 2: teacher and students work together on completing the graphic organizer. Students might suggest information to add. The teacher writes student suggestions on the board or overhead; students complete their copies of the organizer. Step 3: students work in pairs or small groups to complete a blank or partially filled graphic organizer. Teachers may need to provide multiple scaffolds at various times to help students master more complex content. Step 4: students practice independently, demonstrating mastery and gaining speed and automaticity. In each step, teacher and students have different roles and responsibilities.

Instructional approaches that emphasize student responsibility for learning

In the inquiry-guided instructional method, students investigate to answer questions, attaining understanding of concepts independently. This not only promotes the development of lifelong research skills, but also places the responsibility for learning with the student. In the learner-centered teaching method, teachers are responsible for facilitating learning, while students take responsibility for learning. This shifts classroom power from teacher to student. In the instructional method of establishing learning communities, every member participates, taking responsibility for accomplishing learning goals. With shared learning, responsibility is collective, not individual. Participants include students, teachers, other educators, staff, administrators, parents, community members, and other stakeholders. Service learning is an instructional approach combining academic content with community service projects. Teachers are responsible for structuring and supervising learning, enabling student reflection. Students learn to take civic responsibility. In team-based learning (TBL), unlike other group activities, students participate as members of permanent teams; group meetings occupy most of class. Students are more responsible for and reliant on each other (interdependent) for learning, and more responsible for arriving to class prepared. Research finds TBL increases both student engagement and responsibility.

Developing higher-order thinking skills

Align learning goals, objectives, ideas, skills, content, tasks, materials, aids, and assessments. Create organized routines and activities: explain established routines, e.g., starting on time and following planned activity sequences; follow them. Conduct task analysis of a thinking skill to learn: identify the specific skill, prerequisite knowledge and skills, related sub-skills sequence, and student readiness with prerequisites. Prepare examples, sample problems and explanations. Prepare questions transcending simple factual information recall, addressing advanced understanding, e.g., how? How well? Why? Plan strategies for diagnosis, guidance, practice, and remediation. Establish a comfortable, non-threatening atmosphere. Communicate clear expectations, genuine topic interest, enthusiasm, and a businesslike approach combined with warmth. Prepare and organize thoroughly to minimize between-activity transition times. Clearly explain tasks: set goals at beginnings of assignments, and furnish finished product examples. Introduce tasks with clear, simple organizing frameworks like single-paragraph overviews, previews, charts, or diagrams. Introduce key terms and concepts before proceeding. Focus attention on important information using questions. Use written signals, repetition, nonverbal behaviors, and verbal statements for emphasis. Use demonstrations, models, pictures, diagrams, examples, etc. to make ideas vivid. Signal transitions between ideas. Give frequent feedback, including clarifying or correcting incorrect responses.

Student development of higher-order thinking skills

Cognitive and learning strategies include organization, elaboration, rehearsal; and metacognition for self-evaluating and self-regulating one's thinking, entailing mnemonics, visualization, diagramming, highlighting; or more complex strategies, e.g., the Multipass reading comprehension procedure. To help students develop critical and creative thinking and learning skills, intentionally design lessons expressly for teaching specific thinking and learning strategies. Teach self-reflection and self-evaluation: give students inexplicable dilemmas, paradoxes, etc., challenging pre-existing beliefs. Guide systematic student inquiry. Encourage reflection and making sense of new information by having students write or discuss in their own words how to integrate it with their existing ideas, approaches, and opinions. Encourage and guide students in forming hypotheses, brainstorming, guessing, speculating about consequences, and discussing how their thought processes have changed their ideas. Monitor inefficient strategies and correct them. Encourage continuous student reflection of beliefs about thinking, thought processes, and evaluating effectiveness. Use advance organizers and cognitive maps to show main parts or steps when approaching various thinking and learning tasks. Teach PQ4R (*preview*, *question*, *read*, *reflect*, *recite*, and *review*) with written materials. Instruction in abstraction, analysis, outlining, summarization, and generalization enhances both reading and reasoning skills. Stress broad algorithms, heuristics, and problem-solving strategies; give enough practice to overlearn for effortless, consistent use. Teach specific strategies using modeling, think-alouds, discussion, and practice. Students develop self-confidence from teachers modeling self-confidence in thinking and reasoning processes.

Name and define each cognitive skill for students; ask them for examples and synonyms. Model steps for applying each skill. Explain appropriate and inappropriate skill application contexts. Assign cooperative learning groups to practice skills. To improve comprehension, problem-solving, decision-making; and concept, principle, and procedure application: ask probing questions to diagnose existing student conceptions and misconceptions. Furnish hands-on experiences enabling students to explore generating new explanations or interpreting raw data. Give question stems or examples requiring higher-order thinking; have students answer in groups, pairs, or independently. Give practice in brainstorming, decision-making, experimenting, identifying and solving problems in art, music, and writing as well as math and science. Incorporate individualized options in lesson plans, e.g., assignment choices, modalities for multiple intelligences, varying instruction and application sequences, open-ended participation tasks with multiple alternatives, multi-ability tasks and varied activities accommodating differences in abstraction, language proficiency, and emotional influences. Give opportunities to discover procedural knowledge; explain procedure goals, applicable situations or problems, and corresponding strategies and rationales; demonstrate stepwise procedure application; give students practice selecting and implementing procedures;

give performance feedback. Promote internal locus of control by helping students perceive themselves as effective learners.

Integrating technology into instruction

Instructional technology integration is effective when it supports curriculum goals. Technology must support four essential learning elements: active student engagement, group participation, frequent interaction and feedback, and connections with real-life experts. In the 1960s, MIT professor Seymour Papert collaborated with cognitive-developmental psychologist Jean Piaget, and then developed Logo, a programming language for children to use without advanced mathematical knowledge. Students using Logo could write and debug programs to control robot movements with minimal instruction. They learned more in-depth geometry concept understanding and programming skills—and were more engaged in learning than in traditional classroom exercises. Papert pointed out the ample overlap of education and fun with computers for promoting all students' internal motivation. Today technology learning tools abound; almost every US public school has Internet connection. When technology is used for more ambitious learning goals than basic skills, studies find it helps students develop creativity, research skills, and higher-order thinking.

Technology can further learning through building local and global communities including students, teachers, administrators, parents, scientists, and others; giving students and teachers more opportunities for reflection, feedback, and revision; offering learning tools and scaffolds, e.g., visualization tools and modeling programs; giving classrooms exciting, real-world problem-based curricula; and expanding teacher learning opportunities. Social media support collaboration, reinforcing learning's social nature. Technology enables learning communities and improves learning cultures. Students learn concepts in ways impossible or impracticable with other instructional methods through social networking, simulations, and digital gaming. Educational technology complements what exemplary teachers naturally do. Experts note that digital games, instead of separating instruction from assessment, constantly assess student problem-solving progress, giving students feedback and further practice. Letting students teach them how they engage with digital media both informs teachers about technology and develops student metacognition. Integration means using technology to learn content and demonstrate content understanding, not simply digital expertise. Students need guided practice and exploration to achieve this.

Computer mediation

Communicating using computers gives students opportunities to access remote data sources, collaborate with students in other places on group projects, and share their work with other students to obtain their responses or evaluations. Research finds that computer-based instruction (CBI) and computer-assisted instruction (CAI) combined with regular classroom instruction enhances student motivation, academic achievement, and attitudes. Moreover, the increasing prevalence, even requirement, of computers in workplaces demands student preparation; and federal and state standards increasingly require integrating technology into instruction and student computer literacy. Studies have shown that the following computer-mediated communication applications are effective for enhancing student learning of prerequisite skills and higher-order cognitive skills: building skills in logical reasoning, inductive reasoning, deductive reasoning, and making verbal analogies; practicing and drilling procedures that incorporate tests or probes; and practicing problem-solving strategies and skills in making inferences. In addition, interactive learning software programs give students more autonomy in learning, allow them to learn at individual paces, engage student interest, and often make learning more entertaining. Moreover, students need immediate, specific, corrective feedback on their learning progress, which interactive software programs can give more consistently than single teachers with large classes.

Active teaching and learning strategies

Active teaching and learning strategies make students active participants in learning. Rather than passively listening to teachers discuss, read about, or observe others perform skills, students practice skills to gain proficiency. Many students learn best by doing. Hands-on activities take students out of books and sometimes their seats, classrooms, schools, or even familiar thinking habits. In addition to engaging student interest and giving actual practice, they have the benefit of integrating subject-area content with all four language and literacy domains—listening, speaking, reading, and writing. Though research consistently shows students learn better through active content engagement, some teachers avoid active learning. Objections and dilemmas include: concerns they will never cover required content; losing class control by not lecturing; having trouble getting students to work in teams—some doing all the work, others none; students' not knowing how to answer higher-order questions; student resistance to active learning or a preference for habituated listening and note-taking; what to do with ELL or special education students during active learning and group activities. Guidelines include: vary partners and small-group teams via randomization, specific rotation schedules, or other systematic schemes. Vary required team tasks and techniques. Clearly identify team member roles, task purpose, outcome, and time allotted. Prepare all needed materials. Determine how to grade tasks. Start small or brief activities early. Establish a signal for students to stop discussion.

Giving students choices among assignments enables them to decide how to demonstrate their learning. For example, some might choose to write compositions, some to make spoken presentations, some to draw illustrations, and some to construct models to demonstrate the same knowledge. A language strategy is A-Z Taxonomy: small student groups write the alphabet vertically on paper and think of vocabulary terms in the content they are studying that start with each letter. This technique is effective as both pre- and post-instruction. Pairing students to debate some controversial issue related to learning content, having pairs explain pro and con positions to each other and agree to an overall recommendation gives students practice in negotiating and compromising skills, plus listening and speaking opportunities. Brainstorming evokes creativity, originality, and quantity: ask open-ended questions; never criticize ideas. Providing a suitable target number of ideas sometimes helps. Some linguistically diverse students may feel more comfortable responding as members of a small student team or group.

In a "carousel questions" strategy, the teacher writes several questions about a content topic being learned on large posters or paper stations posted around the classroom. Small student groups, each with a different color marker, rotate every few minutes among question sets. At every station, teams add ideas, responses, or answers not already included. Then the class shares all student responses, gaining multiple and varied answers to the questions. In case studies, students are given real-world stories about things that happened to an individual, family, school, or community; students apply their content knowledge and skills to authentic situations. In critical explanation, teachers ask students to consider reasons or factors that might explain some content-related issues or problems. Use "might" and "could," not "why" to avoid implying right, wrong, or only one correct answer. In discussion webs, students consider a content-related issue or problem in small groups, then regroup and share their work and information with classmates from other groups. In field studies, students have opportunities to learn about and study issues in their community related to the content they are learning. Health classes might study community nutrition, disease, safety, environmental issues, consumer health, or healthcare services; earth science classes might collect rock samples, identify them, and determine local distribution patterns; social studies classes might study local landmarks and associated history, etc.

Long-term goals, short-term objectives, instructional objectives, and lesson plan objectives

Long-term goals typically are mastered over a school year and are stated in very broad, general terms. Goal areas typically correspond to content areas like reading, writing, math, and other subjects. Teachers derive short-term objectives from long-term goals. Short-term objectives can be completed in shorter time periods, ranging from two weeks to three months. Teachers then derive instructional objectives from short-term objectives. Students can generally master instructional objectives within one lesson. From smaller numbers of long-term goals, teachers should be able to generate a larger number of short-term objectives and even larger numbers of instructional objectives from short-term objectives. As an example, if a long-term goal is for students to read at grade level, then related short-term objectives could include recognizing vocabulary sight words; using phonics, context clues, and structural analysis to identify unfamiliar words; and demonstrating text comprehension on literal, inferential, and critical levels. From these, a teacher could break down phonics into rules for short and long vowels, digraphs, initial and final single consonants, and consonant blends to write individual instructional objectives.

Correctly written objectives include: student orientation, behavioral terminology, a criterion, and a condition statement. "Review long and short vowels in one-syllable words" or "teach fire safety" are teacher-oriented. To clarify their significance and use for students, they should be student-oriented: "correctly read aloud words containing long or short vowels"; "identify fire safety rules." Behavioral terminology is observable and measurable. This is why Bloom's taxonomy supplies action verbs for each complexity level in the hierarchy and each domain. Experts remark that while knowledge-level objectives, e.g., to read sight words aloud or recite multiplication tables, are prerequisites for more advanced learning, teachers should still not dwell primarily on these as most easily observable or identifiable, but ensure they give equal time in their lessons to higher-level cognitive skills. Experts also remind teachers not to confine objectives to Bloom's cognitive domain, but include the psychomotor and affective domains as well. Objectives can include all three. For example, an instructional objective for a student to answer comprehension questions orally with 90 percent accuracy after silently reading a passage from a grade-level basal text can include requesting assistance by raising one's hand, using a person's name to get his or her attention, asking a question, and saying "please" or other social amenity.

SWOT

SWOT analysis stands for *strengths, weaknesses, opportunities*, and *threats*. While frequently used by anyone analyzing market trends, identifying target markets, and/or developing marketing plans (which includes not only salespeople, but also therapists and other practitioners who must promote their services), it is also useful to apply to education. For example, teachers can use it with high school students in career counseling to identify the job-relevant skills they possess (strengths) and those they lack (weaknesses); jobs open, job growth probabilities, and chances for advancement in a student's preferred career field (opportunities); and competition for jobs, dead-end positions, and downsizing probabilities (threats). Accompanying the SWOT analysis, a gap analysis tool identifies employer needs and job requirements; student and candidate knowledge and skills; differences between these, which represent gaps; an action plan to fill gaps; a timeframe to complete the plan; and people who can help. For example, an employer might require knowledge of Excel or other spreadsheet software; the student might only know Word or other word-processing software. The action plan is to learn Excel or other spreadsheet programs through a short community college course, school enrichment program, library-offered class, interactive computer tutorial, etc. Teachers can also use these tools to identify and address other, non-career-related academic gaps.

Hypothetical situation wherein a teacher identifies and analyzes student knowledge gaps

Suppose a teacher has designed a unit on a content subject and has taught the class a number of individual one-day lessons within this unit. The teacher's regular practice is to conduct formative assessments, e.g., pop quizzes, oral Q&A sessions, whips (going around the room quickly, having every student answer an open-ended content question), etc. near the end of each day's lesson. So far, each formative assessment has shown 80-100 percent of students grasped main lesson concepts, facts, and points. But on this day, the teacher finds 90 percent of the students fail to demonstrate knowledge or understanding of lesson content. It is highly unlikely 90 percent of students did not pay attention or lacked cognitive ability to comprehend the lesson, and highly likely the lesson was ineffective. Also, the 10 percent displaying knowledge and understanding may have been the most conscientious students and/or had the highest cognitive ability levels; and/or some, most, or all of the 10 percent may already have had existing knowledge of the lesson topic. Therefore the teacher re-teaches this lesson, using different instructional strategies than the first time. This time the formative assessment shows 95 percent of the class knowing and understanding key concepts and information.

Teacher assessment literacy, practices, and needs

Various research finds teachers viewing learning as memorization assesses student information recall; teachers viewing learning as constructing knowledge and understanding use formative assessment to create continuous information flow about student understanding and adapt instruction to be more effective. Studies also show assessment-literate teachers do not limit assessment to multiple-choice or true-false questions but apply many, varied strategies, selecting those strongest and most relevant for specific learning goals. Pre-service teachers are found having inadequate repertoires of assessment strategies. One study showed the teacher asking the most conceptual questions and having the biggest variety of ways to adapt instruction according to assessment results had the highest student performance level. Also, some researchers (Gottheiner and Seigel, 2012) conclude others frequently overlook how teachers interpret formative assessment data in their studies, and more resources for doing so are needed. Teachers in their study reported that, although student group discussions of questions could contribute to new misconceptions, they also triggered discourse—building on classmate ideas and enabling concept discovery and construction before even learning corresponding terminology.

Addressing student conceptions, misconceptions, and preconceptions

Multiple teachers agree to the value of having students discuss scientific concepts and struggle to define these on their own before teachers supply them with the scientific terminology. They find this process enables students to construct and own their knowledge. Teachers also observe students from diverse cultural backgrounds may have different ways of making sense of problems, making it important to provide real-life contexts giving them personal relevance to students and accessing prior student knowledge for understanding them. Teachers emphasize structured activities, which afford students chances to develop their thoughts before sharing them; and allowing each student time to share ideas increases participation. Starting with small groups and progressing to whole-class discussion allows teachers to circulate, monitoring or assessing many more student responses; allows students to exchange and develop ideas in smaller, non-threatening groups; and improves subsequent whole-class discussion levels. Teachers emphasize needing to address previous student knowledge. They realize misconceptions can be based on cultural beliefs and personal experiences, making them resistant to change. Researchers report that, although teachers can often predict common student misconceptions, students frequently give wider response ranges than teachers can predict; and that many teachers propose re-teaching for preconceptions, but more experienced teachers try different instructional strategies.

Differentiated instruction practices effective for enhancing student literacy

Teaching experts advise using common instructional texts for read-alouds to facilitate differentiation. Teachers can use teaching text read-alouds to build background knowledge, demonstrate strategy application to students, introduce issues and invite student journal responses, and assure every student access to the information and skills they need to improve their reading. Researchers find that using multiple texts at varied reading levels—not just one—to teach units enables all students to obtain information from materials they can read best. Rather than teaching "the textbook," teachers need to organize every individual instructional unit around a topic, issue, or genre. This applies whether teachers assign students to small-group work, or use whole-class differentiated instruction approaches. By organizing for instruction this way, teachers can meet all student reading levels. Because students can only become better readers if they understand how to construct meaning while they read, teachers must show them this process by modeling the ways in which they think about texts during read-alouds; work with small reading groups; and one-on-one instructional conferences with individual students. This gives students multiple opportunities to learn how to construct meaning from text.

Expert teachers find discussion particularly important when differentiating reading instruction. Student discussion effectively builds on every individual student's factual knowledge and understanding, and gives students opportunities to build comprehension and clarify meaning. Students deepen recall and understanding when teachers ask them to progress past fact memorization to discussion applying those facts to problems and issues. In-depth small-group or whole-class topic discussions demonstrate how classmates think and reason, build background knowledge, and can make information relevant to students' personal lives. Teachers must never assume every student absorbs the same information from a lesson or demonstration; also, students not having absorbed lesson content can write little or nothing about it because they can only write what they know and understand. Writing strengthens comprehension and enables thinking, exploration, and learning. Teachers can glean insights from reading student journals about student text analysis and inferential thinking skills, supporting intervention planning. Ongoing assessments enable teachers to reveal individual student need areas and successes and target instruction accordingly to support every student. Experts also advise teachers to think through every unit to determine what they want students to learn about genres, issues, and reading strategies; carefully plan units accordingly; and assemble appropriate read-aloud texts, plus reading materials to meet every student's needs.

Culturally responsive teaching

Culturally responsive teaching utilizes diverse students' cultural background knowledge, previous experiences, and performance styles, increasing the effectiveness and appropriateness of learning for them by teaching through and to their strengths. Culturally responsive instruction recognizes various ethnic groups' cultural heritages as legitimate—both as legacies influencing student attitudes, approaches, and dispositions to learning; and as content worth including in formal curricula. Culturally responsive approaches establish meaningful connections—both between students' school and home experiences, and between abstract academic concepts and the sociocultural realities that they live. It employs a broad range of instructional strategies addressing different student learning styles. It teaches students not only knowledge about their own and others' cultural traditions and heritages, but moreover to praise one another's cultural legacies and practices. Instructional practices that are culturally responsive incorporate multicultural information, materials, and resources in all skills and subjects schools routinely teach. Classroom environment considerations include using literature reflecting various literary genres and ethnic perspectives; incorporating everyday living concepts like jobs, economics, and consumer behaviors of different ethnic groups into math instruction; and activities that reflect a range of visual, auditory, tactile, and other sensory experiences to accommodate different student learning styles.

Culturally responsive teachers maintain cultural identity and heritage as well as academic performance. They teach the whole student, using cultural references to develop cognitive, affective, social, and political learning. Students develop interpersonal relationships, acting as extended family members supporting, encouraging, and helping one another. Group accountability makes individual success everybody's responsibility in academic communities. Teachers satisfy student needs regarding human dignity, sense of belonging, and individual self-concepts. Multidisciplinary teacher teams may collaborate, teaching single cultural concepts; students can actively participate in their own evaluations. Classroom climate, learning context, student-teacher relationships, curriculum content, instructional techniques, and assessments are included in culturally responsive teaching, which is multidimensional. It empowers students as learners and people by sharing teacher and student authority; relating personal growth to public life; developing critical curiosity and inquiry habits as well as strong knowledge and skills; and treating individual development as a social, cooperative, active process wherein students explore society, power, inequality, and change. It uses varied cultural experiences, not traditional practices, as teaching and learning resources. Students learn reflection, decision-making, and effective action—personally, socially, economically, and politically; more humane, caring interpersonal understandings and skills; more insightful, clearer thinking; and continual knowledge criticism, revision, renewal, and sharing.

Cooperative learning

Cooperative learning requires positive interdependence (students sink-or-swim together): assign assembly line-style and synergistic task completion. Establish collective goals, resources, and rewards; assign group roles; arrange group furniture and environment; have groups compete against each other. Face-to-face interaction entails seating groups in circles or pairs facing each other. Promote individual accountability through checking with random group members, assigning individual tasks, bonus group credit or rewards if all members perform well individually, and having students bring individual work to their groups. Social skills including decision-making, communication, trust-building, leadership, and conflict management must not be assumed but taught. Teachers should record their observations of students on observation forms to provide feedback. Social skills include categories of group formation and assembly, group functioning, and the formulation and fermentation of ideas and knowledge. Group processing can be accomplished orally and/or in writing by small group reflection; teacher provision of feedback to small groups or whole classes; teacher and small group observations; and goal-setting, by students with teacher guidance as needed, for students' next work sessions, e.g., regarding further social skills development.

Promoting student use and refinement of higher-order thinking skills

To get students to explore ideas from diverse perspectives, plan and ask questions prompting them to use their imaginations. For example, during a lesson on agriculture, ask students what they would think and feel about certain policies and practices if they were, respectively, legislators, corporate executives, factory farmers, small farmers, migrant farm workers, consumers paying for groceries, families eating groceries, etc. In a history lesson, ask students to take the perspectives of Native American tribes and of European settlers; or consider both the viewpoints of American revolutionaries and British colonial governors, etc. To promote problem-solving, instead of telling students how to solve problems—mathematical, scientific, economic, logistical, creative, etc.—ask students how, also promoting inquiry; have them brainstorm to generate many ideas as a group; guide their consideration of alternatives and speculation about potential consequences; and let them practice implementing solutions, analyzing and discussing results. Rather than "yes" or "no" questions, asking open-ended questions allows for many varied responses. To develop research skills, have students form research questions, guiding revision of overly broad or narrow questions; guide them through steps of formulating hypotheses, conducting experiments testing hypotheses; collecting, analyzing, and interpreting data; reporting results; and drawing and communicating conclusions.

Areas of executive functioning that commonly pose challenges for students.

Parents frequently identify <u>time management</u>, <u>planning</u>, and <u>organization</u> as challenges for their children. These are three among many areas involving executive function. Executive function skills start developing during infancy, continuing development into adulthood. Considering this duration for full development, children need solid foundations. Executive functioning involves cognitive skills utilized for executing tasks. A single task requires several executive function skills. For example, to get dressed for school, a student must plan ahead for the weather, sustain attention long enough for task completion, manage emotions regarding wanting or not wanting to go to school, and start and finish the task in a timely fashion. Students use executive functioning skills to help them do homework and chores, keep track of belongings, follow rules, save money for things they want, and many other things. Some signs that a student may be experiencing difficulty developing and/or applying executive function skills include: the student has trouble estimating how long it will take to complete a school project, and/or planning the project; telling a story with the details sequenced correctly; or remembering information while performing an activity.

Helping students develop time management, planning, and organizational skills

<u>Time management</u>: have students color portions of a clock face using dry-erase markers to represent time segments, e.g., five minutes, 15 minutes, etc., helping them visualize elapsed and remaining time; and check in halfway through time allotted. Give students halfway-point questions, e.g., are they halfway finished? Are they still focused on the task's goal? Are any distractions robbing them of on-task time? Must they speed or slow their work pace? <u>Planning</u>: one application is helping students plan homework. Ask them what a given homework assignment would look like; have them sketch it on paper divided into two columns, e.g., with a vocabulary assignment, students write vocabulary words and definitions in the left column, and draw pictures illustrating each definition in the right column. This helps them identify where to start, what they need, and how completed homework will look, promoting more independent work. Post-it note calendars help students visualize longer-term assignment due dates, and divide assignments into more manageable chunks. <u>Organization</u>: workspaces with Post-it notes or baskets labeled "Prepare," "Do," and "Done" support both planning and organization. Dual-pocket folders, one pocket for

homework or materials to take home and another for completed homework to turn in, facilitate organization.

Procedural steps for teaching that follow direct instruction principles

(1) <u>Introduction and review</u>: get student attention to introduce new information, or review or build on previously learned information. Identify the lesson's learning goal and relevance or significance. (2) <u>Development</u>: model the skill, knowledge, or behavior students will need to demonstrate. Clearly explain and give sufficient examples of material to be learned. Check for understanding by asking key questions or otherwise eliciting student questions. Use visual aids, multimedia presentations, or other prompts to facilitate successful student information processing. (3) <u>Guided practice</u>: once students respond positively to modeling, explanations, and examples, assign tasks for student practice and monitor them closely. Offer help and additional direct instruction (repeating the second step) to students not having mastered the material yet. (4) <u>Closure</u>: conclude the lesson, recapping what it covered; remind students of the learning goal; prepare them for the next step: (5) <u>Independent practice</u>: assign tasks or activities to students who demonstrated proficiency and competency in step (3) to eliminate any teacher prompts and assess degrees of student mastery. This can include homework. (6) <u>Evaluation</u>: assess progress formatively through classroom assignments, worksheets, etc.; and/or summatively through projects, tests, etc. Determine if learning goals are met or need revisiting in future lessons through evaluation feedback.

Indirect instruction strategies

Indirect instruction is student-centered. Students actively discover or construct knowledge through inquiry, hands-on exploration, experimentation, and problem-solving activities. Teachers are facilitators assigning and guiding student activity selection, supervising and supporting work. In inquiry learning, students formulate, ask, and answer questions and solve problems rather than teachers' giving answers or solutions. Students apply content knowledge and skills analyzing and explaining teacher-supplied case studies—detailed, in-depth histories and observations of individual real-life persons, families, groups, schools, communities, etc. Concept mapping facilitates students' visualizing, organizing, and applying learned concepts. Teachers guide student project and assignment preparation, identifying focus, participants, schedules, etc.; idea generation and listing; idea sorting and rating for structure; developing maps using software for multidimensional scaling, cluster analysis, etc.; interpreting; and applying maps. Reading for meaning involves active reading, previewing and predicting before, seeking relevant information during, and reflecting after reading. Students identify explicit textual messages; make logical inferences; identify main themes and ideas; analyze development, connection, interaction of people and characters, events and plot, and ideas; evaluate purpose or viewpoint influences on text content and style; differentiate objective and subjective; integrate and evaluate visual and numerical as well as verbal content; comparatively analyze multiple text topics, themes, approaches, and information. Cloze procedures—requiring student meaning determination from context to supply missing words—teach sequencing awareness, linguistic relationships, searching, prediction, and reconstruction.

Independent instruction promotes individual student autonomy, initiative, self-determination, self-direction, self-reliance, self-improvement, self-confidence, self-efficacy, and self-esteem. Students can pursue individual interests using individual styles and paces. Its applications are highly flexible and adaptable. One caveat is that teachers must ensure students have acquired the skills necessary before beginning. In learning contracts, students agree to complete specified tasks within designated conditions and schedules and sign them, promoting accountability and responsibility. In research projects, students independently develop research questions; locate, access, and consult multiple information sources; use the information to answer research questions; and write reports or papers organizing and communicating results (with teacher guidance as needed). Learning centers are self-contained areas within classrooms containing easily accessible, varied learning materials where students independently engage in self-directed learning activities. They include skill development centers, exploratory and interest centers, and enrichment centers. In computer-mediated instruction, students interact with software programs rather than teachers or classmates, working more autonomously at their own paces. In distance learning, students access information remotely, eliminating restrictions from geographic locations.

Field trips, experiments, simulations, role-plays, games, and observations

Students generally love field trips for getting them out of classrooms and providing real-world adventures, experiences, and materials. However, they also benefit from applying knowledge and skills acquired in classrooms to real-life situations for authentic, hands-on learning experiences. For example, in a geology lab, rock samples are usually distributed equally; but on field trips, students discover some rock types (e.g., quartz) are far more plentiful; find samples with mixed types; and enjoy independence and excitement in seeking and procuring samples—while additionally interacting with nature. In experiments, instead of reading or hearing about scientific concepts and procedures, students practice these, encountering and solving involved problems and challenges first-hand. They experience direct ownership of their learning. Instead of abstractions, concepts become real to them. Simulations, while not real, are realistic, enabling students to engage in activities not experienced in real life, e.g., developing military strategies, planning battles, and fighting wars; working in various occupations; marrying, raising families; building and managing cities, farms, corporations, etc. Technology makes simulations increasingly accessible, interactive, and vivid. Role-plays enable students to envision different perspectives, developing understanding, empathy, and social interactions. Games apply skills and knowledge in entertaining contexts, structured by rules. Observations develop student perception, detail-orientation, and objectivity.

Interactive strategies

All interactive strategies promote interpersonal and social skills. Brainstorming eliminates or minimizes student inhibitions and promotes self-expression, originality, and creativity by asking students to generate and express as many different ideas as possible without teacher or classmate criticism, censure, or rejection. Quantity supersedes quality. Students acquire more ideas from classmates than they could produce alone. Cooperative learning groups promote both collective and individual accountability, responsibility, and teamwork. They access and utilize the cooperative, noncompetitive orientations of students from collectivist cultures; and enable ELL and LEP students to ask classmates questions their cultural backgrounds might inhibit their asking teachers. Interviews help students learn about one another, show them they can serve as helpful resources for one another, and develop student communication skills. Discussions let students exchange ideas, information, and opinions; ask and answer questions; consider problems, questions, or ideas classmates propose that did not occur to them; use evidence to support their arguments; learn to disagree civilly; and consider differing perspectives. Peer practice affords classmate support, interaction, and greater comfort levels and identification than individual or teacher-led practice. Debates teach students to apply logic, support arguments with evidence, attend and respond to opponent arguments, take turns, follow rules, and interact formally.

Helping students develop complex thinking processes

When students learn concepts, they are not merely memorizing facts, the lowest level of Bloom's taxonomy. They also understand ideas, which is the next level. Problem-solving involves multiple steps: first, students must identify the specific problem, requiring observational and analytical skills. Then they generate multiple possible alternative solutions, requiring understanding relationships between needs and actions, plus independent and divergent thinking. Third, they anticipate various potential consequences of different alternatives, requiring abstraction, imagination, relating hypothetical situations to their own background experiences, and speculation. The next step, implementing solutions, requires active, hands-on, experiential learning. Then students evaluate solution results, requiring analytical thinking, cost-benefit analysis, judging effectiveness, value, etc. Analysis is Bloom's fourth level, evaluation Bloom's fifth. Metacognition involves thinking about one's own thought processes, requiring objectivity, analytical skills, reflection, and application—using metacognitive insights to inform, self-improve, and refine one's own learning strategies and processes for greater effectiveness. Critical thinking requires intellectual standards; discipline; open-mindedness; fairness; empathy, humility, and integrity; distinguishing objective from subjective information; evaluating and judging information and sources for validity and quality; applying logic and reasoning to unfamiliar or new ideas; informing thought with evidence; accuracy, clarity, precision, relevance, consistency, depth, and breadth. Transferring knowledge and skills requires application—Bloom's third level—to different contexts and situations.

The directed reading and thinking activity (DR-TA; Stauffer, 1969) helps students analyze text, determine purpose, question, clarify, and predict in all content subjects. Students examine the title to predict text subject matter. Following reading, open-ended questions elicit student predictions, opinions, and opinion-text connections. Comparison-contrast: make students develop questions about similarities and differences, writing them in graphic organizers, e.g., students might ask, "If circles were squares, what would happen?" "How are dogs and cats different and similar?" "How are gloves like hands? How are they not like hands?" Inferring: provide political cartoons or comic strips, and ask students to infer meaning. Student pairs or small groups identify inferences and connections they must make to interpret the cartoonist's point. Categorizing: with younger students, play 20 Questions or "animal, vegetable, mineral"-type games; provide manipulatives, having them sort objects into three different category containers. Give older students a controversial question or statement; have small groups research the topic; sort information into columns headed "Pro," "Con," and "Interesting Facts"; form opinions, and discuss. Summarizing: model first; have student partners or small groups read, stopping regularly to paraphrase; have them summarize key ideas in three or fewer textbook sections in no more than 20 words. Synthesizing: have students contribute to an idea web mural, adding and connecting ideas and comments about a central topic or question.

Modeling, developing self-regulation skills, scaffolding, guided practice, and coaching

Modeling: many students learn better from witnessing demonstration than only hearing or reading verbal description, particularly when learning procedures they must execute physically. Modeling also allows teachers to demonstrate correct techniques and sequences. Additionally, modeling helps students develop self-regulation skills including managing emotions, overcoming discomfort, taking turns, listening, demonstrating, and communicating. Teachers modeling appropriate behaviors show students how to perform tasks, and use self-regulation to complete them. They also teach self-regulation through hints, cues, and scaffolding: temporary support students need to complete tasks that are gradually removed as students gain skills. Differentiating instruction:

teachers recognize diverse student experience and expertise levels in content knowledge, thinking, problem-solving, listening, speaking, reading, and writing; through ongoing assessments, develop differentiated lessons to meet each student's needs. Having students learn in pairs or small groups promotes meaningful discussion, observation, and learning from each other. Differentiation focuses on concepts and issues, not chapters or books, encouraging students to expand concept understanding and explore so-called "big ideas." Choices of experiences and tasks or projects motivate students. Guided practice: after modeling, explaining, and examples, assign tasks or activities, monitoring closely; offer assistance as needed. Coaching: helps students understand impacts of time management, organization, and disorganization on studies; examine and strengthen study skills, problem-solving, strategic thinking, and effective interaction and collaboration.

Phases of self-regulated learning

One popular model of self-regulated learning defines three phases. (1) Forethought and planning: students analyze learning tasks, setting specific goals for completion. Students learning new or unfamiliar material may not recognize appropriate goals, best task approaches; teachers instruct them about these. (2) Performance monitoring: students apply strategies for task progress, monitoring strategy effectiveness and their motivation to continue. Students may react to discomfort with new strategies by falling back on more familiar, less effective strategies. Teachers help students overcome frustration and gain fluency with new strategies through close monitoring and specific feedback. They also support self-monitoring by having students keep records of how many times they worked on specific tasks, amounts of time working, and strategies they used, enabling students to visualize progress and make needed changes. (3) Reflections on performance: students evaluate strategy effectiveness, their task performance, and manage emotions regarding outcomes. Self-reflections influence subsequent planning and goals. Encouraging setting short-term goals helps students track progress. Goal-setting and planning are complementary: planning includes and supports establishing goals. Teaching students to approach tasks with plans promotes self-regulation and learning. Self-monitoring involves goal-setting and planning. Instructional strategies promoting self-regulation include direct instruction, guided and independent practice, reflective practice, social support, and feedback.

Instructional grouping configurations

The whole-class group configuration is the traditional, most widely used model. Teachers deliver lectures or lessons, assign classwork to, ask questions of, and lead discussions with the entire class at once. Small-group instruction, a more recent development, divides classes into groups, usually three to six students each. Each group collaborates, researching and discussing topics. Group members may be assigned different group roles, e.g., leader, facilitator, recorder, summarizer, timekeeper, presenter, errand monitor, etc. Teachers may assign individual tasks to each group member or have everyone contribute to a larger task. Students benefit from sharing, discussing, developing, and preparing their ideas in less threatening smaller groups before doing so in the whole class; and learning and practicing social interaction skills with fewer classmates under more controlled conditions. Small groups can benefit ELL/LEP students culturally intimidated about questioning teachers by enabling questions of classmates, and students with autism spectrum disorders (ASDs) overwhelmed by larger group interactions. Independent learning allows proceeding at students' own paces, using their own learning styles and strategies. One-on-one instruction benefits students needing intensive, direct instruction, remedial intervention, and/or personal student-teacher interactions and relationships. Think-pair-share structures student discussion, limiting off-task thinking and behavior, and builds in accountability through reporting to partners and the class.

Cooperative learning groups are very structured, typically containing three or four students working several days or weeks. Teachers clearly define assignments, goals, and plan of operation, and spend time teaching member roles, e.g., questioner, reporter, recorder, etc. Within designated roles, team members share leadership. All must contribute for team progress: group interdependence dictates groups win or lose together. End products represent whole teams. Cooperation, goal achievement, task completion, and group process awareness are equally important. Highly individualistic or creative students may chafe at restrictions and students preferring whole-class anonymity feel pressured, but learn cooperative teamwork skills. Collaborative groups feature three to six students working days, weeks, or months on open-ended problems or tasks which can cover much content. Flexible student roles can change throughout assignments and projects. Students help others, observing, evaluating, critiquing, explaining, and suggesting improvements. Team goals, product, and collaborative communication process awareness is constant; meeting goals justifies changing direction. Students honestly discuss ideas, information, resources, procedures, results, their own and/or others' work; multiple approaches and open communication are important. Students needing structure may prefer cooperative teams, but collaborative groups learn flexibility and communication. Homogeneous groups may feel more comfort and commonality than heterogeneous, gender-inclusive and multi-age groups, but lack their exposure to diverse perspectives expanding experience. Multi-age grouping can facilitate helping and mentoring relationships.

Short-term, working, and long-term memory

When we temporarily retain information for about three to 20 seconds, this involves short-term memory—a receptacle for visual and auditory information we rehearse, consider, analyze, interpret, or otherwise manipulate using working memory. For example, repeating a phone number to oneself silently or under one's breath until dialing or telling it to someone is in short-term memory. When we encode or consolidate and transfer information from short-term memory to long-term memory, that information is stored for an indefinite time period. Depending on individual cognitive characteristics, relative importance and meaningfulness of information, its affective impacts and associations, whether and how often one accesses the information, etc., long-term memories can last a lifetime, years, or less. Via top-down processing, prior knowledge in long-term memory strongly influences sensory perceptions; expectations about sensory experiences influence their interpretation, contributing to bias. Instructional design implications include making information sufficiently meaningful and relevant for transfer to long-term memory; and dividing information into chunks to facilitate transfer. Chunking enables the brain to automatically group some items for better retention and learning. Long-term memory, organized into interrelated schema networks, enables recalling relevant knowledge and relating new information to existing knowledge, which teachers activate using curiosity-piquing questions, graphic organizers, video, etc.

Teachable moment

Teachable moments, unlike instruction teachers plan in advance, are unplanned situations arising in classrooms, offering teachers ideal opportunities to impart some understanding or insight to students regarding some concept or topic. Teachers cannot design or plan for teachable moments. They occur momentarily; therefore, teachers must be observant, notice them, and seize the opportunity to take advantage of them. Because they are unexpected, making use of teachable moments can insert temporary detours into a teacher's original lesson plan in order to explain some idea which has aroused collective student curiosity and/or captured their interest. As an example, a teacher describes a morning class meeting wherein one student asked why the previous day had been a school holiday to observe Veterans Day. The teacher took advantage of this question as a teachable moment to discuss military service personnel's historical and current sacrifices on behalf of our country. Students were so fascinated with this topic, they discussed neighbors, relatives, and friends serving and the meaning of the military to the country's future for 20 minutes. The benefit of following such tangents is their maximal impact on students through their natural timing. Teachable moments can ultimately develop into complete lesson plans or instructional units.

Useful feedback

Useful feedback must be consistent, formative, timely, and ongoing to enable student performance adjustments. It must be user-friendly: students must understand feedback to apply it, so it must be age-appropriate or developmentally appropriate, not containing excessive or overly technical information for students to handle. Expert educators communicate observation of one important behavior, which changing can produce noticeable improvement immediately, not offering advice until ensuring students understand the significance of observations. Effective feedback is actionable: grades, "wrong," and "good job" are not feedback. Inferences from data without presenting data are not descriptive enough. For example, "Many students were bored in your class" is judgment, not observation. "Twelve of 25 students texted or passed notes during your lecture; only one did during the small-group activity" is less arguable, more neutral and useful. Feedback must include explicit goals and tangible, goal-related results. Students can be too occupied with performing to attend to results: video recordings help. Most school district "formative" test grades refer to recently taught objectives, not final performance standards. Evaluating fall and winter performance against spring standards, measuring progress using more pre- and post-assessments, and using item analysis to identify individual student performance improvement needs are more effective.

Diverse student backgrounds and needs

Today's classroom diversity includes students with different native languages, cultural backgrounds, previous educational and personal experiences, and knowledge. Disabilities are also a possibility. Regardless of background, gender, or other characteristics, all students need teachers to behave and communicate in considerate ways. Teachers who consider how peers and faculty may misjudge some students and how this affects them, and are aware of stereotypes and their consequences, can develop true awareness of others' perspectives. Using language, examples, and behaviors to treat students with interest and consideration and encourage others to follow suit facilitates establishing welcoming environments where students feel comfortable participating, enabling their success. Even though teachers may have student records, they need to inform themselves of individual students' background knowledge. They can begin school years surveying student knowledge prerequisite to their subject or class; give students lists of basic content-area vocabulary they expect students to understand, asking them to identify unfamiliar or problematic words; consult Individualized Education Program (IEP) information, special educators, and parents about how student disabilities can affect attendance and participation; and ask students, parents, school social workers, and/or others about student religion, family obligations, and other unique factors to consider.

Motivation theory

Self-determination: student propensity for initiating activities independently, as opposed to only doing what teachers tell them to do. Achievement motivation research finds student motivation to learn and perform is stronger based on internalized motives, e.g., interest in subject matter, self-efficacy, desire to know things, desire to succeed, career ambitions, etc. By comparison, externalized motives, e.g., to gain rewards from teachers, schools, or parents; to avoid punishment; to impress teachers, classmates, friends, parents, etc. are not as effective. Attribution: how and where we assign cause. Students with more internal locus of control attribute their success or failure to personal abilities and actions; students with more external locus of control attribute successes or failures to people, actions, events, or situations outside themselves. Cognitive dissonance: discomfort with contradictory information; we adjust our schemas (mental representations) to reflect new information, form new schemas, or reject the information to restore congruence and resolve the discomfort. Classical conditioning: associating an unrelated stimulus with one that elicits a certain reflexive reaction can condition it to evoke the same reaction. Pavlov repeatedly paired bell-ringing with meat powder to make a dog salivate; eventually bell-ringing alone evoked salivation. Operant conditioning: manipulating antecedents and consequences shapes behavior; positive reinforcement strengthens probability of repeating behavior; punishment weakens it. Negative reinforcement removes a reinforcer or reward, decreasing behavior repetition.

Promoting student motivation

Teachers delivering instruction with enthusiasm and energy are role models: demonstrating their motivation and passion motivates students. Teachers showing why they are interested in subject content personalize it for students. Getting to know students, belief in student ability, strong interest in their learning, and personal interest in student backgrounds and concerns inspire personal student loyalty. Many students want to know the application, utility, or real-life relevance of content before further engagement. To do this, use many examples and explain how it prepares them for future opportunities. Design activities directly engaging students in material, offering mastery opportunities: discovery learning requiring reasoning through problems to discover underlying principles independently satisfies students. Positive social pressure makes cooperative learning activities effective. Design assignments with challenges appropriate to student abilities and experiences. Set realistic performance goals; help students set and achieve reasonable goals. Tests and grades should show mastery, not shortcomings. Allow all students opportunities to achieve the highest grades and standards; avoid grading on curves. Make criticism constructive, feedback nonjudgmental. Criticize specific performances, not performers. Seek means of stimulating advancement; emphasize improvement opportunities. Avoid classifying students as leaders or followers. Give students as much choice and control over their learning, assessment, and performance as possible.

Intrinsic motivation

Students intrinsically motivated to learn are attracted to and fascinated by subjects, recognize their relevance to real life, feel a sense of accomplishment from mastering them, and feel called to them. Their reasons for learning are typically because the content interests them, they find it improves their thinking skills, and/or they find school success rewarding. Advantages include that intrinsic motivation sustains itself and has more longevity than external rewards; teacher efforts to build internal motivation typically involve efforts to further student learning as well, typically focusing not on rewards or punishments but on subject matter. Disadvantages include more specialized preparation, taking longer to produce behavior change, and requiring teachers utilize a variety of approaches in different students. Getting to know individual students and what interests them, connecting student interests to subject content, and strong teacher interest in subject content (and demonstration thereof) support developing intrinsic motivation in students.

According to one model, students offered opportunities to engage in learning activities first decide whether an activity is interesting to them or not. They engage in activities that interest them. If not immediately finding interest in an activity, they then evaluate it according to two criteria: whether or to what extent it is stimulating, i.e., it attracts their curiosity, affords a challenge, and/or appeals to their sense of fantasy; and whether or to what degree it affords them personal control—i.e., it is not too difficult for them to accomplish, and allows them some measure of free choice in the specific topics, learning styles, methods, procedures, materials, and forms of assessment they can use to acquire knowledge and demonstrate understanding. If students perceive an activity as both stimulating and controllable, they consider it potentially interesting or valuable and engage in it. If either or both conditions become inadequate, students disengage unless influenced by some extrinsic motivation. Students are more likely to repeat engagement in activities they find repeatedly stimulating and controllable, and discard those repeatedly not satisfying these criteria. Research finds the more constructive teacher criticism is and the more freely and often teachers praise student efforts, the more encouraged and self-motivated students become.

Including students in instructional decisions

All human beings want some control over their circumstances and activities. This is especially important to K-12 students: as minors, they have less legal and practical power and control over their lives than adults. Students perceiving teachers as having all the control over their instruction are more likely to respond only to external rewards and punishments and less likely to develop internal motivation to learn and achieve academically. When teachers include students in instructional decisions, students feel ownership of the content and their learning. For example, teachers can ask students which aspects and topics within curriculum subjects interest them and let students choose topics they are interested in for papers and projects. They can give students choices among working independently, in pairs, or in small groups for some learning activities. Teachers can offer students options for how to weigh different assignments and assessments to determine their grades. Including papers, projects, tests, presentations, and other varied ways of assessing students allows them more control over how they demonstrate their learning. Participation and control in their instruction increases student motivation for acquiring and demonstrating knowledge.

Internal vs. external motivation

External motivations include teacher and parent expectations of students; rewards students can earn by demonstrating learning; and grades, which determine passing, promotion, retention, graduation, future opportunities, college admissions, scholarships, etc. Applying external motivators typically requires little preparation or effort, frequently does not require much teacher knowledge about individual students and their interests, and produces more immediate behavior changes. However, designating appropriate rewards and punishments becomes challenging when students become habituated, requiring escalation over time. External rewards frequently distract students from learning subject matter. They are not durable: students lose motivation once rewards and punishments are discontinued. Additionally, multiple experiments (e.g., Lepper, Deci) show external rewards can decrease internal motivation: students of all ages continued to engage in activities without rewards as they found them inherently interesting, whereas those given rewards for engaging in them discontinued engagement when rewards ceased; extrinsic rewards apparently reduced intrinsic interest. Internal motivations, including student interest in subject matter and learning and desire for knowledge and success, require more teacher time and effort and take longer to change behavior, but are durable, not dependent on rewards or punishments. Additional factors affecting student motivation include how stimulating activities are and how much control students have over them.

Contrasting with internal motives that students have for learning and succeeding academically, grades are external motivators. While they provide an index of how a student performed in classroom activities and assessments—which can vary in accuracy—grades by themselves do not give students intrinsic reasons to learn or achieve. Students displaying extrinsic motivation might say they need certain letter or number grades to pass courses and accomplish graduation from high school, to the next grade, receive rewards promised by teachers or parents, or avoid punishment. This differs from students saying that certain grades prove they know, understand, or have mastered subjects. Though some view formative assessment grades as feedback, these often do not inform adjusting performance. In an expert's (Wiggins, 2012) analogy, suppose a student's goal in PE is to run a five-minute mile, already having achieved 5:09. Suppose at the end of the first lap of a mile race, her coach yelled, "B-plus on that lap!" This does not support progress toward the goal. But the coach's yelling individual lap times, feedback, and advice: "You're on pace for 5:15," "You're not swinging your arms," "You need two seconds off the next lap to finish under 5:10—pick it up," provides specific information and advice for progress toward the goal.

Showing students the appeal of instructional content

Teachers can encourage student interest in subject content by showing its appeal. To show novelty, comment how you have not seen anything quite like a certain topic or activity. To show utility, describe a topic as including valuable ideas you will use later in the course and being a topic they will use over and over in both school and life. To show applicability, point out how relevant certain subject matter is to the course and everyday life. To show anticipation, prompt students to ask themselves while reading what next logical step the text foreshadows. To show surprise, remark that the class has used some subject matter in many different ways, and then whet their interest, saying, "If you think you've seen them all, just wait until our next activity." To show challenge, suggest students will find the upcoming material very interesting and invite them to rise to a challenge. To show feedback, predict that when students try an assigned activity, they will discover whether they really understood the previous lesson or not. To show closure, announce that many students have asked about a topic or phenomenon, telling them they will now finally find out more and why.

Ways in which individual student differences influence classroom communication

Younger students need concrete terms, examples, and materials; older students can handle increasing abstraction. Teachers should give students of all ages concepts and vocabulary slightly above their current levels for challenge and growth. Both student and teacher communication can be influenced by gender, e.g., volunteering, calling out, or waiting to be called on regardless of knowledge and preparation. Teachers may perceive or treat identical student responses differently according to student gender and/or race, e.g., as assertive vs. aggressive or enthusiastic vs. disruptive. ELL and LEP students may know content, but lack English to express it, or feel uncomfortable with their ELP levels. Numerous studies show when teachers communicate high learning expectations for all students, including ELLs and students with disabilities, they perform better. Emotionally engaging anecdotes, examples, and connecting topics to student prior knowledge, experience, interests, value, and utility stimulate student curiosity and interest. To clarify class goals and purposes, focus on major points, letting students find additional information in other activities. Repeat key concepts and ideas, compare and contrast, summarize, use analogies and metaphors to aid student comprehension and emphasize importance. Structure classes logically: present problems, then develop solutions; frame topics as stories; chronologically recount processes and events; show interconnected ideas' relationship to overarching themes; share outlines; explicitly transition between topics using mini-summaries, connections, or verbal signals.

Ensuring engagement and understanding of all students

Verbally, vary vocal speeds and tones to keep speech interesting to students. Vocal projection facilitates student hearing and also demonstrates teachers' confidence in what they say. Pausing strategically gets student attention, emphasizes transitions in topics, and gives students time to process information. Give ELLs and students with hearing, cognitive, learning, and other disabilities more wait time to allow for translating and processing teacher questions and formulating and translating their answers. Nonverbally, stand up straight and maintain eye contact to project confidence. Smiling communicates valuing what you say. While avoiding distracting apparel and excessive gestures, use movement to express enthusiasm, excitement, and energy. To help explain, illustrate, or clarify complex ideas, use media—not to distract from but to enhance instructional communication. Use chalkboards, dry-erase boards and overheads to demonstrate reasoning behind derivations, illustrate processes, and teach dynamically. Use slide presentations to organize varied visual, audio, and animated content, summarize ideas, and emphasize key points. Animations and videos offer sense of scale and illustrate dynamic processes. Audio can illustrate sounds associated with physical processes and introduce new, historical, or remote voices into classrooms. Artifacts can incorporate real-life elements, and print or electronic handouts give students detailed images and information. Redundant and multimodal presentations benefit ELL, exceptional, and all students.

Classroom question types to access different levels of Bloom's taxonomy

Levels, question types: knowledge and comprehension: what are the main points? What happened when...? Why did...? Application: can you think of other words meaning the same thing? Can you use this word in a different context? Can you think of another example of this? Does the same idea apply to...? Analysis: what effect does this achieve? Why do you think the author chose to do this? Does this fit into a pattern? What is suggested by...? How...? Why do you agree or disagree with this? Evaluation: which of these are most effective? What do you think of this? Do you think this works well? What are the strongest and weakest aspects of this? Synthesis: can you create your own version of this? How can you change the audience, features, etc. of this text? Where else can you see examples of this? Student activities, levels: analysis: debate a topic. Create text-based questions. Draw concept maps exploring connections. Mind-map aspects of a topic or text. Synthesis: study pastiche and parody. Analyze authors and writing styles closely; adopt styles. Experiment with genres, audiences, and text type features. Evaluation: devise reader expectation criteria for various text types. Apply assessment criteria to own and others' work.

Active listening strategies

Effective, active listening strategies accomplish multiple goals: teachers show students they care about them, demonstrate attention to their concerns, make them feel understood, establish and develop student-teacher relationships, give students emotional connections with school, model effective listening strategies for students to learn and use, and motivate student learning. Research shows student learning motivation requires feeling connected. In active listening, the listener uses verbal and nonverbal signals, asks questions to clarify, and restates main points for the speaker to confirm or correct. Restating in one's own words can also involve interpreting the speaker's message. For example, a student says, "I don't like this school as much as my other school. People aren't nice." The teacher responds, "You're unhappy here?" The student answers, "Yes. I haven't made any friends. Nobody includes me in anything." The teacher responds, "You feel left out here?" The student confirms, "Yes, I wish I knew more people." Questions, restating, and interpreting clarify factual and emotional message content. When speakers refine listener interpretations, they feel heard, gain insights into their own feelings, and may experience catharsis. Listeners enhance their skills in focusing on speakers and considering implied meanings.

Nonverbal communication

Open postures communicate receptivity; crossed arms and legs or similar averted body positions communicate the opposite. Ways of walking, sitting, standing, holding one's head, and subtle movements all convey attitudes and feelings. Gestures supplement speech, often unconsciously. Because different cultures assign different meanings to the same gestures, awareness is important to prevent misunderstanding or misinterpretation. Vocal tones and inflections express confidence, affection, anger, and sarcasm; and can even indicate understanding, agreement, and many more. Listeners also attend to speaker loudness, speed, and timing. Eye contact demonstrates interest in our culture; in some other cultures, it is perceived as confrontational and avoiding it shows respect. We communicate affection, attraction, or hostility as well as interest through eye contact; gauge others' responses; and maintain conversational flow. Facial expressions universally show happiness, sadness, anger, fear, surprise, disgust, and other emotions. Personal and social physical space or distance vary by individual, relationship, situation, and culture and can communicate intimacy, dominance, or aggression. Nonverbal communication informs verbal communication by repeating verbal messages; contradicting them; substituting for them; complementing or adding to them, e.g., patting on the back while verbally praising; accenting them; or emphasizing them, e.g., pounding the table, desk, lectern, dais, or pulpit with spoken points.

Questioning students

Questions cognitively lower on Bloom's taxonomy—for knowledge and comprehension—are better when imparting or retaining factual knowledge. Open-ended, higher-cognitive questions—for application, analysis, evaluation, and synthesis—should be more than half of those used in higher grades, but elementary-grade students need smaller proportions of these too. Research finds combining higher and lower questions more effective than using either one exclusively. Studies show older students' on-task behavior, response length, number of relevant contributions and questions, peer interactions, complete sentences, and speculative thinking correlate positively with using greater than or equal to 50 percent higher-level questions. Teachers may still need to include explicit instruction, not just many more questions, for complex concepts. Pre-reading questions are effective with older, higher-ability, and interested students, but not with poor readers and younger students, who focus only on material for answering them. Slightly increasing wait-time promotes achievement. Studies find teachers paradoxically allow less wait time for students perceived as poor or slow learners than those perceived more capable. Teachers encourage participation by inviting student responses non-critically, addressing incorrect answers with redirection, and partial answers with probing—both explicit to student answers. Vague feedback, e.g., "Wrong, try again" is ineffective for achievement. Active listening restates student responses, helping clarify student understanding and meaning and encouraging participation.

Teachers ask students questions for varied purposes, e.g., actively involving students in lessons, regardless of questions' cognitive levels. "When did this author live?" "In what period is this work set?" Even low-level knowledge questions involve students as they consider and/or respond. "Why do you think the author did...?" require cognitively higher responses. Teachers might ask "Have you ever...?" or "Do you know anybody who...?" This relates textual events and experiences to students' own lives. Connecting new material to prior knowledge increases motivation and interest. Questions can evaluate preparation and check on assignment completion: in classes with many students not typically hesitant to speak, if nobody answers basic questions about assigned reading, they likely did not do it. Students completing math assignments successfully can likely answer specific questions about the operations they used or solutions they got, while those not doing or understanding it cannot. Questions develop critical thinking skills when requiring students to apply concepts and analyze them, separate inference from fact, evaluate or judge ideas and products, and synthesize components to construct new meaning. Questions help teachers review prior lessons to assess, increase, or refresh student comprehension and retention. They cultivate insights by making students think about topics, assess goal achievement, and stimulate independent learning.

Managerial questions facilitate classroom operations. Rhetorical questions reinforce or emphasize statements and ideas. Closed questions check retention and focus thinking. Open questions promote student discussion and interaction. Probing questions, based on student responses, require students to go beyond first answers. Clarifying: "What do you mean? Can you elaborate?" Increasing critical awareness: "What are you assuming? What are your reasons? What would an opponent say?" Refocusing: "Then what are the implications for...? Can you relate that to...? Let's analyze your answer." Prompting: "What's the square root of 94?" (Student: "I don't know.") "What's the square root of 100?" (Student: "10.") "Of 81?" (Student: "Nine.") "Then what do we know about the square root of 94?" (Student: "It's between nine and 10.") Redirecting to another student: "Do you agree? Can you elaborate on his/her answer?" Factual questions elicit simple information, e.g., "Who wrote this? Who is the main character?" Or they elicit event sequences: "What are the steps for a bill to become law?" "How is hydrochloric acid produced?" "How did Robinson Crusoe react to discovering footprints?" Divergent questions have no right or wrong answer, eliciting exploration of possibilities and both concrete and abstract thinking. For example: "If the Spanish Armada had defeated England in 1588, how would it have changed history?"

Rather than remembering answers, students must figure out answers by higher-order questions, which require generalizing in meaningful patterns relative to facts. Evaluation: requires valuation, judgment, or choice via comparing things and ideas with established standards. Assuming equal resources, would you rate General Ulysses S. Grant or Robert E. Lee more skillful? Why? Which of these two books do you think contributed more to understanding this era? Why? Inference: requires deductive or inductive reasoning. Deductive: if gas temperature remains constant but altitude is increased 4000 feet, what happens to gas pressure? Why? Inductive: considering these world leaders' shared qualities, what can we conclude about required leadership qualities? Why? Comparison: requires discerning similarities, differences, contradictions, and non-relations – How are Social Darwinism and late-19th-century Supreme Court rulings related? How are Pericles' Funeral Oration and Lincoln's Gettysburg Address similar or different? Are clams and mussels the same? Application: requires transferring concepts and principles to different contexts – How did Germany's Weimar Republic demonstrate Gresham's Law? Problem-solving: requires using acquired knowledge, seeing relationships, relating parts to whole – Imagine you grew up thinking dogs were bad, but none bit you; how would you react now? Would the dog's characteristics matter? Explain the idea of prejudice using this example.

Supporting students in articulating ideas

One strategy teachers use to support clear student expression is prompting. Verbal prompting: when a student does not know the answer to the teacher's initial question, the teacher asks additional questions to which the student does know the answers, leading the student to discover more about the answer to the original question. For example, a teacher asks a student a square root s/he does not know; the teacher asks the student two more square roots, one higher and the other lower; the student realizes the unknown answer is between the other two. Nonverbal prompting: nodding or making affirmative sounds and gestures indicating agreement to encourage continuing, pointing at objects or information to give hints, hand-over-hand guidance with manipulatives, etc. Restatement: repeating a student's message in the teacher's own words, either affirming the message or allowing the student to deny or correct the restatement or clarify the message. Student: "This assignment took me all night!" Teacher: "It was too hard?" Reflective listening statements mirror student messages, not just restating them but moreover interpreting implicit meanings. Student: "I will never get this right!" Teacher: "You feel frustrated?" Wait-time enables student processing: understanding questions, recalling information, formulating responses. Research finds three minutes optimal for factual or low-cognitive, and longer for high-cognitive questions.

Methods that promote higher thinking levels

(1) After assigned reading or video viewing, ask students what they would have done in a fictional character or nonfictional individual's situation. After students complete projects or assignments, have them write (a.) what they could have done differently, (b.) how, (c.) what they will do differently or additionally next time, and (d.) what they learned during the process of the project or assignment. These both require students to reflect on their experiences and articulate insights and thoughts. (2) In class discussion, have students identify a book or movie's main assumption(s). Ask how they know these are true. Have them research for proof or disproof, teaching the habit of questioning and investigating rather than simply accepting others' assumptions. (3) Have students compare similarities and contrast differences between or among books, movies, experiments, natural phenomena, etc., guiding them to find relationships. Have them make cause-and-effect graphics identifying relationships among events or actions in history, fiction, or drama. Ask how fictional characters and historical or current figures influence(d) one another; how chemicals interact, causing reactions; why, etc. (4) Ask students to explain how information relates to current study topics. For examining validity, see (2) above; also have students test claims directly when feasible. (5) Review information identified in lessons and classwork, ask what students conclude based on it, and have them explain the logic leading to conclusions. (6) Assign applying newly-learned skills in other classes, field trips, homes, communities, and workplaces.

Setting the stage for effective classroom discussions

For teachers to get all students engaged in discussing a topic, they need to make it appealing. One way is connecting topics to existing student experience and knowledge, making them more personally relevant. Ask if they have encountered similar situations or felt similarly in other situations: find some commonality between the topic and every student's life experience. Teachers also need to show respect for all student opinions. Experts note teachers' natural inclinations to evaluate, approve or disapprove, and judge student contributions, increasing student fears against expressing thoughts. To create climates welcoming participation, teachers must suspend judgment; instead of responding with "Right," "Wrong," or "That wasn't what I was thinking about," etc., they can respond, "Tell me more about that," "Thank you for sharing your ideas with us," etc. Asking students to elaborate without judging makes them feel safe to progress in their thinking and share it. This teacher acceptance establishing safety also supports student risk-taking. In safe, non-threatening, non-judgmental atmospheres, teacher acceptance encourages students to express potentially controversial or minority views. Making all students feel safe and invited to participate facilitates collaboration: teachers model respecting others' ideas; students with non-judgmental teachers are less likely to fear classmates' judgment.

Problem-solving learning tasks and learning project activities

Technology is an enormous asset to both teachers and students. For example, word processing programs, e.g., Microsoft Word, streamline teachers' work creating instructional documents like learning units, lesson plans, student handouts, worksheets, rubrics, checklists, progress reports, written parent communications, etc. Students can write essays, research reports, papers, short stories, plays, poetry, books, etc. They can type and save preliminary notes and outlines, then easily copy and paste portions into compositions. Students benefit from being able to delete and restore text paragraphs and sections instantly, and easily move paragraphs and sections to other locations as they learn how to organize their writing. Spell-checkers and grammar-checkers, while not substitutes for student knowledge, alert students to typing and mechanical errors for correction. Microsoft Excel and similar spreadsheet programs facilitate organizing numerical data and verbal information. Students can type in figures or lists with little or no editing and Excel displays and prints them in spreadsheet format. Databases give teachers and students large amounts of easily accessible information about specified topics, enabling them to search and sort it. Graphic tools enable students and teachers lacking artistic ability to create colorful, effective, professional-looking visual images to illustrate, organize, and understand information and concepts. Students and teachers can establish, use, and contribute to online communities to communicate and share information remotely, often instantaneously.

Communicating and publishing information with various technology tools

Teachers and students alike can use available technology productivity tools to organize, share, and present information in different formats. For example, in preparing a lesson plan, a teacher might create a PowerPoint slide presentation to project while delivering a lesson. By entering summary statements of main ideas, important concepts, major facts, etc. on each slide, teachers call student attention to the most significant aspects of the lesson, reinforcing these even as they provide additional information and details through lectures, discussions, textbooks, etc. Not only are slide presentations good for identifying main points, they also reinforce information presented in other ways (speech, textbooks, handouts), providing the redundancy students need to learn and retain it. In addition to PowerPoints, slide shows are good ways to illustrate lectures, lessons, and student presentations with visual imagery that engages viewers. Teachers can make videos of class for objective feedback and analysis; students can produce videos for class projects. Teachers can create multimedia presentations to access different student learning styles, helping all students benefit from instruction. Teachers can write parent newsletters, and students can create and publish classroom or school newsletters. Students, parents, and school personnel can view documents via websites and programs on monitor screens and/or print copies.

Assessing learning that students demonstrate through technological activities and projects

Teachers newly integrating technology into student work often wonder how to grade it. Evaluating student processes and actions is the same as with traditional written work, though it differs with the divergent potentials and unique features of each medium. For example, a notebook contains handwritten notes and drawings; a blog can contain hypertext, interactive imagery, embedded video, etc. Teachers must distinguish a technology tool's capabilities from the performance of the student using it. For example, iMovie has built-in, user-friendly professional effects enabling anybody to produce visually impressive video presentations. Hence teachers cannot grade the end product but the process, i.e., the student's research, writing, image selection, and other activities. In this sense, assessment must be more formative than summative to avoid focusing only on flashy end products and observe learning activities throughout the project. Teachers can create assessment rubrics using online generators like Rubistar, Digital Media Scoring Guides, Matrix Rubric with Points, PBL Checklists, Scholastic Rubric Maker, and Common Core Rubric Creator; or use available rubrics designed for general assessment; student blogs, wikis, websites, digital portfolios, social media, effective technology use, videos, digital storytelling, podcasts, graphic organizers, programming, coding, and gaming.

Providing unique growth opportunity for modern students

Many technologies (e.g., calculators and iPads) are student-centered. They were developed to provide a one-on-one interactive experience with some form of learning. Research has shown that learning technologies act as cognitive amplifiers. Students can learn more efficiently and effectively with technology. Technology, however, is not a silver bullet. Simple access to technology will not empower students to learn better. Teachers will require training to learn how to properly implement classroom technology (in coordination with pedagogy) and students will have to learn to appropriately and responsibly use technology. In coordination with technology and new pedagogical innovations (e.g., flipped classrooms, collaborative problem solving, or inquiry-based learning), teachers are able to provide their students with engagement opportunities previously unavailable. Students who have access to technology are able to directly engage with concepts and contexts any time of day or night. No longer are teachers the sole facilitators of quality learning. With traditional pedagogies (e.g., lecture), technology may be more distracting and less helpful. Technology is not best utilized as a replacement for old modes of knowledge transfer (e.g., note-taking or board presentation). A professional educator can adapt to both the new devices and new modes of thinking that empower student learning at trajectories not previously attainable.

Incorporating social media in the classroom

Social media is virtually ubiquitous in 21st century America. Our students are immersed in a society dominated by social media and this offers teachers an opportunity to model asynchronous (i.e., outside the time and vicinity constraints of standard class periods) learning processes that help students become lifelong learners. Examples of positive classroom social media outlets include *YouTube* where students can view or develop podcasts directly applicable to classroom topics. Teachers can use *Twitter* to post updates about assignments or deadlines. Teachers and students can blog about classroom experiences and practice academic writing skills. Students can receive more immediate feedback on academic pursuits with *Facebook*. Through all of these social media interactions, teachers can monitor students and model appropriate etiquette for online interactions as they help students become responsible and respectful citizens in a digital world.

Although there are a number of great benefits of social media in the classroom learning environment, these benefits do not come without the possibility of distractions. Students may try to tweet or snapchat with friends during class time. Teachers can always use less common social media tools to provide an opportunity for technologically empowered student engagement without the distraction associated with the most popular social networking platforms. For example, *Edmodo* enables educators to communicate with students, share materials, and distribute assessments in an efficient and non-distracting manner. Teachers and students can share work and gain efficient feedback through shared *Google Docs* that allow limitations on who contributes to social interactions. *Edublogs* allow teachers to share materials, encourage student contributions, incorporate videos, and facilitate online discussions.

Relationship between academic instruction and classroom management

When educators teach and encourage students to take responsibility for their own behaviors rather than taking total responsibility for guiding student behaviors, teachers and students approach and understand content differently. Moreover, when instruction is more demanding (e.g., students address novel problems and/or create products), teachers must make more complex management decisions. This relationship between instructional activity levels and management complexity supports research evidence of the inseparable, complex interrelationship of instructional curriculum and classroom management. Teachers must help students learn to meet concurrent academic demands for comprehending and manipulating content, and social demands for interacting with others to demonstrate that content knowledge effectively. This broader view of classroom management has redirected research from controlling behavior to creating and sustaining learning environments—including furniture arrangements, classroom decorations, developing and communicating rules and routines, and interacting with students. Research shows teachers implementing systematic classroom management approaches when school years begin have students demonstrating higher task engagement and academic achievement. Researchers also identify strategies eliciting low misbehavior and high involvement as communicating awareness of student behavior, overlapping activities, smooth transitions, instructional momentum, and whole-class-focused attention alerting.

Understanding student group dynamics and managing their behavior

Be aware of individual students' group roles, e.g., leader, instigator, conscience, intimidator, enforcer, procurer, or negotiator; develop friendly relationships with the first three, and keep the first two on-task. Know group-required behaviors, conversation topics and interests, and what maintains a group's cooperation and unity. Place a daily "do-now" activity on the board or students' desks to start upon arrival before lessons, preparing students for lessons and continuing ongoing group or team tasks and activities. Greet and converse with students, always respectfully. Pleasantly remind and encourage desired behaviors before classes begin. Engage group leaders in task preparations (equipment setup, writing assignments on boards or overheads, reading assignment directions, handing out worksheets): others follow. Include cooperative learning groups, and allow collaborative team answers. Recognize and reward good behavior. Never embarrass students in front of classmates, which provokes individual and group rebellion. Determine behavior reasons and functions, e.g., boredom, overly easy or difficult assignments, confronting or embarrassing students, favoritism, group leader behavior contagion, pre-existing issues, distracters, etc. Prevent escalation using low-impact interventions: interest in student work, encouragement, good-natured humor, physical proximity, touch, interrupting oneself mid-sentence and using the "teacher glare," reminding classes and groups of times they did well, and changing lesson presentation to become more interesting than any distraction(s).

Productive classroom environments for students at different developmental levels

Teachers must take into account the developmental levels of their students to establish positive classroom environments for them. For example, teachers should not expect young children to begin preschool having already learned to share with other children. Teachers can model sharing and cooperation for them, and encourage and reward their imitating teacher examples as well as spontaneous prosocial behaviors, which researchers have observed in young children. Teachers can also observe whether young students engage in unoccupied behavior; independent or solitary play; onlooker behavior; parallel, associative, or cooperative play; and influencing factors, e.g., how well children know each other, offer matching activities, and introduce experiences at the next higher level. Teachers can offer peer collaboration opportunities to older elementary and middle school students by assigning study buddies, partners for peer tutoring, working together, or think-pair-share and similar activities. Small groups can also be formed for planning, organizing, and implementing team or group learning projects, although teachers must remember that students have typically not developed social interaction skills to the extent of high school students, and so must guide them accordingly. In high school, teachers can extend productive learning environments beyond classrooms to surrounding communities, engaging students' abstract cognitive skills to promote respect, social conscience, and action through service projects.

Respecting diversity and promoting the active engagement of all students

Honor student experiences: create safe spaces, enrich curriculum using student experiences, and give students opportunities to learn from each other's perspectives and experiences. View different identity groups from asset-based orientations, let students define their own identities, and avoid or challenge stereotypes. Select texts reflecting demographics of and relevant to specific classes, and assign discussions or reflective writing about reading. Share personal anecdotes inviting student sharing. Student-centered classroom setups should include multicultural decorations or imagery reflecting our society's diversity and student backgrounds. Arrange furniture and materials to support comfort, ownership, dialogue, and collaboration. Structure classrooms for maximal student voice and participation. Involve students in setting norms and expectations, considering gender, language, and cultural and communication differences. Give students daily classroom jobs accommodating different learning styles, innovative student approaches, and real-life responsibility and work skills. Use gender-neutral categories and practices and let students choose group identifications. Build shared inquiry and dialogue through respect, trust, voice, humility, and active listening skills. Revisit participation norms: include and value small-group participation, written and artistic responses, and active listening as well as verbal communication. To create safe climates, actively teach emotional-social skills, work to create positive relationships, build community, prevent or intervene with bullying, focus explicitly on understanding and appreciating differences, practice and teach meaningful conflict resolution, and teach students to challenge exclusion and bias.

Instructional strategy for communicating high expectations

Experts (Marzano, 2010) advise: (1) as early as possible, identify students for whom you have lower expectations. Once formed, negative expectations are hard to admit and change. (2) Identify student similarities. Though teachers resist admitting they automatically form expectations based on student appearance, speech style, or ethnicity, research finds early expectations based on such characteristics. Expectation patterns do not indicate bigotry or racism when people actively work to keep biases from controlling their thoughts and behaviors. (3) Identify your differential behaviors toward low-expectancy students, which are far more important than your expectations. Students observe and make inferences based on teacher behaviors. Affectively, teachers make less eye and physical contact, smile less, and lightly or playfully converse less with low-expectancy students. Academically, they ask them less challenging questions, call on them less frequently, explore their answers in less depth, and reward less rigorous responses from them. (4) Consciously treat high-expectancy and low-expectancy students the same way. Affectively this is relatively easy, but academically more challenging: students habituated to low teacher expectations may experience discomfort when teachers challenge them more. However, ultimately this enables students to ask clarifying questions and risk communicating new ideas.

Responding to all student cultural, linguistic, and familial backgrounds and needs

Students learn more when challenged by high teacher expectations, including open-ended questions and assignments requiring critical thinking skills. Explicitly teaching skills for studying, working with teachers, and completing college applications to students whose parents never attended college fills "cultural capital" gaps, preparing underrepresented students for college. Give students adult responsibilities for collaboratively contributing to planning, coaching, financial activities, etc. Diversity becomes a resource; students learn varied skills. Teacher knowledge and caring about individual students promotes their participation. Understanding student home cultures aids educator understanding of student behavior inside and outside classrooms. Encouraging active parental participation greatly supports student academic success through mutually understanding parent, classroom, and school expectations of teachers and students; helping parents converse to prepare children for classroom communication; helping parents pursue GED or ESL programs; and referring parents to community resources for arts, sports, science programs, and homework help. Eliciting and validating student background experiences, e.g., using semantic webbing to inform lesson planning and increase student engagement. Selecting curriculum for cultural relevance—student ethnic groups' contributions to US history and culture—enhances student self-esteem, makes lesson topics meaningful, and enables authentic, interactive language, literacy, and thinking skills. Culturally compatible social learning organization and communication expectations and norms make teaching and learning more effective.

Developing student oral and written communication skills

Oral: the inside-outside circle – students, facing each other in two concentric circles, pair up; take turns speaking and listening; and rotate partners. Choral response – teacher asks a question, gives a signal, allows wait-time, says "Everyone..." and initiates signal, and the students respond in unison. Think-pair-share – students rehearse responses with partners, getting corrective feedback or elaboration help before whole-class sharing. Dialogic reading – teachers read books with individual students or small groups using "CROWD" prompts: sentence *completion*; asking questions requiring student text *recall*; *open-ended* questions about book pictures; *w-questions* (who, what, when, etc.) about pictures; and *distancing* book pictures and words to students' own life experiences. PEER prompts: *prompting* students to talk about text, *evaluating* responses, *expanding* responses, and *repeating* prompts at higher levels. Written: written responses, same answers – teachers ask questions; students write answers on whiteboards; teachers allow wait-time, say "Everyone..." and students hold up written responses. Written responses, varying answers – like same answers, but students check answers with partners, revise as needed; teachers call on individual students. Think-pair-share activities also enable students to get peer feedback about written responses before sharing them with the whole class.

Communicating expectations to students

By always behaving fairly and consistently in class, teachers model integrity for students, who understand better what is expected of them by witnessing the teacher meeting his/her own high expectations. Reinforce expectations daily, and repeat continually—sometimes through gentle reminders, other times interrupting instruction to discuss expectations as indicated—to change student attitudes. Support and inform student success through parent-teacher collaboration by communicating to parents your expectations of both students and parents. Prepare "achievement contracts" outlining mutual expectations students sign when the school year begins. Give students time to find answers themselves, only giving hints or ideas, not supplying correct answers immediately. Periodically, have students write about how they think they are doing and suggestions for improving the class. Always speak to students positively, emphasizing their ability to learn your instruction. Let students view you as a real person; get to know them. This attitude motivates some students to work harder to please teachers. However, avoid the trap of being students' friend; maintain authority as their teacher. Tell students exactly what you expect, making activity and assignment standards perfectly clear. Ensure every student knows s/he can earn high grades by working hard enough. Let students revise poorly-graded work, promoting mastery learning.

Good student-teacher interactions and relationships

Good student-teacher interactions and relationships enhance classroom atmosphere. Research has generated a significant body of literature showing that the quality of teacher-student relationships influences student academic achievement and behavior. Teachers showing students respect and guiding them to respect each other encourage active learners. Learning more about students, interacting and communicating with them, and providing appropriate feedback establish relationships promoting effective teaching and learning. When students have opportunities to communicate with one another, they share responsibility for learning, discuss diverse viewpoints, and shape class direction. Classes with predominant lecture formats are frequently well-organized; teachers typically know content well and clearly present material, but student-student interaction opportunities are lacking. More student-focused classes present small-group, paired, and whole-class discussion opportunities. Tasks having multiple potential solutions or answers can shift lesson direction, generate deeper thought processes, and enhance discussion quality. Small-group discussions particularly enable enough chances to listen, consider others' ideas, and all students to have a voice. Gallery walks, professional communication projects, classroom data explorations, structured academic controversy discussions, open-ended teacher questions, cooperative learning methods, structured jigsaw activities and other discussion exercises, conceptual multiple-choice questions about lesson themes combined with peer instruction, and in-class think-pair-share assignments are all ways to improve classroom interactions.

Teacher enthusiasm

Numerous studies identify teacher enthusiasm as a behavior which prominently affects student learning. Research also shows that a combination of teacher enthusiasm and constructive feedback enables students to learn more. Investigators find more enthusiastic teachers spend more time on presentation and positive performance feedback. Enthusiastic teacher behaviors include the following: variation in vocal tone, pitch, volume, and pace is important. Teachers with monotonous, droning voices inspire student boredom. Teachers reflect their excitement with teaching and learning through their eyes by making eye contact with students; using their eyes expressively, e.g., raising eyebrows, opening eyes wide, etc.; and using their eyes as well as their ears to listen to students. Judicious teacher use of body language, gestures, and other nonverbal communications also communicate enthusiasm. Effective teachers clap hands, give high-fives, make OK signs, thumbs-up, etc. Sweeping arm motions, energetic body swinging, hand gestures, and facial expressions showing pleasure or displeasure, amusement, disappointment, and approval express enthusiasm. Moving around the classroom not only enables teachers to monitor students, but also makes them less predictable and boring. Nonverbal behaviors also reinforce verbally encouraging students.

Instructional skills and practices that foster innovation

One expert (Hiam, 2011) identifies "five I's" as components of innovation curriculum: imagination, inquiry, invention, implementation, and initiative. Initiative is the foundation enabling the four others. Although daydreaming is discouraged in classrooms, teachers must learn creative expression skills to encourage student imagination. Master teacher collaboration with invention and creativity experts on curriculum design is one recommended solution. To fuel imagination, educators must connect seemingly unrelated topics, skill-sets, and ideas. Most inventions are innovative combinations of multiple domains. Writing across the curriculum, combining arts and sciences, etc., stimulates imagination. To encourage inquiry, students—not teachers—must ask most of the questions. Students must question, explore, and research curiously to innovate. Teachers can incorporate student question-asking exercises following activities into established curricula. Educators must challenge students to invent new and better ways to solve problems and apply learning to real life more often—weekly, not once or twice throughout school or only through science fairs. Implementation must also be increased: students get insufficient practice putting ideas into action, learning from mistakes, refining plans, and persevering. Initiative is more common in non-hierarchical and individualistic societies. Teachers need preparation for mentoring and coaching students in initiative-based learning; schools must support teachers' guiding students by supplying resources and valuing decentralized activities. Challenge, encouragement, and support develop self-efficacy and agency, promoting invention.

Aspects of how information and communication technology (ICT) supports student learning

Education is socially oriented and greater teacher-student personal contact is associated with quality education; ICT is compatible with and supportive of student-centered learning environments. ICT can have a transformational role in teaching and learning. Student-centered learning incorporates experiential and hands-on learning, self-directed student learning, and flexible learning activities. Students must not simply remember information to understand and apply it; they must question, grapple with ideas, discover things on their own, and construct knowledge, with teachers not being information presenters but facilitators—which also enhance their attention, interest, and motivation. Contrasting with teacher-directed learning, student-centered learning is more congruent with constructivist learning. Researchers conclude that to make complex information their own, students must individually discover and transform it. As facilitators, teachers provide opportunities for students to discover ideas, apply them, and consciously utilize their own learning strategies. Thus curriculum design is shifting from emphasizing informational content to competencies and how information will be used. Teachers use ICT in lesson planning and presentation; students use ICT for exploration, practice, and preparing assignments and presentations; administrators and teachers use ICT to complete administrative tasks more efficiently. Technology-facilitated, student-centered approaches facilitate multimedia presentation, enhancing learning; and encourage student responsibility for learning.

Assistive communication technology

Some students have speech and language disorders; some with autism spectrum disorders, cognitive, or other disorders may have limited communication skills or be completely nonverbal. Because academic success depends on communication, assistive communication technology can help students overcome learning obstacles. Visual representation systems are effective for students having difficulty with auditory receptive and verbal expressive, but greater visual processing abilities. augmentative and alternative communication (AAC) systems and devices are assistive technologies facilitating communication. They range from low-technology to high-technology. Low-tech systems and devices are typically easy to use and inexpensive, including dry-erase boards, albums, folders, binders, and other ways of storing and transmitting images. Mid-tech systems and devices include simple, battery-operated or electronic voice output communication aids (VOCAs); overhead projectors; and tape recorders. High-tech systems and devices are more complex and expensive, including computers; software programs, e.g., speech-to-text and text-to-speech software; adaptive keyboards and other hardware; and more complex VOCAs. Special education student Individualized Education Programs (IEPs) must include any kinds of assistive technology required for them to achieve learning objectives and succeed in school. AAC systems and devices enable interactive student-teacher communication, effectively giving voices to students appearing to lack them.

Inclusive classroom environments that promote equity and respect for students

When teachers initiate open dialogues, they engage students in a democratic process and provide opportunities for group decision-making requiring compromise, not competition. Teachers can rearrange classrooms to facilitate group decision-making and student interaction, e.g., sitting in circles, moving all desks to one side, reversing the room's front and back, and letting students learn from their decisions to democratize classroom spaces. They can assign group projects, which should be multidimensional, equally emphasizing textual, graphic, creative, presentation, and other components to address different skills and learning styles. Group projects also require member interdependency for successful completion, and vary in group composition. Rather than the typical forms of talking and writing for classroom sharing, wherein the loudest or fastest student gains the floor, teachers can vary protocols, e.g., visual art; paired and/or small-group sharing; allowing more time for reflecting, organizing their thoughts, and writing; and activities enabling thinkers, talkers, writers, and visual artists to share ideas. During class discussions, creating conflict regarding topics gives students more realistic experiences of complex issues. When students take various views of issues, not for competition or winning but for consensus, it affords experiences that demonstrate the complicated, messy nature of real-life democratic processes.

Organization ofclassroom desks

The classic rows and columns model of student desk placement facilitates a teacher-centered learning environment. All students are facing the teacher who, because of the orientation of student desks, is the fulcrum of every discussion. Eye-contact between dialoguing students in rows and columns of desks may be impractical or impossible. Students can be easily distracted and hard to monitor. Alternatively, teachers might choose to use a U-shaped configuration in which every student has a "front-row" seat. U-configurations are conducive to lively discussion; any student can maintain eye contact with any other student. However, U-configurations may not allow a teacher to reach every student's position. A third option might be pods of three or four. Although pods are not good for lectures and whole class discussions, they are particularly useful for student-centered pedagogy incorporating group projects or collaborative problem solving. Pods will most efficiently allow students to be in close proximity to their neighbors while also allowing a teacher more efficient access to every student and the opportunity to coach them through difficulties when they arise.

Flipped classrooms

A "flipped" classroom is a pedagogical model in which the traditional uses of time inside and outside of the classroom are reversed. Traditional time inside the classroom is devoted to teacher-centered (i.e., passive) activities like lecture. In a "flipped" classroom passive learning exercises are reserved for outside of the classroom. Either the teacher will record audio or video segments for students to consume at home or the teacher will make use of pre-existing content (e.g., Mometrix Academy or Khan Academy). Traditionally time outside of the classroom is devoted to more student-centered (i.e., active) experiences such as problem solving. Because traditional homework is generally individual, problems are often less challenging and less instructive. In a "flipped" classroom, problem solving and other traditional homework is done inside the classroom allowing students to collaborate on more challenging problems with additional assistance from the teacher.

In the student-centered "flipped" classroom model, student learning effectiveness is increased because both halves of the reversal facilitate deeper understanding. Students have more time to digest material at home and can pause or replay lectures as often as they like. In the classroom students can solve more challenging and instructive problems through the assistance of classmates and their instructor.

Establishing and managing productive classroom learning environments

For students to take risks, engage effectively in challenging activities, and collaborate, teachers must make classrooms emotionally safe. Establish a rule for students and yourself, e.g., "We do not laugh at others, tell them to shut up, put them down, or insult them." For all students to participate, teachers must make classrooms intellectually safe. Habituate them to starting work whenever you say, "Please begin," starting with easier tasks, ensuring they know more challenging tasks will follow. Make tasks complex and rich, giving diverse students opportunities to excel and assist peers. Accomplished teachers establish active-learning environments—students thinking, speaking on-task, and working collaboratively near 100 percent of the time—and not only closely observe and measure the quantity (number or proportion of students, amount or proportion of time) of on-task behavior, but also the quality (strength, depth) of student attention and engagement. Newer teachers can start developing lessons and skills for creating ongoing active-learning environments by analyzing which activities really engage their students. Make participation inclusive every day by identifying some questions every student can answer simply; have them raise an index finger when ready; when all do, have them whisper answers or signal, e.g., thumbs-up, thumbs-down, or thumbs-sideways.

Facilitating student conflict resolution

Researchers (Crawford and Bodine, 2001) from the National Center for Conflict Resolution Education report most major conflicts escalating into violence begin as more minor incidents, e.g., unprovoked contact, using others' belongings without permission, etc. Few interactions are initially predatory, yet conflicts rapidly escalate. Most conflicts happen between or among acquaintances, either at school or in the home. Violent behaviors commonly share a retribution goal. Violent acts reflect not lack of values, but value systems accepting violence. Based on these findings, experts (Concordia Online Education, 2013) offer four instructional strategies for effective classroom conflict resolution. (1) Role-playing requires viewing behaviors from others' perspectives, teaches empathy, can add humor to resolving conflicts, and enable examining conflicts more objectively for insights about sources. (2) Have students track conflicts they partake in or witness over time, recording observations in journals (keeping identities anonymous), and discuss student reactions pros and cons. (3) Teach good listening behaviors: eye contact, not interrupting, asking questions, avoiding giving suggestions or advice, nodding and smiling as positive reinforcement, and restating messages in one's own words. (4) Have involved students write about conflicts, providing cooling-off or time-out periods and requiring reflection, including how they felt and retrospectively better alternatives. For example, listing three things they would do differently; model and teach using conflicts as learning opportunities.

Student behavior management approaches

To curtail misbehavior by exercising authority while eliciting minimal emotional distress, and additionally model reasonable, respectful use of authority, a "simple authority statement" promptly and authoritatively expresses disapproval as objectively as possible. If it is either unnecessary or unwise to confront students directly, teachers can redirect student energy to other behaviors, e.g., learning activities. This stops or interrupts misbehavior without provoking student hostility. For example, younger students or those with attention deficit hyperactivity disorder (ADHD) may not be intentionally misbehaving, but lack impulse control; redirection can restore on-task behavior without damaging a student's self-esteem or self-image. Reminding students calmly of assigned tasks enhances their understanding of target behaviors without communicating unpleasant emotions or judgments. Telling students what they should do "next time" gives students behavioral correction, but avoids discouraging them by focusing on the future instead of what they did wrong this time. Teachers can prevent responding inappropriately in haste by responding with silence to misbehaviors not significantly disrupting class. Silence also enables teachers to make mental notes and consider later which actions (if any) apply, and gives students opportunities for solving their own problems.

Helping students develop and exercise accountability, responsibility, and self-regulation

Any time students display careless or unacceptable behaviors, responding with a "check yourself" message advises students to check what they just did, implicitly communicating that by checking, they will realize what they must do to correct their behavior. This reminds students to practice responsible self-management. When students, especially younger ones assigned individual classwork, become restless and off-task, settle them down and increase their concentration powers through a "clock focus" strategy: on the teacher's prearranged cue, students stand and watch the clock's second hand complete full one-minute rotations, choose how many to watch, and then sit down and resume working once the last rotation is complete. This provides scaffolding for students to develop better behavioral self-awareness, self-management, and self-control. Clock-watching, standing, and teacher cues can be gradually eliminated toward independent on-task self-regulation. Placing a student near the teacher in a "visitor's chair," with returning to regular seating allowed whenever the student feels ready to self-manage responsibly, avoids expressing disapproval. When upsetting emotions arise, model honest communication and interpersonal skills without provoking guilt or defensiveness through "I" statements about personal feelings and needs; avoid "you" accusations or comments.

Classroom transitions between activities and lessons

During transitions, students frequently become distracted, restless, and misbehave because the lessons and activities before and after, and the transitions themselves, are not standardized. Hence teachers must build bridges for students for efficient transitions. Bridges must be totally consistent, using the exact same prompts, cues, and steps in exactly the same way every time, so students can rely on them. This makes activities and events both before and after transitions immaterial because students always know what teachers expect of them. Teachers can design a uniform transition by chaining several mini-routines, which they must model, teach, and practice. (1) Signal for class attention. (2) Once all students are attending and making eye contact, start directions with "In a moment… (e.g., we're going to start another lesson)" to maintain student attention. (3) Give precisely detailed directions, including prearranging cues, e.g., "When I say 'go,' you will put away your materials, clean off your desks, and quietly meet me in the learning center." (4) Ask if anybody does not know what to do. Once everybody understands, use the prearranged cue (e.g., "go") to impel students toward learning objectives. (5) Observe student activity and confirm they are following directions. Avoid interrupting transitional activity. To address noncompliance, have students repeat the sequence.

Classroom routines and procedures

Effective teachers devote school's first few weeks not to teaching content, but to establishing classroom routines and procedures: research finds lacking these causes most behavior problems. Routines and procedures decrease instruction interruptions, increasing smooth class flow. Experts advise handing out copies of routines and procedures to every student on the first day, retaining extra copies for new students arriving later. Do not expect compliance after merely handing out and going over them once. Teach key procedures once or twice daily over several days. Explain reasons for each routine and procedure, model each for students, give students non-examples of compliance, and have one or more students model each. Go over less important routines and procedures, monitor, and reinforce as needed. Consistency is critical: teaching, monitoring, and reinforcing routines and procedures, and firmly establishing these over the first three weeks of school offers enormous benefits; do not give up after a few days. Routines and procedures include entering and exiting; starting work; attendance; lunch counts; announcements; lateness; absence; makeup classwork and tests; out-of-seat; teacher attention signal; assignments; pencil-sharpening; collecting supplies; carrying, handling, or using equipment; forming groups; group, learning center, and independent work; lining up; restrooms; water or snacks; other school locations; submitting homework and papers; exchanging papers; getting help; asking questions; finishing classwork early; classroom visitors; fire drills, codes, and alerts; sudden illness or injury; checking out materials; end-of-day cleanup; organizing materials; changing classes; homework; dismissal.

Theoretically based classroom behavior management and monitoring techniques

Based on behaviorism, functional behavior analysis identifies functions, reasons, and purposes of behaviors, enabling identifying and teaching preferable replacement behaviors meeting the same needs and functions. For example, pay attention to students who raise their hands, but not to students who call out answers. Behavior contracts specify precisely what students agree to do, and for what reward. For example, a first-grader becomes bored with teacher read-aloud story time after three minutes, wandering around the room. An initial two-week contract specifies s/he stay seated and attend for five minutes in return for quietly playing with a toy nearby for the remaining time. Future contracts gradually increase attending durations. Contracts teach students verbal obligation, responsibility, self-control, self-monitoring, negotiation, and compromise. Applying the behaviorist principle that positive reinforcement is more powerful than punishment, and the social learning theory principle of vicarious or observational learning, the "catch them being good" technique involves identifying disruptive and non-disruptive behavior instances. At class beginnings, use a randomized beeper or recording; ignoring disruptive student behaviors (whenever possible) and praising nearby students displaying appropriate behavior. (Use time-outs for severe disruptions.) Instead of a teacher singling out or scolding a student and thereby reinforcing disruptive behaviors, students imitate praised classmates for similar rewards. This teaches students they receive no attention of any kind for disruptive behavior, but favorable attention for appropriate behavior.

Establishing developmentally appropriate behavioral expectations of students

Teachers may observe some developmentally unrealistic parental expectations for their children, e.g., expecting them to "do as I say, not as I do" when their own behaviors are not positive models; expecting children to predict how present behaviors will influence future outcomes. While teachers should involve students in behavior changes, teachers cannot expect students to implement changes autonomously. Teachers should consider developmental, not chronological ages of students with cognitive delays or disabilities regarding appropriate expectations. School-aged children and adolescents generally share these cognitive characteristics: they are present-oriented, i.e., they focus on the here and now; usually cannot consider future consequences, which do not seem real to them; have difficulty anticipating consequences of their behaviors beforehand; can understand basic cause-and-effect relationships, provided these are sequenced closely together; have still-developing concepts of time, and difficulty with planning skills. Not standing out as different but fitting in—particularly for adolescents—is a major concern. Expect students to help track goals, not create and track them without reminders; and learn about and select among various choices, not independently make positive choices without concrete rewards and positive parental and adult models.

Promoting ethical academic work habits

Rather than threatening students with punishment for cheating, teachers can better promote ethical work habits by serving as positive role models; explaining and initiating class discussions about honesty and responsibility, how these are compromised by using others' work without giving credit, etc.; and praising and otherwise rewarding individual student work as examples of ethical academic practices. Research finds that, just as with academic expectations, having behavioral expectations high enough to challenge students, but realistic enough that they can achieve them with effort, is more effective than lowering expectations—including for mainstreamed students with disabilities. Rather than doing all the work for students in monitoring their behavior, teachers can engage students in monitoring processes and procedures, gradually teaching them the skills and responsibilities needed to self-monitor and self-regulate their behaviors. Teaching monitoring skills also supports teaching students about conflict management and resolution skills. Teaching students active listening skills reduces miscommunications, misunderstandings, and thus conflicts. Having them role-play opposing positions teaches empathy, objectivity, and insight; and advances conflict resolution, as does having them reflect and write about actual conflicts and potential alternative responses.

The Professional Environment

Partnering with students' families to support education

Family involvement improves student attitudes, test scores, grades, post-secondary enrollment, self-esteem, attendance, and behavior. Research finds teacher practices and school policies predict parents' educational involvement more than race, marital status, or education levels. Avoid preconceptions or judgments about families; respect and make them allies in helping students. Contacting and building rapport with families at the beginning of the year, communicating the importance of their contributions and partnership—not meeting only if or when problems arise—sets an inviting tone. Give all families information about ways of creating positive home learning environments, e.g., limiting TV, creating homework spaces, scheduling homework times, and making homework-checking plans. Contacting families at the first signs for concern shows teachers care and respect family contributions. Regular communication—via newsletters, phone calls, meetings, individual and mass emails, etc.—sustains partnerships. Ask about family expectations for children, how they currently support them with schoolwork, how you and the school can help, if hardships are emotionally affecting students, and sibling childcare or other student home responsibilities. Encourage family questions about students, classroom practices, and contacting you. Include families and students in goal-setting, problem-solving, and creating student consequences and rewards. Focus not on inadequate-appearing family involvement, but helping students succeed. Encourage collaboration among parents and families, particularly considering time constraints.

Helping students, teachers, and families with educational processes

Guidance counselors can help parents and families by interpreting student scores on standardized tests, identify individual student strengths and needs, counsel students on school programs and career paths, collaborate with teachers on programs supporting student career interests, listen to student academic and social problems and concerns, and make suggestions to improve and support student study habits and social interactions. IEP team members can offer ways to incorporate classroom activities enabling students to address IEP goals and objectives, contributing expertise from their respective disciplines and knowledge about individual students. Special education teachers provide ways of adapting and modifying curriculum and instruction to accommodate special student needs, strategies for inclusive and differentiated instruction, and knowledge about assistive devices. Speech-language therapists can inform teachers of student therapy goals, therapeutic techniques, and how to integrate or connect these with classroom instruction. Physical therapists inform teachers of exercises for gross motor skills development, and make or adapt devices. Occupational therapists inform teachers of fine motor skill development and daily living skills activities. Library media specialists help students and teachers locate, access, and evaluate information resources in various formats, and keep them technologically current. Teachers of the gifted and talented provide accelerated and enrichment activities and compressed and streamlined curricula. Para-educators can complete many routine classroom duties and work one-on-one with individual students.

Factors that impede school-home communication and parent and family participation

Collaborating with families makes teachers' jobs easier and raises student odds of succeeding. Higher family involvement in children's education correlates with higher student achievement.

Teachers impede communication when they only tell parents and families what to do; they facilitate communication when they spend equal time listening to families, share teacher and parent or family expertise equally, and brainstorm together for strategies that best support each student. Diverse family member educational backgrounds can impede communication and participation when parents and families had poor school experiences, feel ineffectual due to their own histories as unsuccessful students, feel alienated from school processes by differing cultural or linguistic backgrounds, and/or experience language barriers to communicating. Parental availability and participation can be affected by family dynamics including number of children, work schedules, transportation, custody arrangements, etc. Teachers who collaborate non-judgmentally can address such constraints with appropriate solutions. Teachers should initiate positive parent and family communication when school years start, not wait for problem-related contact; not wait for problem escalation to contact parents; give every family suggestions for establishing positive learning environments at home; maintain regular communication using phone calls, conferences, meetings, emails, and newsletters; inquire about home conditions and parent and family expectations; encourage family questions; and collaborate on student goals, effective reinforcers, and consequences.

Strategies for effective parent-teacher conferences

Experienced teachers advise always starting with some positive student aspect, working into needed improvements, and sandwiching criticisms between positives. Some teachers send conference invitations with forms requesting parents write and return questions or concerns before meeting; and include lists of major topics covered and expectations for each student, so parents are prepared for collaborating during conferences on plans to help students. Keeping student work samples handy for conferences is another strategy. Some teachers design games and ideas parents can use at home with their children. Some write pre-conference notes on student strengths and needs. Teachers emphasize the importance of thanking parents for attending conferences and listening to parents. Administrators also encourage teacher conference preparation, including having specific suggestions prepared for parents asking how they can help. Teachers advise reviewing two or three things students can improve, and asking parents to contact them in the weeks following conferences to report whether students have improved. Tactful phrasing prevents antagonizing parents and students. Some teachers include students in parent conferences. Some agree on one or two goals with students and parents early, then stay in communication throughout the year about goal progress and future plans. Some include student-led conferences about report cards, portfolios, etc.

Benefits of teacher participation in school and district committees and activities

By participating in school functions and projects, teachers access opportunities to work with professional colleagues. Collaborating on committees enables teachers to solve problems for both their students and themselves. Committees work both during school days and during extracurricular events and activities, e.g., PTA (or PTO) nights and school open houses. Teacher participation in such events and committees enables both communication with parents and demonstration to students their interest and support for them beyond academics. Whether students have extracurricular activities frequently depends on teacher support. Numbers and types of committees available for teacher participation expand opportunities for professional development; keep teachers engaged in school activities; and benefit those with whom teachers share their time, individual expertise, and special interests. In addition to traditional department, faculty, staff, and PTA meetings, teachers help other committees decide school rules; disciplinary actions; furnish leadership for athletic and intramural events, concerts, recitals, plays, musicals, book fairs, carnivals, field trips, talent shows, awards, hospitality, holiday programs, and fundraising; safety maintenance and crisis management, child abuse prevention, gang and/or drug awareness and prevention; multicultural awareness; tutoring; new teacher mentoring; technology; school spirit; special population admission, review, and dismissal; instructional continuity; curriculum design, textbook identification and adoption; needs assessments; and faculty professional development and individual content-area training.

Teacher appraisal systems

Experts maintain that reflective teachers fear neither self-evaluation nor evaluation by others, but seek experienced other educators' opinions to inform their self-improvement to serve students best. Teacher performance appraisals are typically conducted annually by trained administrators who observe individual teachers throughout the school year and apply established criteria for identifying acceptable performance. Appraisal systems evaluate teachers in areas including: student-centered instruction; successful, active student participation in learning; student progress evaluation and feedback; time, material, instructional strategy, and student discipline management; professional communication; professional development; requirement, policy, and operating procedure compliance; and improvement of all students' academic performance. Administrators evaluate and score teachers separately in each area. In addition to scores and teacher observations, documents and procedures can include teacher self-reports, annual printed summative appraisal reports (which administrators share with teachers), and annual summative conferences. Typical rules include not making classroom observations right before holidays or at the very beginning or end of the school year, time limits for assessors to provide feedback following observations, and time limits for teachers to dispute assessments in writing. Teachers receiving unsatisfactory ratings typically must follow growth or improvement plans. Teachers can prepare by requesting mentor observation and feedback, and planning lessons according to prescribed formats aligned with appraisal systems.

Working with mentors

Mentors provide newer teachers insights, resources, and strategies developed through years of experience, reassurance regarding challenges, and non-judgmental support. In student relationships and classroom management, they help teachers identify ineffective and inconsistent responses to student misbehavior, arrange classrooms for lesson activities, and organize material distribution and collection. They help with gaps in subject-area content knowledge, specialized vocabulary, information-accessing resources, and content-area emphasis decisions. They also help with unit planning addressing performance standards; incorporating lifelong learning skills; connecting lessons coherently; and including varied challenges, activities, and experiences for extending and applying text and teacher information. Mentors help teachers understand appropriate per-lesson material amounts and student need for clear directions, spiraling material, and regular review; include techniques activating and building on existing student knowledge and relating content to student experiences and interests; activities related to real-world experiences that apply learning; challenges with gradually increasing difficulty requiring individual and cooperative student discovery and work; and questions requiring higher-order cognitive skills. They help teachers implement lesson plans effectively by timing activities properly, anticipating and incorporating student responses into additional questions and discussions, and determining when to diverge from plans regarding student responses; and design, select, and refine and manage assessments. They help teachers contact and interact with supervisors, school staff, and parents; meet supervisor expectations; self-evaluate and pursue professional development.

Findings about the benefits of teacher collaboration

Evidence is mounting of positive correlations between teacher collaboration and student achievement. Researchers have found lower rates of turnover among new teachers at schools providing support through induction and mentoring programs. Teachers report strong collegial relationships, decision-making involvement, and self-efficacy beliefs afford greater personal satisfaction. Though all teachers' sharing responsibility for all students' success and support for new teachers enhance teacher satisfaction and retention, this occurs at the minority of schools. In the majority, teachers plan and teach alone; even in states that fund mentoring programs, new teachers are not guaranteed the support they need or want. Experts recommend school leaders earmark resources for supporting collaboration in classroom observations, planning, and mentoring; engage experienced teachers in both professional development and inducting and mentoring new teachers; and cultivate shared responsibility. Studies find teacher collaboration often dramatically turns around student achievement at chronically low-performing schools within a few years. Case studies find teachers collaborate by meeting to review student work relative to standards and target instructional improvements, form teams for aligning lessons across grade levels and self-plan professional development, receive regular lead teacher and coach support, access data guiding instructional decisions and planning, and share planning time.

Teacher roles in shaping policy and advocating for the teaching profession

Teachers play important roles in nurturing and preparing not only students, but also the next generation of teachers. Secretary of Education Arne Duncan stated public education for coming decades will be shaped by attracting and retaining "the best talent... to elevate and strengthen the teaching profession," which he said would require "massive cultural change" but have "extraordinary" long-term impacts. The US Department of Education (ED), in efforts to enlist this next teacher generation, started the TEACH.org project, subsequently reforming it as a public-private partnership with Microsoft. ED's related Project RESPECT (Recognizing Educational Success, Professional Excellence and Collaborative Teaching) temporarily employs active classroom teachers for input about federal budget proposals, widespread teaching reform efforts, and redefining teaching in the global economy. Elements include attracting and preparing diverse, high-performing talent; creating a professional career continuum with competitive compensation; creating conditions for success; supporting and evaluating teacher and leader development and success; providing highest-need students with the best educators; and transitioning to a more effective educational system beyond the project grant. Duncan identified RESPECT goals as elevating teacher voices in federal, state, and local education policy; collaborating with educators to rebuild teaching; and making teaching "not only America's most important... but most respected profession."

Benefits, characteristics, and elements of school partnerships with community members

Schools' broad-based community involvement, and development and implementation of strategies promoting effective partnerships strengthen schools, families and communities and improve all students' learning. When schools share responsibility for student learning with families and communities, students can see how school curriculum and skills required in the real world are connected. They have more opportunities for engaged, meaningful learning. Schools can use meetings, interviews, and surveys to identify not perceived, but true family and community strengths and needs to develop policies and programs for involvement and partnership. Community needs assessments help school action teams develop involvement program goals leading to full policies reflecting supported involvement levels and types, school priorities for formal partnerships with community businesses and agencies, outreach approaches, and developing parent education and support programs. Some partnerships include learning compacts ensuring shared stakeholder responsibility for education and defining school, parent, family, and community goals, expectations, and responsibilities. Local needs, resources, and interests determine each specific community's most applicable strategies. Important elements include identifying varied means of community member involvement; activities mutually valuable and meaningful to students, schools, and community; emphasizing two-way communication; school outreach soliciting community constituencies' involvement and support; and redefining schools as community learning centers.

Research vs. practice

Educational researchers and educators alike agree that the gap between research and practice, while varied and complex, requires more cooperation between researchers and practitioners. Some researchers propose professional learning communities, and/or design-based research models (rather than only research-based design) as solutions. Some, distinguishing research-based knowledge published in journals vs. classroom teachers' pedagogical knowledge, perceive researcher-practitioner tension attributable to researchers' seeking new knowledge vs. practitioners' seeking new solutions to operational problems. Others distinguish fundamental gaps, i.e., disagreements about vocabulary, reward systems, and the nature of theory and knowledge; from practical gaps, i.e., different time and resource allocations, authority issues, and lack of cross-organizational collaboration. From literature reviews, some researchers have identified four interrelated issues characterizing research-practice gaps. (1) Education research yields insufficient valid, reliable, or conclusive results. (2) Education research has limited practical applications. (3) Teachers find educational research not meaningful, conclusive, or practical. (4) Teachers either lack the skills to apply research findings, or seldom apply it appropriately. Proposed solutions include more researcher-educator cooperation and collaboration; more educator involvement in research processes; including research training in educator preparation; and replacing top-down, linear models of disseminating research knowledge and developing and disseminating educational innovations with mutual, two-way, circular models.

Interpreting the results, data, and conclusions of research

Authors of educational journal articles, speakers at teacher education conventions, and others frequently cite research in support of opinions about learning and teaching. However, as researchers themselves point out (e.g., Ediger, 2000), apparently those citing or even quoting research do not necessarily determine a particular study's quality. For example, a study may examine teaching practices and student outcomes in only one school district, county, or state, but not nationwide. If a study references a conclusion "according to" a specific standardized test, the conclusion stated by that instrument was contextual; different instruments could reach different conclusions. Hence to interpret educational research, teachers should consider researchers clearly state their study's purpose without pre-study opinions or vague assertions. They must remember study participants vary in intelligence, motivation, reasons for learning, achievement capabilities, socioeconomic levels, etc.; researchers cannot always control for all variables. Hypotheses must also be stated clearly. Teachers may need to accept statistical formulas, e.g., for determining significance levels, on faith as these are often too difficult for non-statisticians to understand. Experimental study averages, such as those of student scores, do not reflect individual high and low extremes. Student scores on specific tests and in studies may contradict their typical performance.

Purposes, characteristics and benefits, and teacher uses of educational research

Purposes: research informs educational policy and practices; supports high-quality instruction for all students; and stimulates discussions among educators, parents, business leaders, legislators and other stakeholders. Characteristics and benefits: teachers do not passively receive research findings; they actively decide its implications for classroom practice, give researchers guidance, and conduct their own classroom-based research. Research explicitly describes its guiding beliefs and assumptions, enabling teachers to inform instructional practices with varied theoretical orientations and viewpoints, e.g., research into writing as an individual cognitive process and a social process, respectively. Research also explicitly describes its methodology and explains how methods address classroom realities, enabling teacher insights. Research benefiting teaching and learning is trustworthy and plausible via utilizing methods appropriate to research questions and applying those methods rigorously enough. Such research must also be ethical. Teacher uses: teachers study research to inform instruction, critique research by asking evaluative questions, strategically select research most promising for enhancing teaching and learning based on their knowledge about theory and the relationship of theory and research, apply research to their own classroom practice, and conduct research to answer their own classroom questions and concerns systematically.

Teacher self-assessment model

One teacher self-assessment model (Silver Strong & Associates, 2011) synthesizing much of the best instructional design research from constructivist perspectives has nine dimensions, resulting from combining two main component categories: (I) Instructional Design and Delivery, containing five elements; and (II) Four Cornerstones of Effective Teaching, containing four elements. The five elements for category (I) are: (1) preparing students for new learning (knowledge anticipation), (2) presenting new learning (knowledge acquisition), (3) deepening learning (practicing and processing new knowledge), (4) helping students reflect on and celebrate learning (reflecting on new knowledge), and (5) applying learning (knowledge application). The four elements for category (II) are: (1) organization, rules, and procedures; (2) positive relationships; (3) a culture of thinking and learning; and (4) engagement and enjoyment. Teachers rate themselves on each dimension using a four-point scale of (1) novice, (2) developing, (3) proficient, or (4) expert (or "NA" for self-assessment questions not applicable to an individual teacher's work). The model includes checklists of student behaviors indicating teacher effectiveness in each dimension. For example, for category (II), element (1), organization, rules and procedures, student behaviors include demonstrating respect for the classroom and one another, understanding and following rules and procedures, access to needed resources, using time well, self-direction, responsibility for learning, positive attitudes, and conflict-resolution techniques. Teachers also write ideas for improvement.

School and community

No single person educates a child. Everyone in a child's community (both inside and outside of school) helps that child develop into the citizen he or she will be as an adult. Although schools have the primary responsibility of educating children, community engagement is a vital aspect of any truly successful school. Teachers can always use additional classroom resources to improve the effectiveness of education inside of the classroom. That might entail borrowing a book from a local library or bringing in a professional guest speaker from the community. In a large number of ways, community resources contribute to the development of students each year. One characteristic of a successful teacher is his or her ability to build and maintain positive partnerships with members of the community. Effective school-community partnerships are marked by a sense of ownership and pride of a school, its students, and its successes. A supportive community will come out to support its school at athletic contests, musical/theatre performances, and other events throughout the year. An involved school can give back to its community through service and volunteer projects in coordination with local institutions (e.g., hospitals, nursing homes, shelters, and soup kitchens).

Acceptable use policies

Like many businesses, most schools have acceptable use policies (AUPs) in place to stipulate the practices and constraints that users must agree to when accessing the Internet or local network. Many schools require students and staff to sign their AUP document before providing them with a network ID to gain access. AUPs are also required by Internet service providers (ISPs) of users when they sign up for the company's Internet access services. Users who sign AUPs agree to comply with such rules as not using the service to contribute to violating any law, not trying to violate any user's or network's security, not posting commercial messages to Usenet groups (sets of collected messages or notes on various topics submitted by users and posted to servers on a global network) unless they have obtained permission in advance, not trying to send spam or junk emails to anybody not wanting to receive it, and not trying to "mail-bomb" websites by flooding their servers with mass numbers of emails.

Electronic information

To locate information on digital networks, many search engines exist, e.g., Google, Bing, Yahoo, Lycos, Excite, AltaVista, McAfee Secure Search (from the anti-virus program publisher), Trovi, and DuckDuckGo (a "trackless" search engine keeping search history and information private); and search engines offered by websites known as online marketplaces, social media, or information sources like eBay, Amazon, Twitter, Wikipedia, etc. These user-friendly sites create huge databases indexing millions of websites, locating sites relevant to the search terms (words or phrases) that users enter. Software applications enable accessing and manipulating information from remote devices. Similarly to how technical support agents access user devices remotely to resolve technical issues, users with applicable permissions and software can access information remotely. Both software programs and websites commonly include help features: the user clicks a *help* button loading a window, webpage, or website with information like step-by-step instructions, FAQs, and answers; indexes to look up specific Help topics; interactive tools; and chat windows. To evaluate e-information, first appraise author credentials, publication date, revision and edition, publisher, and journal title. Then critically analyze content, including intended audience, objective reasoning, coverage, writing style, and consult evaluative reviews.

Evaluating electronic information critically

Initial appraisal: what are the author's education, degree(s), experience, publications, and institutional affiliation? Is the institution reputable? Is the source about a topic in the author's expertise area? Look in the source's biographical information and/or *Who's Who* publications. Is the author cited frequently in multiple bibliographies or other sources? What is the publication date? Is the information current? Is the publication a first edition or a revision? Are revision dates given? Who is the publisher? University presses are typically scholarly and reputable. Is a journal scholarly or popular? These differ in complexity levels. Content analysis: read the preface, foreword, or abstract to discern author intent. For a broad overview of covered material, scan tables of contents, indexes, and bibliographies. Read chapters specifically addressing your topic. Is the intended audience general or specialized? Is the source too advanced, technical, or elementary? Or is it suitable for your needs? Is the information fact, opinion, or propaganda? Good writers can convince readers their interpretations are facts. Is information valid and well-researched, or questionable and unsupported? Are assumptions reasonable? Are ideas or arguments fairly consistent with other works on the topic? Is author viewpoint impartial, objective, and unbiased? Does it substantiate, update, or supplement other sources? Are sources primary or secondary? Is the style logical, organized, clear, and readable? Read critical reviews of the publication in online reviewing sources.

Equity issues arising from differences in technology access and use

Although most schools have Internet access and some policies targeting minority, low-income and rural schools have succeeded, recent research still observes "digital divides" between poor and rich countries; differences in access among ethnic groups; unequal distribution of technology across regions and schools by socioeconomic status, minority enrollments, rural and urban vs. suburban schools; more access to computers in schools and homes for boys than girls; and slower Internet connections and unreliable, outdated hardware in poorer schools. Schools often poorly integrate and underuse available technology in classrooms. Even though technology can help students with disabilities access educational content, girls, disabled, rural, urban, poor, and minority students do not receive educational technology's full potential. Most homes have computers, but they are middle-class; in other families, lack of home access exacerbates gaps in school access when students with home access have more technology experience and confidence, dominate school technology, and reap more educational achievement and advancement. Parental support, modeling, and influence are also affected by socioeconomic status, lack of home access, and lack of parental digital knowledge. Girls use Internet and computer technology more confidently and often at home than in school. Even with apparently equal access, boys dominate home equipment, free access, and school computer clubs.

Legal rights and responsibilities of teachers, students, and parents

Teachers have Fourteenth Amendment rights to due process receiving termination notice; protection from discrimination based on race, gender, and nationality; privacy; setting student behavior rules and directions, training students to follow rules, requesting support with student behavior; First Amendment academic freedom of expression, limited by student age and grade level, teacher experience, subject content—specifically prohibiting political or personal class discussions; rights and responsibilities to correct, guide, or punish students to meet educational objectives; student custodial responsibilities; training students in moral values and civilized citizenship. Federal rights include for students with disabilities to free, appropriate public education in the least restrictive environment under the Individuals with Disabilities Education Act (IDEA), which gives parents due process rights to advance notice and refusal of identification, evaluation, and placement for special education and related services; to appeal school decisions about their children, etc. Other student rights and responsibilities vary by state and district. An example (Fairfax County Public Schools, Virginia) includes rights to attend safe, welcoming schools; property safety; fairness, respect, and courtesy from school staff and other students; freedom of expression; advocacy for change in laws, regulations, and policies; complaint and response; expulsion and suspension disputes; responsibilities for timely attendance, dress, rule-following; respecting others' rights, property, beliefs, and differences; staff authority; peaceful dispute resolution; not bullying, hurting others, or using violent, obscene, disruptive, or disrespectful words, gestures, and images; and reporting dangerous behavior to staff.

Teacher roles at progressive levels of qualification, experience, and expertise

While specific districts and schools must determine teacher roles and responsibilities, ED provides an example: <u>resident</u> teachers are beginners—not teachers of record, but paid; not student teachers, but completing a (typically 1-year) Master teacher-supervised residency or practicum. <u>Novice</u> teachers are certified, but still developing; paired with master teachers; not tenured, but may receive tenure; typically promoted after two to five years, possibly after two consecutive years' of effective ratings. <u>Professional</u> teachers are tenured, lifelong learner exemplars, academic coaches and advocates. Many teachers spend whole careers at the professional level. <u>Master</u> teachers, key school leadership team members, work in classrooms, lead school teams, and are teaching resources for the whole professional team, modeling effective teaching practices for resident and novice teachers, teaching both students and colleagues—sometimes dividing hours between classrooms and faculty support. They typically have worked at least five years in classrooms, being rated highly effective at least three years. <u>Teacher leaders</u> also divide time between classrooms and working with leadership teams and principals, e.g., sharing distributed leadership, designing peer evaluation and review systems, and developing communities of practice. They have at least five classroom years, demonstrating effectiveness at least three consecutive years. Each level earns more. With development, master teachers and teacher leaders may become principals.

Instructing special-needs students

With legal mandates for inclusive education and mainstreaming being today's prevalent trend, special education students frequently end up in regular education classrooms, whose teachers are required to instruct them. This can happen even when students are found eligible for special education and related services, assigned a special education teacher, educational specialist, various therapists, other service personnel based on individual student needs, or Individual Education Plans (IEPs) and learning goals. Teachers collaborate with special educators, who provide knowledge and expertise about classroom accommodations and modifications, differentiated instruction, etc. However, teachers are still responsible for special-needs students' instruction unless student IEPs specify otherwise. Diverse student needs including disabilities; ELL or LEP status; and varied cultural, racial, ethnic, and socioeconomic backgrounds require teachers to ensure all students receive educational equity by making curricular, instructional, and classroom environmental modifications and/or accommodations, including selecting or adapting materials to reflect multicultural perspectives; differentiating instruction; consciously avoiding bias, offering equal opportunities, and treating all students fairly. Teachers are both legally and ethically required to keep student records confidential and protect their personal information's privacy. By copyright law, teachers must also request and obtain author or publisher permission to use copyrighted materials as teaching resources.

Family Educational Rights and Privacy Act (FERPA)

FERPA applies to all schools receiving federal funds under applicable ED programs. Parents and eligible students (aged 18 or attending post-secondary school) have rights to inspect and review schools' student education records; to request school corrections of misleading or inaccurate records; to formal hearings if schools refuse to amend records; and if schools still refuse following hearings, to file statements contesting information with records. Schools must generally obtain written parent or eligible student permission to release information from student education records. However, records disclosure without consent is allowed by FERPA to these parties or under these conditions: school officials having valid educational interests, schools where students transfer, specified auditing and evaluating officials, appropriate student financial aid-related personnel, accrediting associations, those conducting certain studies on school behalf, by legal subpoena or judicial order, appropriate personnel in safety and health emergencies, and by specific state laws and local juvenile justice system authorities. FERPA allows schools to disclose student names, addresses, phone numbers, birthdates, birthplaces, attendance dates, honors, awards and other "directory" information without consent. However, schools are first required to inform parents or eligible students and allow them enough time to request non-disclosure. FERPA requires schools to notify parents or eligible students annually of their FERPA rights.

Equal Access Act (1984)

The federal Equal Access Act (1984) prohibits discrimination against student religious groups in public high schools receiving federal funds. Such schools having at least one non-curriculum, student-led club meeting outside class hours ("limited open forum") must allow organization of additional such clubs and equal access to school meeting places and publications. Groups interfering with orderly school activities are exceptions. Technically, schools can prohibit all non-curriculum clubs to "opt out" of this law. In *Westside Community Schools v. Mergens* (1990), the Supreme Court declared this law constitutional, ordering the school let a Christian student group meet. It has been invoked in lawsuits against school administrations denying Gay-Straight Alliance assembly and privileges. State Supreme Courts have always ruled in favor of these alliances, saying schools must either allow them or ban all non-curriculum group assembly. Two major legislative acts governing privacy and confidentiality of student education records in schools are the Family Educational Rights and Privacy Act (FERPA, 1974) and Individuals with Disabilities Education Act (IDEA, formerly PL 94-142, 1975). Both grant similar rights to parents and eligible students (aged 18 or attending post-secondary schools) to review or inspect records, request correction, have formal hearings, document contested information, and advance notice and non-disclosure of directory information.

American Association of Educators (AAE) Code of Ethics for Educators

<u>Principle I</u>: Ethical Conduct toward Students – Educators interact justly, considerately with every student, resolving disciplinary and other problems by school policy and law; eschew intentionally exposing students to disparagement; protect student information confidentiality unless laws require otherwise; constructively endeavor to protect students from conditions harming safety, health, or learning; and seek to present facts without bias, personal prejudice, or distortion. <u>Principle II</u>: Ethical Conduct toward Practices and Performance – Educators meet appointment or contract terms and apply for, accept, and assign positions and responsibilities based on professional qualifications; maintain physical and mental health and social judgment to perform professional duties; continue professional growth; follow laws, regulations, and school policies; avoid intentionally misrepresenting official school or educational organization policies; distinguish these from personal opinions; account for all funds in their charge; and never use professional or institutional privileges for partisan or personal advantages. <u>Principle III</u>: Ethical Conduct toward Professional Colleagues – Educators protect colleague information confidentiality except required by law, make no willful false statements about colleagues or school systems, do not interfere with colleague free choice, and fight coercion violating professional integrity. <u>Principle IV</u>: Ethical Conduct toward Parents and Community – Educators work to communicate to parents all information in student interests; respect diverse cultural values and traditions in classrooms and communities; and take active, positive roles in school and community relations.

Suspension or revocation an educator's certificate

The Education Practices Commission may suspend an educator certificate for up to five years, or revoke it for up to 10 years or permanently for: fraudulent certificate pursuit or acquisition; knowingly not reporting suspected or actual child abuse, alleged administrator or instructional staff misconduct affecting student safety, health, or welfare; proven incompetence to teach or perform duties in public school or teach in or operate private school; acts of moral turpitude or gross immorality; suspension, revocation, or surrender of certification in another state; conviction or guilty plea to a felony, misdemeanor, or any criminal charge except minor traffic violations; being found guilty of personal conduct seriously decreasing district school board employee effectiveness; breach of contract; Department of Revenue notice or court order of certificate suspension due to noncompliance with a written agreement, subpoena, or order to show cause or child support order; violation of Principles of Professional Conduct for the Education Profession according to State Board of Education rules; other law provision violations penalized by certificate revocation; violation of any Education Practices Commission order; plea agreement or court order in any jurisdiction requiring permanent certificate surrender or relinquishment, pursuant to commissioner probable cause finding; or disqualification from educator certification under any of the felony or misdemeanor offenses prohibited under any section of the statute on disqualification from employment (s. 1012.315). There are six additional provisions, three with two, three, and two respective subsections.

Provisions included in most school district policies for using technology in schools

Individual school districts establish policies for technology use. For example, district policies may include Internet safety terms like software filters blocking access to material that is pornographic, obscene, harmful to children, otherwise inappropriate, or disrupts the educational process. Typical disclaimers include that filtering software may block access to other materials, may not succeed in blocking access to all inappropriate or disruptive materials, and does not cancel user obligations not to access such materials. Terms and conditions of use for curriculum and instruction include using district technological and telecommunications resources consistently with district curriculum and diverse student developmental levels, abilities, instructional needs, and learning styles; adhering to selection criteria for instructional and library media center materials; and permission for school staff to use technology and Internet resources throughout the curriculum, consistently with district guidelines and goals. Terms and conditions may define district electronic resources as part of curriculum, not a general-use public forum; stipulate that staff give students developmentally appropriate guidance in using digital information resources for district curriculum-related study and research; and inform students of their network user rights and responsibilities before giving them access. Acceptable use prescriptions and proscriptions, including regarding copyright laws and software licensing agreements, are typically parts of these policies.

Use and maintenance of student records and information

Permanent, cumulative student records—physical or electronic—can vary by school district in kinds of information they contain. Student records include student information, curriculum information, annual standardized test scores, Individualized Education Program (IEP) records, ELP levels, academic background, recent report cards, conference information, teacher comments, and other pertinent information. Teachers should check their school's policy and procedures regarding student records; check cumulative records first when they have questions about individual students; open and update cumulative records when school years start; update IEPs, ELP level changes, and conference information throughout the year; add final attendance, curriculum covered, report cards, comments, and close records at years' ends. Every student cumulative record is a confidential, legal record. Parents and students aged 18+ can request access to their records in writing. Otherwise, only school officials whose professional responsibilities require it can legally view cumulative records. Keep all information safe, intact, and confidential. When working on secure or shared computers, always log out after accessing electronic cumulative records to protect their security. Paper cumulative records should always be kept in school fireproof cabinets unless staff is directly working with them. Replace checked-out cumulative records nightly, never taking them home or leaving them in classrooms.

Ethical responsibilities for a classroom teacher (CAPTAIN)

1. **Confidentiality**: A teacher must not reveal confidential information regarding a student, unless for a professional purpose or as required by law.
2. **Advantage**: A teacher must not use professional relationships with students for private advantage.
3. **Protection**: A teacher must protect a student from harm to his or her health, safety, or welfare. A teacher's duty includes reporting any suspicion of abuse or neglect and taking the proper care not to expose a child to inappropriate disparagement or embarrassment.
4. **Truth**: A teacher must faithfully render reports regarding either students or colleagues. A teacher must never knowingly make false or malicious statements about a student or a colleague.
5. **Authenticity**: A teacher must not distort or suppress elements of his or her subject matter. A teacher must not deny a student's access to different viewpoints and must not impede a student's independent action in pursuit of learning.
6. **Integrity**: A teacher must not misrepresent his or her educational credentials or those of another person.
7. **Non-Discrimination**: A teacher must not unfairly deny benefits from (or grant benefits to) a student on the basis of race, gender, personal beliefs, family, cultural background, or sexual orientation.

Role of the education system in a democratic society

American education systems arose, in part, as a mechanism to prepare students to become responsible citizens in a democratic society. Historically, decisions regarding schools were made in deference to the common good. The school system is open to every student and every student is entitled to an education that will allow him or her to have a fair opportunity to become a successful adult. As a cornerstone of the American democratic society, schools have sometimes been at the center of controversial social questions. For example, 1954's *Brown vs. Board* Supreme Court decision forbidding segregated schools was a crucial part of the larger civil rights movement. Since 1954, Congress has passed legislation (such as 1973's Individuals with Disabilities Education Act) promising each student a free and appropriate public education. This phrase is particularly meaningful for exceptional students who may not be served well by standard educational offerings. Exceptional students may be entitled to an Individual Educational Program (IEP) that provides access to the general curriculum otherwise unavailable due to disability. Educators at every level (national, state, and local) work in collaboration so that every student can have access to a quality education and the promises of a democratic society.

Suspicion of abuse or neglect of a student

The exact guidelines regarding the reporting of child abuse or child neglect will vary by state. In many states teachers who suspect abuse or neglect are required by law to report the suspicion to local authorities within a set timeframe (e.g., 48 hours). Reports of suspected abuse are most likely confidential and educators who make a report of suspected abuse in good faith are typically immune from criminal or civil repercussions. Although you may wish to talk about the situation with a mentor or administrator, reporting to an educational superior will not satisfy a teacher's legal reporting requirement. All reports must be made to the proper local authorities (e.g., Child Protective Services).

Classroom fair use of copyrighted images, sounds, and videos found on the internet

Images found on the internet may be used for in-classroom purposes by a teacher or student. Images found on the internet may not be reposted to the web without permission. No more than 15 images or 10% (whichever is less) of a given collection may be used. Up to 10% (up to a maximum of 30 seconds) of a copyrighted musical composition may be used by educators or students as part of a multimedia presentation. Videos may be used in the classroom for instructional purposes and may not be used for entertainment. No more than 10% of a video or three minutes (whichever is less) may be used.

Professional organizations

In addition to research, mentors, supervisors, and colleagues, professional development resources for educators include professional organizations. Discipline-specific and other organizations enhance educator knowledge, expertise, and skills through conventions, conferences, workshops, trainings, publications, online courses, networking, local chapters, etc. Organizations include: the American Association of School Administrators, National Association of Elementary School Principals, National Art Education Association, American Counseling Association, American School Counselors Association, National Association for the Education of Young Children, American Library Association, International Reading Association, National Council of Teachers of English, American Council on the Teaching of Foreign Languages, Teachers of English to Speakers of Other Languages, Council for Exceptional Education, National Association for Gifted Children, National Council of Teachers of Mathematics, American Association of Physics Teachers, National Association of Biology Teachers, National Science Teachers Association, National Council for the Social Studies, Council for Exceptional Education, National Association for Sport and Physical Education, American Educational Research Association, Association for Educational Communication and Technology, American Federation of Teachers (AFL-CIO union), National Education Association (union), Association for Childhood Education International, Association for Supervision and Curriculum Development, National Middle School Association, National PTA, National School Boards Association, and National Staff Development Council.

Determining professional development goals

US states typically certify or license college graduates to teach in public schools for two years or similar periods with the expectation they will attain master's degrees or some other additional certification during that time. Teachers meeting state-established goals earn more advanced licensure. Even teachers with advanced graduate degrees must continue throughout their careers to set and achieve goals. Mentor teachers help new teachers set personal goals, develop personal development plans (PDPs), and document ongoing professional activities. Goals can include reading professional literature, attending educational conferences and seminars, etc., as well as taking college and graduate courses, accruing continuing education units (CEUs), etc. School district professional development committees (PDCs) work with new teachers and mentors to assure goals meet established district guidelines, sometimes paying workshop tuition. Teacher PDP approval by PDCs gives state licensure boards documentation of new teacher efforts to meet state requirements. PDCs and district administrators collaboratively set district-wide professional teacher goals, both subject-specific and interdisciplinary—e.g., aligning curricula with state standards and raising standardized test scores. PDCs offer all teachers training that targets district goals. Teacher, mentor, and PDC goal-setting must meet state education department standards. Goals should also be SMART—*specific*, *measurable*, *attainable*, *relevant/result-oriented*, and *time-limited*.

Professional development resources

Educational research studies often evaluate the effectiveness of various instructional practices. Educators benefit from many available literature reviews, meta-analyses, compilations, or other syntheses identifying consensus on effective practices to implement. Federal and state education departments, boards, and local school districts frequently adopt research-based instructional practices for individual teachers to follow. Professional organizations also disseminate research findings and provide courses, workshops, and conferences where members can learn additional information, insights, skills, and techniques to improve their teaching and student learning. A common route for teachers to improve knowledge and practical expertise is through graduate courses. Some teachers begin with bachelor's degrees, then complete master's degrees while working, obtaining more advanced knowledge of pedagogy and specific subject-area content, higher-level teaching certification, and salaries. Some certified in general education subsequently complete graduate courses in educational specialties. Some get degrees or certificates in additional subjects and specialties, e.g., math plus science, multiple languages, English plus ESL, special education plus early childhood education, etc. Mentors personally and individually advance PD, helping educators with PD plans; observing and providing feedback; sharing their knowledge, experience, and expertise; and providing reassurance, encouragement, and support. Pre-service internships provide closely supervised on-the-job practice and experience. Study groups and learning communities enable information sharing; learning communities also allow workshop and presentation collaborations, etc.

Helping educators utilize and integrate technology into instructional design and delivery

Contemporary technology not only greatly facilitates and enhances instruction, learning, and education overall, but integrating technology into instruction has become a necessity now that society depends on and requires its use so heavily. Among many available resources, one is the International Society for Technology in Education (ISTE), offering consulting services and helping educators develop customized PD learning programs. Workshops include one providing in-depth examination of worldwide educational initiatives using technology. Another, for teachers and educational leaders with advanced technology skills, teaches ISTE Standards and how to teach others these in schools or through peer coaching. A virtual workshop gives lead teachers hands-on experiences in designing learning activities embedding ISTE Standards, measuring activity effectiveness, and working district-wide with faculty teams to integrate these standards across the curriculum. A three-day onsite leadership academy provides in-depth PD knowledge and understanding of ISTE Standards; and instruction from experts in these standards regarding the conditions essential to implementing them at district, school, and classroom levels. ISTE mobile learning support services help educators and stakeholders apply prevalent (and popular with students) mobile technology for learning. ISTE's classroom observation tool measures effective classroom technology integration. ISTE offers school administrators and principals digital citizenship, technology leadership institutes, a standards readiness workshop, and essential conditions readiness Survey.

Reflection

Reflection enables teachers to gain some distance and objectivity to analyze their instructional practices and interactions with students, which in turn enables them to identify, plan, and implement measures to improve these for improved student learning. To track their effectiveness in the classroom, teachers should establish baselines early in the school year. They can keep journals, writing their reflections about classroom interactions as often as possible. Selecting one high-achieving and one low-achieving student in a class and charting how the teacher's professional relationship with each student develops can often accurately reflect learning opportunities the teacher provides for all students. Writing honestly and rereading previous entries regularly help teachers change their behaviors to improve student-teacher relationships, hence learning. Many pre-designed self-assessment checklists, questionnaires, and tools help teachers evaluate their practices systematically and use their responses to reinforce or expand teaching strengths and address weaknesses. Through peer assessment, teachers have colleagues observe and provide feedback on their instruction: others often see behaviors and omissions we cannot, and/or provide alternate perspectives. The "critical friend" method is similar. Systematic incident analysis enables teacher insights into student behaviors and teacher-student interactions and how changing teacher behaviors can change student behaviors. Portfolios enable teachers to review work development and changes longitudinally.

Reflection questions that a teacher might ask him or herself after a classroom activity

1. What were the learning objectives for this experience? Did I expect too much or too little of the students?
2. Did this experience work well? Did the students react positively or negatively? What data do I have that this experience was (un)successful?
3. What can I change about this lesson? Is it possible to better prepare my students for this lesson next year?
4. What questions should I have asked before the experience? Which questions should I have asked after the experience?
5. What student behavior was most notable? Did any circumstances from outside the classroom affect this behavior?
6. How do my students learn? Would my students learn better in some different way?
7. Were all my students actively participating in this experience? How can I adapt my lesson to make it more student-centered?
8. What data do I need to make an informed decision about this activity's effectiveness? What plans should I make to get this data in the future?
9. What do my data tell me? How can I adjust my expectations and my activity based upon the data I got?
10. Can my students meet the objectives in a more efficient manner? Does this activity need less time or more time? How can I adjust for next year?

Practices that apply research data finding them effective for instructing students

Cognitive research studies have established that comparing, contrasting, and classifying help students understand complex concepts. Teaching students to identify idea similarities and differences applies these findings. Research shows students' higher-order cognitive skills for analysis and synthesis, in-depth analysis, and reading comprehension improve through effectively summarizing information and note-taking. Teaching students how and assigning them to summarize and take notes efficiently applies research to improve instruction and achievement. Educational achievement motivation research demonstrates the impact of recognition for reinforcing and monitoring student effort, e.g., symbolic or abstract recognition is more effective than concrete rewards; rewards contingent on meeting some performance standard are most effective; 8-year-olds' learning strategies differ radically from 12-year-olds' and adults' strategies; and 8-year-olds learn mainly from positive feedback, not negative. Teachers raise student achievement by recognizing, rewarding, and praising specific goal achievements. Studies show learning occurs linguistically and non-linguistically; visual or other non-linguistic representations help students understand, retain, retrieve, connect, and apply knowledge; and the more students combine linguistic and non-linguistic systems, the better they learn and think. Teachers apply these findings using multimodal instruction. Additional research-based effective teaching practices include practice, homework, objectives, feedback, generating hypotheses, testing hypotheses, advance organizers, questions, cues, cooperative learning, and teaching and assigning nonfictional writing.

Feedback

Teachers receive feedback from a number of sources (e.g., students, parents, colleagues, department leaders, and school administrators). Some (but not all) of the feedback will be useful. Feedback like "I don't like your class" does not give a teacher the opportunity to improve his or her classroom practice. Other feedback like, "Try to allow more wait time between asking a question and calling upon a student to answer" is more specific and teachers can act on this. Helpful feedback and less helpful feedback both provide a teacher with the opportunity to initiate a conversation on his or her pedagogy. In response to non-anonymous feedback, a teacher can ask follow-up questions to clear up any vagueness. Feedback can be something to talk over with a mentor, an invitation to initiate a discussion within a professional learning community, or even a starting point at which to begin a process of action research in the classroom. Unfortunately the feedback a teacher receives (particularly from students) is not always helpful and in some cases can be hurtful. A beginning teacher must remember not to take feedback personally. A professional teacher is only expected to do the best that he or she can to improve based upon the appropriate feedback he or she receives.

Characteristics associated with helpful feedback (TOTAL)

1. **Targeted**: Feedback should be targeted towards a goal and allow the subject of the feedback to adjust his or her actions in an effort to improve. Vague or imprecise feedback is not only unhelpful but can also be misleading.
2. **Ongoing**: For feedback to be useful, individuals must have the ongoing opportunity to improve.
3. **Timely**: Feedback must be timely. Late arriving feedback deprives an individual of the opportunity to improve recent behavior or efficiently affect better results.
4. **Actionable**: "Great Work" or "This is not right" are not examples of good feedback. Both lack the specificity necessary to be useful. Good feedback can be acted upon. Adjustments can be made in response to specific and useful suggestions on how to improve.

5. **Level-Headed**: Feedback must be genuine, trustworthy, and not overly ambitious. Improvement in any endeavor is an incremental process that is best accomplished slowly, in short increments over long intervals of time. A feedback recipient must be able to trust that a critique is both sensible and prudent.

Resources available to help professional development and enhance effectiveness

Every educator in the world (at universities, colleges, and schools of every type) is a part of a professional learning community, in the broadest sense of that phrase. The growth of the internet and data resources have made teacher professional development more available than it has ever been before. Websites like *Edutopia* can help a teacher stay current with the latest technology or innovative pedagogy. National organizations (e.g., NCTE, NCTM, NCSS, and NSTA) offer memberships for teachers in every field and each offers publications and web based resources. National and state-based organizations organize conferences at which educators come together to share and collaborate. Numerous research journals are published regularly and are searchable via indexing services (e.g., ERIC and JSTOR). Journals regularly publish peer-reviewed articles featuring the best new ideas in teaching and learning in their fields. A virtually innumerable amount of resources is available for every teacher who wishes to stay current. A modern professional teacher is one that is open to new ideas and is willing to put forth the effort to learn about new pedagogical methods. A modern professional teacher is willing to try to implement new classroom methods based upon new learning about the best practices.

Implicit teacher bias

Implicit teacher biases are stereotypes or attitudes that are manifested unconsciously in the classroom. In some cases these biases may adversely affect student learning. One pervasive stereotype is that girls are not able to do mathematics as well as boys. A math teacher may subconsciously call on boys more often or praise girls less often. Boys may do better in this math class because they are given more opportunities or praise, which may not be available to girls because of a stereotype. As a teacher, awareness of potential biases is the first step in overcoming them. Teachers should reflect on their teaching practice and collect/analyze classroom evidence (data) to determine if biases are present. In order for each student to have a fair chance to succeed, teachers must recognize each as an individual, rather than a member of some stereotypical group (e.g., athletic team, ethnic group, gender, or those with past behavioral issues).

Mentors as a resource for strengthening teacher knowledge, skills, and effectiveness

Collegial collaboration is the basis of quality educational practice. No individual can reach every student or solve every problem. In recent years, a number of school systems have begun formal programs to help train veteran teachers to serve as mentors for younger teachers. A mentor is a veteran teacher who is accepting of a new teacher, is effective in a variety of different interpersonal contexts, and adept at providing instructional support. A mentor is empathetic, optimistic, and open to development in new aspects of the teaching profession. A mentor is a resource who can provide insight into the culture of a school, share tips and tricks that he or she has picked up over the years, and talk about how to resolve challenging circumstances. A mentor is a colleague who can put issues into their proper perspective and reassure a new teacher who may feel isolated or overwhelmed.

Professional learning community (PLC)

Although the phrase "professional learning community" can have multiple meanings, PLCs are most often small groups of educators who meet on a regular basis to discuss and collaborate to improve teaching skills and student academic performance. Professional learning communities might discuss the creation or editing of class materials, completed student work as exemplars of student learning, data from student assessments, or professional literature pertinent to classroom experience. The focus of professional learning communities is learning: student learning and teacher learning about student learning. Professional learning communities can offer an opportunity for teachers to engage in reflection on teaching practice and cycles of action research or other evidence-based adaptations of classroom activities/assessments towards better student performance.

Professional versatility

Education has never been and will never be a one-size-fits-all endeavor. No two learners are exactly the same and no two classes are exactly the same. What works for one student or class may not work for another. Given the diversity of students in the classroom, open-mindedness and a willingness to adapt are arguably the most important characteristics of successful teachers. Both as an individual in the classroom and as a part of a professional learning community outside of the classroom, an openness to the possibility of a new approach allows a teacher to persevere through the most challenging of circumstances. Challenges encountered might arise due to: behavioral problems, learning differences, student exceptionalities, technology, and any of a number of possible distractions originating inside or outside the classroom. A versatile teacher open to collaboration with colleagues, creative problem solving, and trying new methods can overcome almost any challenge.

Action research

Action research is a process of reflective classroom inquiry performed by the teacher. Action research is a technique through which a teacher might refine his or her teaching practice by using available data to inform new methods or mechanisms of student learning. The four generic stages for action research are: Plan, Act, Observe, and Reflect. A teacher plans a learning experience for his or her students and then puts that plan into action. The teacher observes his or her students' reactions during the experience and the learning results (positive or negative) through either formative or summative assessment. After analyzing the available quantitative and/or qualitative data, the teacher formulates a new plan of action for future student learning experiences and the action research process begins again. Action-based research is the most natural mechanism of classroom study for the teacher. The teacher is using the evidence available in a scientific process to improve his or her educational practice. Action research is one example of the evidence-based educational practice advocated by the standards.

Quantitative and qualitative research methods

Quantitative methods are deductive in nature. Quantitative investigators will collect and analyze numerical data with mathematical and statistical tools. An example of a quantitative method would be to compare the results of a pre-test (before a lesson) and a post-test (after a lesson) to determine **if** a lesson was effective. Quantitative methods are commonly applied in scientific fields in which numerical data is available (e.g., biology and physics).

Qualitative methods are inductive in nature. Qualitative investigators will collect and analyze textual data collected from interviews, observations, or conversations. An example of a qualitative method would be to discuss a lesson (after the fact) and ask the students for their perceptions about the effectiveness of the lesson. Qualitative methods will help determine **why** students were or were not successful on a given assessment. Qualitative methods are commonly applied in fields studying human behavior (e.g., marketing and sociology).

Pros and cons of quantitative and qualitative research methods:
- Quantitative methods are number-based. Qualitative methods are text-based. Numerical methods can determine **if** students are learning about a particular concept. Qualitative methods would be required if a teacher wished to understand **why** students were not learning a given concept.
- Quantitative methods are more objective; numerical data is gathered using unbiased measurements. Qualitative methods are more subjective. Researchers must interpret the results of interviews or discussions and can be susceptible to implicit or explicit biases.
- Quantitative methods tend to require more planning time before implementation while qualitative measures require more time after the implementation. Numerical data are more straightforward to analyze but more difficult to collect. Textual data are more challenging to analyze but less cumbersome to collect.
- Quantitative methods are stricter in their design; collected responses must be numerical. Qualitative methods are more open-ended in their design; a greater variety of responses can be accepted and analyzed.
- Both quantitative and qualitative methods can be shown as valid and reliable.

Investigating a problem using a mixed methods study

Quantitative methodologies are adept at answering "if" questions. Numerical-based methods can help answer questions regarding whether there is evidence that a particular pattern is occurring. For example, a study of test scores will tell you **if** your students understand a given concept. Qualitative (number-based) methods are adept at answer "how" or "why" questions. For example, qualitative (text-based) methods would be required to determine **why** students have not learned a given concept well. Mixed method inquiry (including both quantitative and qualitative aspects) can greatly benefit an educator seeking to grow as a professional by providing both direct verdicts and indirect contexts to questions of pedagogical effectiveness.

Practice Test

Practice Questions

1. The educator's code of ethics does not prohibit which of the following activities?
    a. Interfering with the political rights of a colleague
    b. Misrepresenting official district policies
    c. Accepting gifts openly offered in appreciation of service
    d. Revealing confidential student information without a lawful professional purpose or legal requirement

2. Which of the following statements best describes the type of education that the Individuals with Disabilities Education Act of 2004 (IDEA) requires for all students with identified emotional and learning disabilities?
    a. A free and appropriate education, even in cases where the student has been suspended or expelled from school
    b. An appropriate education, except in cases where the student's behavior causes him or her to be expelled from school
    c. A free education that is conducted outside of the general education classroom
    d. An appropriate education that must be paid for by the student's family

3. According to the Family Educational Rights and Privacy Act (FERPA), which of the following is true?
    a. Students of any age can refuse to disclose educational records to their parents
    b. Parents of children under 18 can inspect and request amendments to their children's educational records on demand
    c. Teachers need written authorization from parents in order to disclose a student's educational record a school official with a legitimate educational interest
    d. Written authorization from parents is required before a school releases a student's educational records to a school to which that student is transferring

4. Which of the following is typically the most effective way to state classroom rules?
    a. Rules should be stated negatively (do not speak out of turn)
    b. Rules should be stated positively (students will treat one another with respect)
    c. Rules should be phrased politely (please don't chew gum)
    d. Rules should use detailed and specific language to describe what is prohibited (don't hit, slap, kick, pinch, or shove other students)

5. In resolving behavior problems, a teacher should strive to be:
    a. Consistent and judgmental
    b. Consistent and objective
    c. Patient and collaborative
    d. Authoritative and judgmental

6. Which of the following strategies would foster students' intrinsic motivation to learn?
    a. Helping students to develop a personal connection to and interest in the material they're learning
    b. Emphasizing the rewards associated with academic success (recognition, a good job) and consequences associated with academic failure (shame, punishment by parents)
    c. Both A and B
    d. Neither A nor B

7. According to Jean Piaget's four-stage theory of cognitive development, the distinction between people at the concrete operational stage (approximately 7-12 years of age) and the formal operational stage (approximately 12-16 years of age) of development is that:
    a. Unlike those at the concrete operational stage, those at the formal operational stage can think logically in concrete terms
    b. Unlike those at the concrete operational stage, those at the formal operational stage are highly reliant on sensory and motor skills to learn
    c. Those in the concrete operational stage are capable of abstract thought, while those at the formal operational stage can think only in concrete terms
    d. Those in the concrete operational stage can think logically only with respect to concrete experiences, while those at the formal operational stage can reason in abstract and hypothetical terms

8. A teacher notes a significant gap between a student's intelligence as determined by IQ testing and the student's academic achievement. Which of the following might explain the student's poor performance relative to his or her potential?
    a. The student has a learning disability such as dyslexia or dyscalculia
    b. The student is distracted by a family problem such as homelessness or divorce
    c. The student is an immigrant and is not proficient in the English language
    d. All of the above

9. As students enter adolescence, their social lives will most likely take on which of the following characteristics?
    a. Desire to spend most of their time with immediate family members
    b. Membership in a small social group that has a shared set of values and interests
    c. Marked rise in insecurity resulting from increased threats of violence
    d. Decreased interest in ethnic and cultural identity

10. A teacher assigns his seventh grade students to research their families' cultural heritage by interviewing parents and grandparents. Which aspect of the students' social development would this project most directly facilitate?
    a. Identity formation
    b. Ability to interact cooperatively with peers
    c. Leadership skills
    d. Tolerance for other cultures

11. Ms. Andrews has recently learned that she will have a student in her fifth grade class whose family is currently living in a local homeless shelter. The teacher's most important responsibility to this student is to:
    a. Ensure that she creates an accepting, non-judgmental classroom environment
    b. Screen the new student to see if special education services are needed
    c. Determine whether the student suffers from depression or anxiety disorder
    d. Make sure that the student has adequate food and clothing

12. Mr. Gonzalez has noticed that one of his seventh grade students, Benji, has experienced a rapid decline in his academic performance over the past few weeks. Benji seems unusually sluggish on some days and abnormally restless on other days. He frequently arrives late to school, saying that he overslept. Which of the following is the most likely explanation for this change in Benji's behavior?
    a. Benji has developed a learning disability, and should be screened for special education services
    b. Benji's unpredictable behavior is normal for an adolescent and should not be cause for concern
    c. Benji's behavior signals that he might be using illegal drugs
    d. Benji is probably experiencing depression, and should be referred to the school counselor

13. A survey conducted by a local newspaper reports that most parents of middle school students think that bullying is very common among adolescent boys, but unlikely to occur among girls. What is the most likely explanation for this misconception?
    a. The survey respondents were disproportionately male
    b. The parents who were surveyed do not participate in school-related activities or monitor their children's social development closely
    c. Parents are less likely to recognize bullying among girls because it is usually conducted through gossip and exclusion, rather than outright violence
    d. The level of violence at the school is so high that parents didn't notice the bullying that occurs among girls

14. Each week, Mr. Jackson asks his seventh grade science students to write a brief research report about a different animal. While some of the students turn in detailed, high-quality reports based on Internet research, other students turn in well-written but simplistic reports based on print resources available in the school media center, which does not have Internet access. To address this disparity, Mr. Anderson should:
    a. Tell the students who are turning in less detailed reports that they need to start using the Internet to conduct research, or he won't accept their reports
    b. Ask the students who are using the Internet to stop using it, because it is unfair to the other students who are using the media center resources
    c. Use a less rigorous grading scale for students who can't use the Internet
    d. Provide students and their parents with a list of community resources like libraries that offer free Internet access and training

15. Students who are English Language Learners usually have which of the following traits in common?
    a. A need for special education services
    b. Normal to above-average intelligence
    c. Above-average academic performance
    d. Below-average academic aptitude due to their cultural background

16. Mrs. Li is a sixth grade general education teacher in an inclusion classroom where several students have learning disabilities in writing. To assess her students' reading comprehension skills, Mrs. Li asks them to write in their journals for 15 minutes each day after a period of sustained, silent reading. However, she's concerned that the learning disabled students will become frustrated with this timed writing assignment. How should Mrs. Li handle this dilemma?
    a. She should ask the learning disabled students to write as much as they can during the 15 minute period, although they probably won't be able to completely convey their thoughts
    b. She should let the learning disabled students continue to read during the writing period
    c. She should take the learning disabled students to a quiet area and facilitate a 15 minute group reading discussion while the other students write
    d. She should tell the students to start their journal entries during class, and finish them up for homework

17. Mr. Robinson, a fifth grade teacher, wants to improve his students' motivation by showing them that math and reading skills can be used to learn about important subjects like the environment, history, or multiculturalism. The best approach to achieve this objective would be to:
    a. Ask students to conduct an independent research project on a topic of their choice
    b. Have students practice math and reading skills in groups
    c. Present a thematic unit that incorporates math and reading skills
    d. Use curriculum-based methods to assess students' progress in math and reading

18. Ms. Frank conducts an assessment and discovers that most students in her fourth grade class are auditory learners, while a few are visual or kinesthetic learners. When teaching students a new concept, which of the following strategies would be most effective for the largest number of her students?
    a. Having her students write an explanation of the new concept in their own words
    b. Teaching the students a song that explains the new concept
    c. Writing an explanation of the new concept on the chalkboard
    d. Teaching the students to describe the concept using sign language

19. Of the practices listed below, which would be most likely to promote a productive classroom environment for middle-level students?
    a. Providing opportunities for students to work cooperatively with peers
    b. Frequently changing classroom routines to keep students engaged
    c. Encouraging students to work independently to improve their ability to self-direct
    d. Avoiding kinesthetic and active learning activities that overexcite students

20. Mr. Stratton has assigned his sixth grade social studies class to write a research report about a historical period that they have learned about in class during the year. To ensure that students understand what is expected of them and are able to complete the project on schedule, the best approach for Mr. Stratton to take would be to:
    a. Take time to explain how to do the research and set several 'checkpoints' before projects are due
    b. Pair students who have never completed a research project before with students who have
    c. Hold after-school tutoring sessions to help students brainstorm ideas and conduct research
    d. Send a note home to parents telling them about the project and the due date

21. Mrs. Frances wants to develop a theme-based unit that is interesting and relevant to her fifth grade students. Which of the following approaches would be most likely to help her achieve this goal?
   a. Send a note to the students' parents asking them what theme their children should learn about
   b. Review the success of theme-based units that were used by the students' teachers in previous years
   c. Conduct an informal, open-ended survey to look for interests that the students share
   d. Present three different theme ideas as ask the students to vote on the one that will be used in class

22. Ms. Fremont, a sixth grade language arts teacher, is planning a strategy to help students learn and practice note-taking skills. Which of the following approaches would be the best way to help students adopt this new skill?
   a. Lecturing throughout the class period, and then collecting and grading students' notes at the end of class
   b. Providing an outline of key words and points for students to fill in during the lecture, and gradually providing less and less detail in this outline until students are taking notes without assistance
   c. Having students compare their notes with a partner's notes at the end of class
   d. Providing students with audio-recorded lectures so they can practice taking notes at home

23. Mr. Swanson has implemented a token economy behavior management system for several disruptive students in his class. For each day that the students exhibit appropriate behavior, they earn a check mark, and if they have earned three check marks by the end of the week, they are allowed to play computer games for 30 minutes on Friday afternoon. So far, all of the students have earned enough check marks each week to get the reward, but each student is still disrupting class at least once per week. Which of the following strategies would probably be most effective for further reducing the students' disruptive behavior?
   a. Taking away a check mark that the student has already earned if they engage in disruptive behavior
   b. Explaining to the students that they have done a good job of improving their behavior, but that they can do even better; as a consequence, they now need to earn four check marks to get the reward, which is 45 minutes on the computer
   c. Increasing the reward to one hour of computer time
   d. Implementing a system where students start out with five check marks at the beginning of the week, and lose one check mark for each episode of disruptive behavior; students who still have five check marks at the end of the week earn 30 minutes of computer time

24. Ms. Carleton receives a phone call from one of her sixth grade students' parents. The parent is concerned that her daughter is performing poorly in language arts class, even though she has done well in this subject in the past. Ms. Carleton knows that this student has regularly failed to turn in homework assignments. How should Ms. Carleton respond to this parent's concerns?
    a. She should tell the parent that her daughter clearly doesn't understand the course content, and needs a tutor
    b. She should explain to the parent that her daughter isn't turning in homework assignments, and tell her to make sure that her daughter does so in the future
    c. She should tell the parent that, unfortunately, the Federal Educational Right to Privacy Act (FERPA) prevents her from discussing her students' academic records without their permission
    d. She should explain to the parent that her daughter has missed several homework assignments, and offer to tell the parent about future assignments so that she can ensure that her daughter completes them

25. Mr. Fields wants to design an assessment method for his sixth grade math class that will help his students learn from their assignments and motivate them to improve. Which of the following approaches is most likely to accomplish this objective?
    a. Assigning ungraded homework problems and having weekly tests
    b. Assigning nightly homework problems that are peer-graded in class the next day, and going over the answers after the assignment is graded
    c. Assigning homework problems that are graded by the teacher and returned on the day before the unit test
    d. Assigning nightly homework problems which are graded and returned with a correct answer key within three days

26. An eighth grade student is preparing a research paper for her language arts class, and she has used information from three books, one newspaper, and several websites created by the U.S government and non-profit organizations. For which of these resources should she include a citation in her bibliography?
    a. Only the books
    b. The books and the newspaper
    c. The books, the newspaper, and the websites
    d. The books, the newspaper, and the U.S. government websites only

27. A fifth grade teacher has a mainstreamed special education student in her class who has a behavioral disability. The student has become increasingly disruptive over the past few weeks. Which of the following steps should the teacher take first in attempting to resolve this situation?
    a. The teacher should call the student's parents and ask them to speak with the student about her behavior
    b. The teacher should send the student to the principal's office when the disruptive behavior occurs
    c. The teacher should discuss the problem with the special education teacher
    d. The teacher should isolate the student so that her class is not disrupted

28. A school district has established a help hotline for teachers to call when they have questions about using technology in the classroom, or when they encounter technical difficulties. A teacher has called the hotline for advice on how to create a PowerPoint slide show for his social studies class. A voice prompt asks the teacher to press one if he is calling with a question regarding software, two if he is calling with a question regarding hardware, three if he has a question about using the Internet, and four is he is calling with a question about audio-visual equipment. Which number should the teacher press to learn more about PowerPoint?
    a. 1
    b. 2
    c. 3
    d. 4

29. Ellen, a seventh-grader, has been diagnosed with a serious illness and will be out of school for several months. Ellen's parents have asked her teachers to send her worksheets home to her in electronic form. All but which of the following could be used to send electronic copies of paper worksheets?
    a. Copy machine
    b. Scanner
    c. Flash drive or disc
    d. Email

30. A middle school art teacher has taken his class to the school's media center so that the students can use the Internet to research their favorite Renaissance artists. If students bookmark the websites that they find useful, which of the following statements is true?
    a. The students can use those bookmarks to return to those websites on their home computer
    b. The students can use those bookmarks to return to the same websites only if they are using a computer in the school's media center
    c. The students can only use those bookmarks to return to the same websites if they also enable the computer's pop-up blocker
    d. The students can only use those bookmarks to return to the websites they've selected if they're using that particular computer

31. Mr. Ferris has asked his eighth grade language arts students to submit their 500-word book reports in Microsoft Word format electronically via email. In terms of assessment, the main advantage of this method is that:
    a. Mr. Ferris can grade the term papers more quickly and return them electronically so as not use up valuable class time while passing them out
    b. Mr. Ferris can easily determine whether or not each student's report is the correct length
    c. Mr. Ferris can use the change-tracking device in Microsoft Word to show the students how to improve their papers
    d. Mr. Ferris can tabulate the number of specific grammatical errors the students have made in order to determine areas that he should focus on in class

32. Mrs. Thomas recently taught her fifth grade students a new math concept that they seemed to understand clearly. However, when she administered a unit test of the material, more than half of the students failed. Mrs. Thomas' first reaction should be to:
   a. Give the students another chance to learn the material by re-teaching it the same way as she did the first time
   b. Analyze the test and the results to determine whether the assessment was well-designed and fairly administered
   c. Review the test results to discover exactly which aspect of the material the students had trouble with
   d. Compare her students' test results with the performance of last year's fifth grade class on the same test to see if there is a discrepancy

Questions 33-36 refer to the following scenario:
   The administrators at a middle school are considering implementing a team-teaching model for sixth grade classes in the upcoming school year. The administrators, including the principal and vice-principal, have convened a staff meeting to discuss this possibility with the sixth grade teachers.

33. One of the sixth grade teachers, Mrs. Ling, favors the proposal and wants to convince her colleagues to support it as well. Which of the following arguments should she use to accurately and persuasively describe the advantages of team teaching for sixth grade students?
   a. Team teaching reduces the student-teacher ratio, providing more individualized attention for students
   b. Team teaching provides an effective "bridge" between the single-teacher model of elementary schools and the multiple-teacher model of high schools
   c. Team teaching provides increased opportunities for interdisciplinary teaching
   d. Team teaching allows students more opportunities to develop supportive relationships with teachers and fellow students

34. The teachers and administrators come to an agreement that they should implement a team-teaching model during the upcoming year. However, the vice-principal points out that they must determine how they will divide the students into the various teams. The principal suggests that they divide the students into teams on the basis of their academic ability, so that the higher-achieving students will not be held back by their peers. Mrs. Ling disagrees with this proposal, because she believes that this approach will cause students in the lower-achieving classes to feel stigmatized and fall further behind. What would be the best way for Mrs. Ling to persuade the administrators to agree with her views?
   a. She should simply state how she feels about the ability grouping proposal and why she feels this way
   b. She should tell the principal that she refuses to participate in the team-teaching plan if students are grouped by ability
   c. She should affirm the principal's concerns, but explain why she feels that avoiding the stigmatizing effect of ability grouping is more important than providing enrichment opportunities for high-achieving students
   d. She should not directly confront the principal, but instead resist implementing ability tracking in her own classes

35. In adjusting their lesson plans to accommodate the new team-teaching model, the teachers decide that it would be advantageous to create linkages between the various subjects that they teach. To do this, they want to create a thematic unit that will be taught jointly in math, science, social studies, and language arts classes. What is the best way for the teachers to develop the content of this unit?
   a. Have each teacher create a curriculum map for the year, and compare these maps to find themes, content and skills that are similar
   b. Design the thematic units first, and then have teachers adjust their lesson plans to accommodate them
   c. Ask students to vote on themes that they would like to learn about, and then design the units around these themes
   d. Select one teacher to design the thematic units and deliver them to the other teachers, who will find ways to fit the units into their lesson plans

36. At the end of the year, the teachers decide that they want to evaluate the effectiveness of the team-teaching model for their sixth grade students. Which of the following research strategies would provide them with the best assessment of the model?
   a. The teachers should compare this group of students' performance on standardized tests in previous years with their performance in sixth grade at the end of the year
   b. The teachers should compare the students' performance in classes that are part of the team teaching model (math, science, language arts, social studies) with their performance in classes that are not team-taught (health, physical education, art)
   c. The teachers should compare their students' performance in sixth grade to the performance of sixth grade students at schools that do not use team teaching
   d. The teachers should compare their sixth grade students' performance this year with the performance of sixth grade students in previous years where team teaching was not used; they should also consider the performance history of this particular group of sixth graders relative to previous groups

Questions 37-42 refer to the following scenario:
   During Mr. Aaron's 50 minute class period with his eighth grade language arts class of 30 students, he wants the students to read a short story and discuss their reactions to the story with their classmates. This exercise is intended to help the students develop their reading comprehension skills, as well as their communication skills and their ability to exchange opinions in a respectful manner with other students.

37. Given the learning objectives that Mr. Aaron has set for this lesson, what would be the best way to structure the discussion portion of the class?
   a. Ask the students to write out their reactions, and then call on students and ask them to share these reactions with the class
   b. Go over a list of rules for respectful discussion with the class, and then guide the discussion by calling on students to answer specific questions
   c. Remind the students about rules for respectful discussion, and then provide the students with a list of questions that they discuss in small groups
   d. Provide the students with a structured list of questions, and having the students discuss them in order as a class

38. Mr. Aaron notices that some of the students in his class seem to enjoy discussions and take a natural leadership role. Why might this be the case, and how could Mr. Aaron use this fact to enhance the discussion if he chose to use a small-group format?
　a. These "natural leaders" probably have a high level of intrapersonal intelligence, and Mr. Aaron should be sure to put all of these student in the same discussion group so that they do not intimidate less outgoing students
　b. The students are "natural leaders" because they have a great deal of interpersonal intelligence, and Mr. Aaron should spread these students throughout the groups so that they can help facilitate discussion
　c. These "natural leaders" probably have a high level of interpersonal intelligence, and Mr. Aaron should be sure to put all of these student in the same discussion group so that they do not intimidate less outgoing students
　d. The students are "natural leaders" because they have a great deal of intrapersonal intelligence, and Mr. Aaron should spread these students throughout the groups so that they can help facilitate discussion

39. Another language arts teacher at Mr. Aaron's school prefers not to use discussion in his classes, because he feels that is takes valuable time away from the study of reading and writing skills. In defending his practice of using discussion in his class, Mr. Aaron would be most likely to refer to which of these learning theories?
　a. Hunter's theory of direct instruction
　b. Piaget's theory of assimilation
　c. Vygotsky's socio-cultural theory of learning
　d. Gardner's theory of multiple intelligences

40. Mr. Aaron's discussion session goes well, and he decides to extend this idea and ask students to complete a group project in which they can perform a skit, create a poster, jointly write a book report, or create a collection or invention that relates to a book they're reading in class. The most effective way for Mr. Aaron to group the students would be to:
　a. Allow students to choose their own groups, since they know with which other students they'll work best
　b. Keep the same groups from the class discussion, since they seemed to work well
　c. Create groups that are balanced in terms of the students' academic ability, so that no group will be at a particular disadvantage
　d. Determine students' personal intelligence profiles (musical, interpersonal, mathematical, verbal , etc.) and assign students with similar strengths to the same group so that they can choose a project that fits their abilities

41. In designing the group project, Mr. Aaron wants to implement an assessment system that provides incentives for all students to contribute equally to the project and that is fair to students in cases where certain group members contribute more than others. Which of the following strategies would be most effective in helping him to achieve this objective?
    a. Giving all students in the group the opportunity to confidentially rate the contributions of their fellow group members, and giving lower grades to students who are rated lower by the members of their group
    b. Giving all students in the group the same grade so they'll be motivated to monitor one another's contributions and exercise teamwork skills
    c. Asking students to submit a report detailing exactly what their contribution was to the project, and to provide a self-evaluation of the value of their own contribution
    d. Grading the projects using a pass/fail system, since it is very difficult to equitably grade group projects

42. Ms. Schneider, a fifth grade teacher, has been assigned a paraprofessional who comes to her class three times a week to work with the mainstreamed special education students. For the past week, the paraprofessional has arrived late to the classroom and appeared distracted and disinterested in his duties. What should be the first step that Ms. Schneider takes to resolve the problem?
    a. Ask the school principal to assign a different paraprofessional to her class
    b. Send a note to the special education teacher explaining the problem
    c. Take the paraprofessional aside and explain her concerns
    d. Help the special education students write a letter to the paraprofessional explaining how his behavior is affecting their learning

43. Mrs. Alexander is preparing her seventh grade science class for the upcoming standardized achievement test, but the class has fallen behind. One day she receives a letter from one of her students' parents stating that she is a microbiology researcher and would be interested in coming to class to discuss some of the biology concepts that the students are learning. How should Mrs. Alexander respond to this request?
    a. She should invite the student's parent to come speak to the class as soon as possible
    b. She should tell the parent that she appreciates the suggestion, but her class has fallen behind and there is no time for the presentation
    c. She should tell the parent that she can deliver a presentation after school hours so that students can attend if they chose to
    d. She should explain the fact that the class has fallen behind in preparing for an upcoming standardized test, but that she would like to schedule a time for the parent's presentation after the test

44. The middle school teachers are in the middle of administering the test when the school's fire alarm is sounded. What should the teachers do?
    a. The teachers should tell their students to continue taking the test, since it is probably just a drill
    b. The teachers should ask the students to leave their tests at their desks and follow the usual fire evacuation procedures without discussing the test
    c. The teachers should ask the students to follow the usual fire evacuation procedures, but take their tests with them
    d. The teachers should immediately contact the administration for advice

45. While administering the test, a teacher notices that that a student has erased an answer so vigorously that she has torn her testing booklet. What should the teacher do?
   a. Give the student a new test booklet with the same form number to use for the remainder of the test, and transcribe the student's responses from the torn booklet to the new booklet after the test
   b. Simply ask the student to erase more carefully in the future
   c. Give the new student a new test booklet with the same form number and ask her to immediately transfer her answers into the new booklet and continue the test
   d. Give the student a new test booklet and ask her to continue using that test booklet, since two booklets can be scored as one

46. When the middle schools receive the test results later on, they see that the students' scores are reported in both raw and scaled form. The scaled scores will be most useful for:
   a. Determining exactly how many questions students got right and wrong
   b. Determining which types of questions students had the most trouble with
   c. Comparing students' performance across different administrations of the same test
   d. Predicting students' performance in the classroom and on future tests

47. In preparation for the upcoming school year, the test results shared with the teachers who will be working with the students the following year. How will this information be most useful to the students' new teachers?
   a. It will determine which students should be placed in remedial classes
   b. It will help the teachers plan their instruction based on the strengths and needs of the incoming students
   c. It will help determine which students should repeat a grade
   d. It will help the teachers decide whether or not they should use team teaching

48. After examining the assessment results for their incoming class of students, the teachers determine that about 35% of the students do not meet grade level standards for math. Which of the following approaches would be most likely to improve the overall performance of the class on future tests?
   a. Having the underperforming students take math class three extra times per week, while reducing the number of math classes that students who exceeded the math standard take per week by three
   b. Having all students take an extra three periods of math, while reducing science classes to only two times per week
   c. Creating a compulsory after-school remediation program for the students who are behind in math
   d. Finding creative ways to incorporate math instruction into other subject areas, and offering optional math tutoring during lunch and after school

49. In order to effectively lead a class discussion, what is the best thing for a teacher to do after posing a fairly complex question to the class?
   a. Immediately call on a student to answer the question
   b. Wait two minutes, and then call on a student to answer the question
   c. Engage in another activity like writing on the board while waiting for the students to compose their answers
   d. Tell students that if no one answers right away, she will call on a student

50. During a class discussion, a teacher has posed a question to her seventh grade art class, but no student has responded. What should she do?
    a. Continue to wait until a student answers
    b. Repeat the question
    c. Rephrase the question
    d. Tell the students the answer

51. Which of the following assessment methods is most likely to be used in a learner-centered middle school classroom?
    a. A method that provides different alternatives for students to demonstrate their knowledge
    b. A method that allows students to complete the assessment in groups
    c. A structured method that allows students' mastery to be compared with that of other students
    d. A multiple-choice test which students help to construct and grade

52. Which of the following statements best explains why middle school students' academic performance can be most effectively assessed by focusing on progress, rather than comparisons with other students?
    a. Focusing on progress makes it possible for all students to earn good grades, even if they are struggling academically
    b. Since middle school students are so developmentally diverse, focusing on progress allows teachers to maintain high expectations while meeting students where they are academically
    c. By focusing on progress, it is easier for teachers to justify the fact that many of their students are not meeting grade level expectations
    d. By the middle school level, some students have fallen irreversibly behind, and using a progress-focused assessment approach prevents students from being retained

53. Which of the following characteristics accurately describes authentic assessment techniques?
    a. They are norm-referenced
    b. They are designed to build higher-order thinking skills
    c. They allow students to choose from a set of teacher-prepared responses
    d. They measure students' performance at a specific point in time

54. Josh, a student in Mr. Calloway's seventh grade science class, used to be energetic and outspoken in class, and always participated actively in group projects. Recently, though Mr. Calloway has noticed the other students ostracizing Josh, and as a result, he has become quiet, nervous and withdrawn. How should Mr. Calloway structure his class so that Josh can be academically successful?
    a. He should eliminate group projects altogether because they make unpopular students uncomfortable
    b. He should speak directly to the class and tell the other students to be more friendly towards Josh
    c. He should speak with Josh privately to find out why the other students are ostracizing him
    d. He should take note of which students Josh seems to feel more comfortable with, and allow him to work with those students during group projects

55. Ms. Wilson wants to convey to her eighth grade students the fact that although many of them are starting the year out behind grade level, she believes that they can all improve enough to pass the standardized test they are required to take at the end of the school year in order to move on to ninth grade. Ms. Wilson could most effectively convey her high expectations and motivate her students to achieve using which of the following methods?
   a. Describing other groups of students who have made similar gains within one school year
   b. Reminding them at the beginning of each class that they will fail eighth grade if they do not work hard to improve
   c. Working with students to create a contract that includes both her and the students' goals for themselves, as well as specific steps that she and the students will take to reach those goals
   d. Writing a letter to the students' parents detailing her goals for the students and asking for parents' help in achieving them

56. Which of the following statements most accurately describes the academic potential of students in low-income schools?
   a. They will fall irreversibly behind their wealthier peers because of lack of parental support and resources
   b. They should be presented with lower expectations since they will not need high-level academic skills for their future careers
   c. They may have a poor perception of their academic ability, but this disadvantage can be overcome with effective instruction and high expectations
   d. They cannot succeed academically unless their schools and communities are given vastly greater economic resources

57. The most important quality of a middle school classroom discipline plan is:
   a. Flexibility
   b. Clarity of rules and consequences
   c. Student input
   d. Avoiding harsh punishment as long as possible

58. Each day, behavior problems begin early in Mr. Mencia's sixth grade class while he calls out each student's name to take attendance. The first step Mr. Mencia should take to correct this problem is to:
   a. Ask the disruptive students to come to class after attendance has been taken
   b. Tell the students that they will be considered tardy if they are disruptive during the role call
   c. Find a way to take attendance that is more engaging for the students
   d. Take attendance at the end of class

59. Mrs. Brown is becoming frustrated because her sixth grade students begin packing up their materials in anticipation of the bell while she is still teaching. Students most likely engage in this behavior because:
   a. Sixth grade students tend to have very short attention spans, and the students are bored with her teaching
   b. Students at this age don't want to stand out, so when one student starts packing up her materials, all of the other students are likely to follow
   c. Sixth grade students have difficulty sitting still, and they are anxious to get up and move around
   d. Middle school students, especially sixth-graders, tend to be anxious about completing transitions

60. Mr. Tollison has noticed that many of his eighth grade math students are not completing their homework assignments at all, are partially completing them or are completing the wrong problems. Mr. Tollison's first response should be to:
   a. Call the students' parents if they fail to turn in more than one assignment
   b. Grade whatever problems the students do turn in, even if they are not the right ones
   c. Develop a system to ensure that all students correctly record the homework assignment
   d. Walk the students through a few of the homework problems before they leave class

61. Ms. Kincaid has sent home a note with her fourth grade students asking their parents to sign up for parent-teacher conferences, but after a week, only about ten percent of the students' parents have done so. Ms. Kincaid is concerned that if a student's parents fail to attend a conference this will negatively impact the student's academic achievement. What is the first step that she should take in order to increase the number of parents who attend conferences?
   a. Take the students whose parents have not scheduled conferences aside and ask them whether or not they gave their parents the note about parent-teacher conferences
   b. Call the parents directly and notify them about the upcoming conferences
   c. Give the students another note to take home that emphasizes the importance of conferences to the students' academic development
   d. Tell the students that their grades will suffer if they don't convince their parents to attend the conference

62. Mr. Ivanov has several students in his fifth grade class whose parents have recently immigrated to the United States and who are not comfortable conversing in English. The parents' native language is Spanish, and Mr. Ivanov does not speak Spanish. In order to ensure that these parents can participate in the upcoming parent-teacher conferences, which of the following steps should Mr. Ivanov take first?
   a. He should ask the Spanish-speaking students if they would be willing to serve as translators for the conferences
   b. He should send a note to the parents informing them that they will need to hire a translator if they want to participate in the conferences
   c. He should inform the school principal that he cannot hold the conferences if he is not supplied with a translator
   d. He should find someone to help him write a note to the parents in Spanish explaining that he will help them find a volunteer translator if they do not have a friend or family member who could translate for them

63. Mrs. Fillmore is teaching her fourth grade class about fractions, and she wants to explain to the students why multiplying two fractions together yields a smaller fraction. Which of the following methods would most effectively communicate this concept?
   a. Giving the students a list of proper fractions, and asking them to multiply any two of the fractions together in order to demonstrate that a smaller fraction is always the product.
   b. Explaining that multiplying two fractions together produces a fraction of a fraction, and using manipulatives to demonstrate this
   c. Verbally explaining to the students that multiplying a fraction by a whole number produces a larger number, and multiplying a fraction by a fraction produces a smaller fraction
   d. Demonstrating that when you divide the product of two fractions by one of the fractions, the result is the other fraction

64. A sixth grade science teacher has used a new textbook this year, and she wants to evaluate its effectiveness compared with that of the textbook she used in previous years. Which of the following strategies would be most appropriate?
   a. Comparing this year's students' performance on standardized tests to the standardized test scores of the students she taught in previous years using the old book
   b. Comparing this year's students' performance on norm-referenced in-class tests to the test scores of the students she taught in previous years using the old book
   c. Comparing current students' improvement on a criterion-referenced test administered at the beginning and the end of the year to previous students' improvement on that same test throughout the year
   d. Surveying current students' interest in science and comparing it to previous students' interest in science

65. Mr. Kelley is teaching his eighth grade social studies class about World War II, and he engages his class in a discussion about how U.S. involvement in the war affected ordinary Americans. What is the primary educational benefit of engaging in this discussion?
   a. It will help students remember important details about the war, such as dates of important events and names of important historical figures
   b. It will help develop students' higher-order thinking skills
   c. It will help students use their own experiences to understand social studies concepts
   d. It will help develop students' sense of patriotism

66. Which of the following is an example of a teacher using differentiation in the classroom?
   a. Ms. Morse divides her fourth grade students into ability groups and spends at least one hour each week working with this group in a way that meets the members' unique needs
   b. Mr. Stillwell only holds parent-teacher conferences with the parents of students who are struggling in his class
   c. Mr. Karl and presents each of his reading lessons in ways that target the various academic levels and learning styles of his students
   d. Mrs. Tanner asks her seventh grade math class to complete an assignment in groups, each of which contains at least one student who has demonstrated mastery of the material

67. The school district in which Mr. Copeland teaches seventh grade language arts is in a low-income community with a high adult illiteracy rate, and he knows that the parents of many of his students can only read on an elementary school level. While many of the parents are very engaged in their students' education, they're not able to help their children with reading assignments at home. What is the first step Mr. Copeland should take to ensure that all of his students receive support in completing their reading homework?
   a. He should identify parents who struggle with reading and help them enroll in a local adult literacy program so that they can learn to read and eventually help their students with homework
   b. He should attempt to create a tutoring program in which older students and literate parents volunteer to provide homework support after school or during lunch
   c. He should personally provide tutoring to parents who struggle with reading
   d. He should eliminate homework assignments altogether or provide easier assignments for the students who lack homework support

68. Several of Ms. Holloway's seventh grade math students are in foster care. One student is constantly being shifted among different foster parents, and the students' academic performance is suffering considerably since he went into foster care. Which of the following would be the most appropriate way for Ms. Holloway to respond to this problem?
   a. She should ignore the problem for the time being, since the student is simply distracted by his unstable home environment and will be able to catch up once he returns to his family
   b. She should contact the student's current foster parents to inform them of the problem so they can help the student with math
   c. She should contact the student's social services caseworker about the problem so that he or she can inform each of the students' successive foster parents of the importance of helping the student with math
   d. She should give the student easier math assignments until the student returns home so that his grades will not suffer

69. Which of the following is true of students whose parents are highly aware of and involved in their academic progress?
   a. They are always from high-income families
   b. They typically perform better in school than students whose families are less involved
   c. They are always near the top of their classes
   d. They are typically lower-performing students, because parents are only interested in their children's academic progress if they are not doing well

70. Mr. Mailer recommends that Thomas, a student in his fourth grade class, be assessed for a possible reading disability, but Thomas' parents are strongly resistant to this idea. They say that Thomas is just a "late bloomer," and that testing him for a reading disability will only erode his self-esteem. They insist that the test be put off at least until next year to see if Thomas improves. How should Mr. Mailer respond to Thomas' parents' resistance to his conviction that Thomas needs to be considered for special education services?
   a. Since parents understand their children's needs best, he should simply agree to wait until next year
   b. He should have Thomas tested anyway, and let the parents know the results only if Thomas qualifies for special education services
   c. He should refer the matter to the school principal to avoid possible legal repercussions
   d. He should explain to the parents that the decision is ultimately theirs, but he should also provide them with educational resources about reading disabilities and emphasize that delaying receipt of special education services can exacerbate the problems associated with reading disabilities

71. During her annual review, Mr. Ainsley is told by the school principal that his teaching is good overall, but that his portfolio shows that he does not assess his students as often or as effectively as he should. What actions should Mr. Ainsley take first to correct this problem?
   a. Write a letter to the principal stating that he thinks this assessment of his teaching is unfair, and explaining his reasons for his failure to assess his students adequately
   b. Use available professional development resources on assessment to develop a plan to improve his use of assessment in the classroom and present it to the principal for review
   c. Confer with other teachers to find out if the principal made similar suggestions to them about improving their assessment techniques
   d. Sign up for an assessment workshop that will occur in a few months and let the principal know that he will need to take a few days off work to attend the workshop

72. Ms. Mattingly has received her fourth grade class' standardized test results, and they show that her students are significantly behind the other fourth grade classes in the district in both reading and math. She didn't realize her students were so far behind, because they had been doing well on in-class assessments. How should Ms. Mattingly respond to this situation?
    a. Since standardized tests are an imperfect measure of achievement, she should ignore the results as long as her students are doing well in her class
    b. She should confer with her principal and other fourth grade teachers to determine whether her grade level expectations for academic achievement align with those of the district as a whole
    c. She should change her instructional methods to "teach to the test" and include more practice taking multiple choice tests for her students
    d. She should send a letter to her students' parents informing them that their children need tutoring in reading and math

73. In middle school students, sudden declines in academic performance may be caused by:
    a. Parental divorce
    b. Drug use
    c. Eating disorders
    d. All of the above

74. Mrs. Cranston, a seventh grade science teacher, tries to provide her students with several options when assigning projects. This approach is useful because it fosters emotional development in which of the following areas?
    a. Development of a variety of learning approaches
    b. Development of self-concept
    c. Developing a sense of autonomy
    d. Developing identification with peer groups

75. Each year, Mr. Caldwell holds a debating contest in his eighth grade language arts class. He does not tell the students which side of the argument they will be debating until the day of the debate, so the students must prepare to argue both sides. Which of the following best describes why this is a useful exercise for middle school students?
    a. Practicing argumentation helps promote students' growing sense of autonomy
    b. Public speaking improves students' self-esteem and assertiveness
    c. Preparing to argue both sides of the debate develops students' higher-order thinking skills by promoting awareness of competing viewpoints
    d. Researching both sides of the argument develops students' organizational skills

76. At the beginning of each school year, Mrs. Bonner, a middle school principal, asks all of the teachers in her school to write out a broad set of learning objectives for their students and compare these objectives with those stated for their subject and grade level. Which of the following statements best describes the purpose of such an exercise?
    a. Ensuring that the teachers' learning objectives align with district standards
    b. Assessing the clarity of the learning objectives
    c. Determining whether teachers from the same grade level and content area have comparable learning objectives
    d. Evaluating the learning objectives in terms of their ability to be assessed

77. Which of the following is the best example of a learning experience that would prompt middle-schoolers to explore educational content from varied and integrated perspectives?
   a. Taking a computer-administered test
   b. Reading about life in a different country
   c. Using flashcards to study for a vocabulary test
   d. Writing a research report about an animal of the students' choice

78. All but which of the following are critical values that are formed during the middle school years?
   a. Respect for diversity
   b. Commitment to continued schooling
   c. Tolerance of those who are different
   d. Higher-order thinking skills

79. Mr. Reid has assigned his seventh grade science students to complete a group project that he thought would engage them, but so far they have shown a marked lack of interest in it. How can Mr. Reid best use his knowledge of middle school students' developmental characteristics to enhance his students' interest in the project?
   a. He can appeal to the students' growing sense of autonomy by providing them with several different options for completing the project
   b. He can appeal to the students' sense of autonomy by allowing them to work on the project individually
   c. He can appeal to the students' growing organizational skills by asking them to write out a timeline showing when they will complete each portion of the project
   d. He can appeal to the growing differentiation in social roles that characterizes middle school students by allowing each group to democratically elect a leader

80. Mrs. Lindsey frequently engages her sixth grade science class in structured problem solving activities. The main benefit of such activities for middle level students is that they:
   a. Foster inquiry and critical thinking skills
   b. Improve organizational and time-management skills
   c. Enhance students' social skills
   d. Teach students to appreciate diversity

81. Middle school students benefit from kinesthetic learning experiences. Which of the following is an example of a kinesthetic learning activity that would be appropriate for middle school students?
   a. Engaging them in an activity that involves sorting different colored candies in order to develop their categorization skills
   b. Asking students to recite a conceptually important pneumonic device at the beginning of every class
   c. Having students write essays about what they want to be when they grow up and how they plan to achieve their goals
   d. Asking students to act out a scene from a play that they are reading in class

82. Middle school teachers are expected to manage their classrooms in ways that respect students' rights. Which of the following classroom practices might violate this expectation?
    a. Publicly posting students' names and test grades
    b. Publically telling a student aloud that she will be assigned to detention if she speaks out of turn again
    c. Assigning students to groups without giving them input in their groups' composition
    d. Punishing a student for being tardy to class, even though the student said he was late because he left a book in his previous class and had to go back to retrieve it

83. Mr. Norton has noticed that some of the students within the sixth grade teaching team that he is part of are in constant conflict with one another. He has tried disciplining the students according to school protocol, but the problem behavior has continued. Mr. Norton has called a meeting of the teachers on the team to discuss a strategy to deal with the problem. Which of the following steps should the teachers take first?
    a. Hold a diversity workshop for their students
    b. Take the students involved in the conflict aside and tell them that some of them will have to be moved to a different teaching team if they do not stop fighting
    c. Refer the students to the school's peer mediation program
    d. Hold a team meeting to renegotiate the team rules with the students' input

84. Mrs. Hanson gives a brief lecture and asks students to discuss a list of questions in pairs before the class as a whole discusses them. This technique is effective for facilitating class discussion primarily because:
    a. It gives students the opportunity to try out their answers in a "safe" environment before stating them in front of the class
    b. It encourages students to compare their answers to those of their classmates and revise them if they are not socially acceptable
    c. It develops students' higher-order thinking skills by demonstrating that there are differing perspectives
    d. It provides Mrs. Hanson with the opportunity to see which questions are most interesting to the students before the classroom-wide discussion commences

85. Ms. Fry, an eighth grade science teacher, gives her class verbal instructions about how to complete an experiment, but when she tells them to begin, the students do not seem to know what to do. Which of the following methods would have been least effective in communicating the directions more clearly?
    a. Asking the students to write down the instructions
    b. Asking students questions throughout her explanation to make sure that they were comprehending the directions
    c. Providing written instructions
    d. Asking students if they had any questions after she had explained the directions

86. Mrs. Alito has a student in her fourth grade class who has been diagnosed with anxiety disorder. Sometimes the student becomes so anxious in class that he needs to go to the special education resource room for brief periods. How can Mrs. Alito best meet the student's needs without making him feel uncomfortable or disrupting the rest of her class?
	a. She can quietly check in with the student once every few hours to see if he is feeling especially anxious
	b. She can ask him to raise his hand and ask to be excused if he is feeling anxious
	c. She can teach him relaxation exercises so that he does not need to leave the class
	d. She can keep an eye on the student and provide him with a nonverbal signal that he can use to alert her if he needs to go to the resource room

87. Mr. Moyer wants to introduce his middle school math students to household budget management, so he gives them a list detailing the cost of common household bills and items, as well as a monthly spending limit. Which of the following computer programs would be most useful for the students in calculating their monthly budgets?
	a. Microsoft Excel
	b. Microsoft Outlook
	c. Adobe Pagemaker
	d. None of the above

88. Which of the following actions is most likely to be considered "fair use" under U.S. copyright law?
	a. Printing out a copy of an e-book for a student who cannot afford to purchase the book
	b. Copying several chapters out of a textbook for a student who lost his textbook
	c. Copying the assigned homework questions from a textbook for a student who was home sick for a few days
	d. Borrowing a DVD movie from the library and making a copy to show to students each year

89. Which of the following activities constitutes plagiarism?
	a. Copying a sentence verbatim from a website and citing the website in your bibliography
	b. Paraphrasing a sentence from a book and citing the book in the text and in your bibliography
	c. Copying a verse from a poem verbatim, placing it in quote marks, and citing the poem in the text and in your bibliography
	d. Paraphrasing a sentence from a website and citing the website in the text and in your bibliography

90. A seventh grade science teacher is conducting Internet research on the latest developments in paleontology to find material for a lesson. She finds a website that is published by a professor at a well-respected local university, and would like to use the information in her class. What other information should the teacher look for before deciding to use the information on the website for her lesson?
	a. Whether the information is also available in book form
	b. When the information on the website was last updated
	c. Whether the professor still works at the university
	d. Whether the information is copyrighted

91. Mrs. Eli is holding a career day for her sixth grade class of 25 students, and has invited parents to come to class and discuss their jobs. Many parents have expressed interest, but most of them have said that they will have difficulty leaving their jobs during the school day. All but which of the following technological solutions might be helpful in addressing this problem?
    a. Holding the presentation by videoconference during the parent's their lunch break
    b. Holding the presentation by teleconference during the parent's lunch break
    c. Asking the parent to create a videotape in which they discuss their job and sending it to school
    d. Asking the parent to create a Powerpoint presentation about their job for their child to present to the class

92. Mr. Shields has been issued funds to purchase a computer software program for the middle school's student newspaper staff to use to publish their paper. Which of the following programs would be most appropriate?
    a. Microsoft Word
    b. Microsoft Access
    c. Adobe Flash
    d. Adobe Pagemaker

93. Acceptable use policies for school computers are intended to:
    a. Deter students and school employees from accessing inappropriate information or engaging in illegal activities using school computers
    b. Ensure that students and teachers do not accidentally stumble upon inappropriate material while using school computers
    c. Teach students about copyright laws and plagiarism
    d. Prevent students from transferring documents created on school computers to their home computers

94. Which of the following correctly describes a skill which should be both introduced and mastered during grades 6-8?
    a. Keyboarding
    b. Understanding the relevance of technology to future job prospects and daily life
    c. Opening, saving, and printing standard documents
    d. Using word processing software

95. Providing opportunities for self-assessment is important in the middle school classroom primarily because:
    a. It increases students' feeling of control over their grades
    b. It helps to foster students' growing sense of autonomy
    c. It prepares students to evaluate their own work in the absence of an instructor
    d. It gives students a stake in the assessment process and fosters their sense of fairness

96. Which of the following assessment methods would be most useful for fostering middle school students' ownership of their learning?
    a. Providing students with charts showing their improvement over the course of a year
    b. Giving the students pre- and post-tests for each instructional unit so that they can see their learning progress
    c. Giving students detailed feedback on their performance and providing opportunities to incorporate the feedback and demonstrate improvement
    d. Creating an environment wherein students openly compete to achieve the best grades, but are also rewarded for improvement

97. Which of the following statements are true of rubrics?
    a. Rubrics are only useful for complex assignments like oral presentations and research papers
    b. Rubrics must include at least three but no more than five categories
    c. Rubrics are effective assessment tools because they provide students with more specific feedback
    d. Both B and C are true

98. Student-led conferences can be effective at the middle school level primarily because:
    a. They encourage students to take ownership of their learning by evaluating their strengths and weaknesses
    b. Parents prefer to hear their children discuss their grades, as opposed to listening to the teacher discuss them
    c. Teachers can gain insights into their students' family relationships by holding student-led conferences
    d. Parents are more likely to attend student-led conferences

99. Effective parent-teacher conferences at the middle-school level:
    a. Should always be student-led
    b. Should be student-led only if the student is performing well academically
    c. Are only necessary for students who are misbehaving or performing poorly
    d. Should provide parents with the option of meeting privately with the teacher, participating in a student-led conference, or adopting a hybrid model

Constructed Response

Ms. Nolan is a first-year English-Language Arts/Geography teacher in a middle school with average test scores and academic standards. In her eighth-grade ELA/Geography class there are 24 diverse 12- and 13-year olds. She is beginning the seventh week of instruction.

Ms. Nolan will have her students work on the following project during this week's class sessions: Short Stories and Their Settings, Group Presentations
Objectives: Students will—
- Review and utilize concepts learned in class about short stories.
- Demonstrate speaking, listening, and writing skills
- Use creativity in the presentation (visual art, music, items from geographic region, etc.)
- Use higher-order thinking skills

Assignment:
- Students will work in assigned groups of four.
- Each group with select one short story from the list.
- The group will plan, gather information and present a group report to the class on the short story and the surrounding geography and its impact on the story.
- Use the short story/geography lesson from the previous week as a model for your presentation's organization.
- The presentation should include some use of visual art, music, cultural objects, etc.
- All students must participate in group presentation and planning.

Activities:
- Present/discuss assignment with class and assign groups.
- Group work: select short story, plan presentation, divide and assign responsibilities
- Group work: prepare presentation
- Group presentations to class
- Writing assignment—compare/contrast the different geographies presented and the similarities/differences in their influence on the short stories.

Assessment:
- In class group work—individual and group grade
- Group presentation to class—individual and group grade
- Writing assignment

Constructed Response Items

1. Identify one strength and one weakness in Ms. Nolan's project plan.

2. Explain how both the strength and the weakness you describe above demonstrate effective planning or the need for it. Your answer should be based on principles of planning instruction.

3. Propose two ways that Ms. Nolan can strengthen her assessment section. Describe how she can help her students have a better chance to show their achievements in this project.

4. Detail how each suggestion you gave above for question #3 can give students a better chance to show their achievements. Your response should be based on principles of formal and informal assessment.

Answers and Explanations

1. C: educators may legally accept gifts that are offered openly by students, parents, supervisors, etc., provided these gifts are offered to recognize or express appreciation for the educator's service. Gifts that influence an educator's professional judgment are prohibited. The code prohibits educators from interfering with the political rights of their colleagues, deceiving others with regard to the policies of the school district or educational institution, and revealing confidential student information (unless the disclosure is for a lawful professional purpose or is required by law).

2. A: IDEA requires schools to provide learning disabled students with a free and appropriate education, even if the student has been suspended or expelled from school for disciplinary reasons. Since some students have disabilities that cause them to misbehave, refusing to educate them on this basis would constitute discrimination. C is not correct because the IDEA requires learning disabled students to be educated in the least restrictive environment possible, so many students are taught wholly or partly in general education classrooms with non-disabled students. D is incorrect because schools are required to pay for accommodations for learning disabled students.

3. B: The FERPA stipulates that parents of children under 18 can inspect and request amendments to their children's educational records on demand (B). However, once students reach the age of majority, they become "eligible students." This means that this right is transferred to them and their permission is required to disclose their educational records to anyone, including their parents. Written permission from parents or the eligible student is not required in order to disclose records to a school official with a legitimate educational interest (C) or to a school to which the student is transferring (D).

4. B: effective rules are usually stated positively. Stating rules negatively, as in answer A or especially D, proscribe specific behaviors, but by definition "allow" all other behaviors not discussed. Further, it sends students the message that they are expected to misbehave, and makes positive reinforcement difficult. (It makes more sense to say, "Class, you can play for 15 minutes because you did an excellent job of working quietly today," than to say, "You did a good job of not yelling and bothering other students, so you may play outside"). While it may be appropriate to phrase rules politely (C), simply doing this does not have the same impact as stating them positively.

5. B: When resolving behavior problems, teachers should strive to be consistent and objective (B). Consistency is important because students will not feel that they are being singled out and treated differently than other students, and objectivity is key because practicing it will prevent the teacher's own biases from affecting his or her students. Together, objectivity and consistency will help the teacher run the classroom fairly and earn students' respect. A is incorrect because teachers should avoid reacting judgmentally to behavior. This can aggravate behavior problems with students who conclude that the teacher just "doesn't like" them or "doesn't understand" them. While patience and collaboration maybe useful in dealing with behavior problems, they are not as important as consistency and objectivity because being patient and/or collaborative alone does not provide a mode for directly addressing the behavior (i.e., one could be patient and collaborative but still inconsistent and ineffective at solving the behavior problem).

6. A: intrinsic motivation can be fostered by helping students to develop a personal connection to and interest in the material they're learning. Intrinsic motivation refers to a person's desire to do something (like a hobby) without any apparent material motivation and without any threat of punishment should the activity not be done. In contrast, answer B refers to extrinsic motivation.

This type of motivation propels a person to do something not because they enjoy the activity for its own sake, but because they fear punishment or desire rewards produced by that activity.

7. D: According to Piaget's theory, the distinction between people at the concrete operational stage (approximately 7-12 years of age) and the formal operational stage (approximately 12-16 years of age) of development is that Those in the concrete operational stage can think logically only with respect to concrete experiences, while those at the formal operational stage can reason in abstract and hypothetical terms. Children at the sensorimotor stage (birth to 2 years old) rely on their sensory perception and motor skills to learn and understand the world around them, and children at the preoperational stage (3-7) think in a literal, symbolic manner.

8. D: When a student's academic performance is poorer than what is predicted by IQ testing, this is often a sign of a learning disability, and indicates that a student should be considered for placement in special education services. Such a discrepancy may also be explained by behavior problems associated with emotional disabilities such as oppositional defiant disorder, or temporary strains associated with family or personal problems. A third possibility is that the student is struggling because of limited English proficiency, and a plan is needed to improve English skills so that the student can succeed in all academic areas.

9. B: As students enter adolescence, their social lives will most likely revolve around membership in a small social group that has a shared set of values and interests. While students maintain interest in family, they will increasingly choose to spend more time with friends. While violence is likely to affect the lives of some students, physical insecurity is not a predominant characteristic of most adolescents. Adolescents also begin to show an increased interest in their ethnic or cultural heritage as part of the identity-formation process.

10. A: exploring their own cultural heritage would directly impact the identity formation process (developing a set of personal values and goals). While such a project may also teach students tolerance if the projects are shared with the class, the actual process of researching one's own background would facilitate identity formation more than tolerance.

11. A: the teacher's most important responsibility is to create an accepting, non-judgmental classroom environment. Since homeless students attending school face many obstacles ranging from transience to lack of appropriate clothing and hygiene tools, they will be more likely to continue attending if they are accepted by their teachers and peers. Since the student is living in a shelter, the relevant social service agency is responsible for ensuring that the student is fed and clothed. Teachers are also not responsible for diagnosing mental illnesses, although the teacher should inform the student's parent or caseworker know if she suspects a problem. While the teacher may want to screen the student for possible learning disabilities, she should not assume that poor academic performance is the result of a disability. Homelessness often results in prolonged absence from school and emotional problems that interfere with learning, and these factors may explain poor performance.

12. C: Benji's behavior signals that he might be using illegal drugs. Students who begin using drugs may suddenly become more sluggish or more restless than usual, and they may begin experiencing abnormal sleep patterns that interfere with school attendance. A is incorrect because learning disabilities do not usually develop "overnight," unless they are caused by an accident or acute medical condition. Benji's symptoms also do not fit the symptoms of depression (D). Also, such rapid and detrimental changes are not normal, even for adolescents whose minds and bodies are changing rapidly (B).

13. C: While bullying among boys is usually displayed by obvious teasing and even violence, girls tend to use bullying tactics that are more discreet. For example, girls might spread false rumors about each other or exclude certain individuals from social activities. While parents and teachers are less likely to notice this type of bullying, it can be just a damaging to the victim's self esteem as violence.

14. D: the teacher should help the students who are not using the Internet find low-cost Internet access and training in their community. While teachers can require students to purchase certain low-cost school supplies like pencils and paper, they cannot expect that all students have the same knowledge or access to more expensive technologies like computers with word processing software and the Internet. It would also be counterproductive to prevent students who do have computer access from using it, because this would hold back their learning. The best solution to this problem would be to try to help all students gain access to the Internet.

15. B: students who are learning English as a second language typically have normal or above-average intelligence, although their academic performance may suffer because most assignments directly or indirectly require English language skills. Because English Language Learners are typically of normal intelligence, and because being an English Language Learner is not considered a disability, these students cannot be referred for special education services unless they have a true learning disability (A). Further, cultural background has no bearing on intelligence, so D is incorrect.

16. C: the best approach would be for Mrs. Li to take the learning disabled students to a quiet area and facilitate a 15 minute group reading discussion while the other students write. Since the objective of the writing assignment is actually to assess the students' reading comprehension, not their writing ability, this can be accomplished orally as well as in writing. Although giving students more time to complete the assignment would be appropriate if this were an assignment assessing writing ability, it would be unfair to ask students to complete extra homework due to their learning disability if there is another assessment method readily available.

17. C: Mr. Robinson can achieve this objective using a theme-based unit. Theme-based units allow students to explore a topic of interest from many different perspectives, and use their reading, math, writing and reasoning skills to learn more about the topic. For example, in a theme-based unit about weather, students might learn how to use number lines by reading a thermometer, read about the devastating effects of severe weather, and write about a time that the weather affected their lives.

18. B: Since most of the students in Ms. Frank's class are auditory learners, she would reach the majority of her students by teaching them a song about the new concept that they're learning. Auditory learners remember and comprehend concepts best using their sense of hearing.

19. A: of the practices described here, providing opportunities for students to work cooperatively with peers is most likely to promote a productive classroom environment for middle-level students. The classroom environment should be planned and structured, as opposed to frequently changed (B), and students should be encouraged to work cooperatively, rather than independently (C). In addition, kinesthetic and active learning activities can be very beneficial for middle-level students (D).

20. A: If Mr. Stratton's goal is to ensure that students understand what is expected of them and that they are able to complete the project on schedule, the best approach for him to take would be to explain how to do the research and set several 'checkpoints' before the final product is due. By explaining the research process, Mr. Stratton ensures that all students understand what they're expected to do. Setting checkpoints, (for example, asking students to submit a brief description of their project one month before it is due and asking them to submit a rough draft one week before it is due), Mr. Stratton can make sure that all of his students are on track to complete the project as scheduled.

21. C is the best answer here. If Mrs. Frances wants to develop a theme-based unit that is interesting and relevant to her fifth grade students, the best approach would be to conduct an informal, open-ended survey to look for interests that her students share. This approach would allow Mrs. Frances to find a topic that would interest the broadest range of students. While presenting several topics for students to vote upon (D) would also come close to achieving this goal, it is a less desirable alternative because it artificially narrows the choices available to students by predetermining the options.

22. B: in order to help students make the transition to note-taking, the best approach would be to provide an outline of key words and points for students to fill in during the lecture, and gradually provide less and less detail in this outline until students are taking notes without assistance. Although the other strategies mentioned also have advantages, this approach is the best because it includes both a method for teaching note-taking techniques (students start out with a template of what notes should look like) and an opportunity to practice the skill.

23. B: The most effective strategy for Mr. Swanson to use would be to explain to the students that they have done a good job of improving their behavior, but that they can do even better. As a consequence, they now need to earn four check marks to get the reward, which is 45 minutes on the computer. This strategy has several advantages over the other options presented here. Unlike A and D, this strategy maintains consistency with the previous plan, and it also increases the reward in proportion to the expected improvement in behavior. C would not be effective because it increases the reward without requiring a commensurate improvement in behavior.

24. D: Ms. Swanson should explain to the parent that her daughter has missed several homework assignments, and offer to tell the parent about future assignments so that she can ensure that her daughter completes them. This answer is better than answer B, because it lays out a clear plan for correcting the problem. Answer C is not correct because teachers are permitted to discuss students' academic records with the students' parents as long as those students are under the age of 18. Answer A is also incorrect because failure to turn in homework assignments does not necessarily indicate that a student doesn't understand the course content. Other causes of the problem should be eliminated before academic remediation is pursued.

25. B: Mr. Fields is most likely to achieve his objective by assigning nightly homework problems that are peer-graded in class the next day, and going over the answers after the assignment is graded. This method offers two advantages: first, students receive immediate feedback on their performance that they can begin to apply to future assignments and tests; second, students have the opportunity to find out why they arrived at wrong answers when the teacher goes over the problems. This makes assessment a positive experience that helps students perform better in the future, rather than making it a negative experience that de-motivates students by making them feel powerless to improve their performance.

26. C: All of the sources used by the student, including the books, the newspaper, and the websites should be cited in the bibliography. Citations should be included for all sources that are used in a research paper.

27. C: The teacher should first discuss the problem with the special education teacher, who may have additional insight on the problem based on information in the student's Individualized Education Plan (IEP). Adjustments to the IEP may be necessary if current strategies are ineffective. The student's parents should also be notified about the problem, but the special education teacher should be informed about any problems first. Punishing a student with a behavioral disability through isolation or any other method must be done after discussions with the special education teacher in order to be effective, and may actually constitute discrimination if not implemented appropriately.

28. A: The teacher should press one for software. Hardware refers to the physical parts of a computer, like the monitor and the keyboard. Software is a term that describes the programs that allow the computer user to perform various functions like typing a document or creating a slide show.

29. A: In order to send Ellen electronic copies of paper worksheets, a scanner and email, a disc or flash drive would probably be needed, but a copy machine would not be necessary. The teachers could scan the documents using a scanner and send them as an email attachment or save them to a disc. The disc could then be sent home and Ellen could download the documents and print them out, or Ellen could open and print the email attachment.

30. D: Bookmarks are saved on a particular computer, so the students would not be able to access those bookmarked websites from home or from other computers within the school's media center. Enabling the computer's pop-up blocker, which prevents additional windows from automatically opening when other websites are opened, would not be necessary in order for bookmarks to function.

31. C: Mr. Ferris can use the change-tracking device in Microsoft Word to show the students how to improve their papers. Answer D is not correct, because Mr. Ferris could still track grammatical errors if the reports were in paper form. Answers A and B are not correct because, although these are advantages, they are not as helpful for assessment purposes as answer C.

32. B: In order to identify and resolve the problem, Mrs. Thomas' first step should be to consider whether there may be a problem with the assessment itself. Perhaps the assessment did not directly test the material that was covered, or perhaps the students were not given adequate time to complete the assessment. Only if Mrs. Thomas finds no problems with the test itself should she analyze the results to find out exactly which aspects of the material the students struggled with.

33. B: Team teaching, which involves a group of students rotating between roughly 2-5 different teachers, is advantageous for middle school students because they are easily overwhelmed by the need to frequently change classes and teachers. The team-teaching model provides more consistency in terms of classmates and teachers, gradually easing students into the more complex model used in high schools (B). Team teaching is also advantageous because it allows teachers to more easily coordinate interdisciplinary lessons (C), and it helps breed familiarity and support between teacher and student members of the team as well (D). Although a 25:1 student teacher ratio is recommended for teams, the model itself does not inherently reduce the number of students assigned to teachers (A).

34. C: Mrs. Ling should affirm the principal's concerns, but explain why she feels that avoiding the stigmatizing effect of ability grouping is more important than providing enrichment opportunities for high-achieving students. This method would be more effective than simply stating her opinion (A), because it addresses the fact that both her own and the principal's opinions are based on important, but competing, values. In order to change the principal's mind, she must explain why she feels that the value she is advocating (avoiding stigmatization) is more important than the value advocated by the principal (providing unlimited learning opportunities for all students).

35. A: the best way to create effective thematic units would be to have each subject teacher create a curriculum map for the year, and compare these maps to find themes, content and skills that are similar. Designing the thematic units first, and then having teachers adjust their lesson plans to accommodate them (B) would not be effective because the units would be designed without reference to the learning objectives that the teachers have in place for their students that year. Having just one teacher design the units (D), or having students choose the units (C) would present a similar problem. It is crucial that thematic units be designed in response to a clearly outlined curriculum map that details what the students should learn and in what order. Otherwise, learning objectives may be overlooked or material may be presented in an illogical sequence that hampers learning.

36. D: In order to assess the effectiveness of the team-teaching model, the teachers should compare their sixth grade students' performance this year with the performance of students in previous years where team teaching was not used. This will eliminate the possibility of differences among schools that would be present if they compared their students to students in other schools (C). It would also rule out the possibility that performance typically increases in sixth grade relative to previous years, which would be present if they only compared the students' performance this year to their performance in previous year. They should also consider the performance history of this particular group of sixth graders relative to previous groups to rule out the possibility that this group of students' performance has been higher or lower overall.

37. C: The best way for Mr. Aaron to ensure that the discussion helps students achieve the learning objectives he has set forth would be to remind the students about rules for respectful discussion, and then provide the students with a list of questions that they discuss in small groups. By providing rules for the discussion, Mr. Aaron both instructs the students in the skill of respectful discussion and gives students the opportunity to practice it. By providing a list of questions and breaking the students into small groups, Mr. Aaron ensures that all students will have the opportunity to participate in the discussion, and provides the small groups with a guide so that they can stay on track without his immediate presence.

38. B: The students are "natural leaders" because they have a great deal of interpersonal intelligence, and Mr. Aaron should spread these students throughout the groups so that they can help facilitate discussion. Students that have exceptional interpersonal intelligence tend to be more outspoken and confident than their peers, but this does not mean that they are overbearing. To the contrary, they tend to be good at mediating and interacting with different types of people, and so it is likely that they would be effective discussion leaders.

39. C: Mr. Aaron would most likely appeal to Lev Vygotsky's socio-cultural theory of learning to explain the effectiveness of including discussion in his class sessions. Vygotsky argued that learning is a social process, and full intellectual development is not possible without social interaction with instructors (parents, teachers, etc.) and peers (collaborative learning). Mr. Aaron could point out

that language arts students cannot learn to fully comprehend the texts they read without discussing their reading in a social setting.

40. D: Mr. Aaron should group the students by determining their personal intelligence profiles (musical, interpersonal, mathematical, verbal, etc.) and assigning students with similar strengths to the same groups so that they can choose a project that fits with their abilities. This method will ensure that all students can contribute effectively to the group and take pride in the group's work while showcasing their own talents.

41. A: Mr. Aaron should give all students in the group the opportunity to confidentially rate the contributions of their fellow group members, and give lower grades to students who are rated lower by the members of their group. This approach will give each student an incentive to contribute equally, because they can receive a lower grade if they do not contribute. This method would allow Mr. Aaron to grade fairly in cases where certain students fail to contribute.

42. C: Ms. Schneider should take the paraprofessional aside and explain her concerns. She should attempt to find out what is causing the behavior, and help the paraprofessional find a way to improve his performance. She should only begin approaching others regarding the problem after she has discussed the problem directly with the paraprofessional and given him a chance to improve his performance.

43. D: Mrs. Alexander should explain the fact that the class has fallen behind in preparing for an upcoming standardized test, but that she would like to schedule a time for the parent's presentation after the test. This way, all students will have the opportunity to hear the presentation, but the presentation will not detract from the students' ability to pass the standardized test.

44. B: The teachers should ask the students to leave their tests at their desks and follow the usual fire evacuation procedures without discussing the test. Students should always follow safety procedures, but if the test is to be resumed after the school building is cleared, it is important to ensure that students do not discuss the test or look at other students' tests.

45. A: The teacher should give the student a new test booklet with the same form number to use for the remainder of the test, and transcribe the student's responses from the torn booklet to the new booklet after the test. Asking the student to transcribe the answers during the test would affect her performance, but the answers must be transcribed because a torn booklet cannot be scored and two booklets cannot be scored together.

46. C: A scaled score is most useful for comparing students' performance across different administrations of the same test. (For example, comparing this year's sixth graders to last year's, or comparing the performance of students at different schools who took different versions of the same test. Raw scores simply indicate the number of questions a student answered correctly (A), and can only be used to compare students' performance on that specific version of the assessment.

47. B: This information will help the teachers plan their instruction based on the strengths and needs of the incoming students. Standardized test information should not be the sole basis on which students are given remedial instruction (A); their class performance should be strongly considered as well. D is incorrect because team teaching can be effective regardless of how well or poorly students perform on standardized tests, and C is incorrect because the decision to repeat a grade typically does not involve a student's future teachers, and should not be based solely on standardized test results.

48. D: The teachers' best option for improving students' overall performance on the test, including students who are not struggling with math, would be to find creative ways to incorporate math instruction into other subject areas, and to offer optional math tutoring during lunch and after school. This approach includes all students, so that students who are meeting the standard also have the opportunity to improve their performance. In addition, it does not detract from students' learning in other critical subject areas, or deprive students who are performing satisfactorily of math instruction.

49. C: The teacher can most effectively lead the discussion by engaging in another activity like writing on the board while waiting for the students to compose their answers. This action removes the pressure that the students feel and allows them time to remember the answer and compose their explanation. While waiting is important, two minutes (answer B) is probably too long, and calling on a student immediately will only make that student feel uncomfortable.

50. C: The teacher should try rephrasing the question before telling students the answer. Often, students fail to answer because they simply don't understand what information the teacher is looking for, rather than because they actually don't know the information. The teacher might try asking the question from a different angle, providing a hint, or using different terminology.

51. A: Learner-centered assessment provides alternatives that allow different students to be assessed differently. Although student participation in assessment creation (D) is also an important part of learner-centered assessment, a multiple choice test does not reflect the goals of learner-centered assessment because it does not provide an authentic assessment experience.

52. B: Since middle school students are so developmentally diverse, progress-focused assessment methods allow teachers to maintain high expectations while meeting students where they are academically. Progress-focuses assessment methods are not intended to "coddle" underachieving students (C and D), but rather to provide them with an opportunity to succeed academically despite having a starting point below grade-level expectations.

53. B: Authentic assessment techniques are designed to build higher-order thinking skills because they require students to construct their own answers instead of choosing from preselected answers. They also allow for the possibility that multiple "correct" answers are possible because students bring different perspectives and prior experiences to the material. They typically measure student performance over an extended period of time and are graded on a criterion-referenced basis (e.g., students are compared to an objective standard, rather than being directly compared to one another).

54. D: Mr. Calloway should take note of which students Josh seems to feel more comfortable with and allow him to work with those students during group projects. While it may also be helpful to speak with Josh privately about the situation (C) and refer him to the school guidance counselor if necessary, this approach is unlikely to resolve the immediate problem that is impeding Josh's performance. It would only increase Josh's discomfort if the teacher addressed the other students directly about the problem (B), and it would also be counterproductive to discontinue an effective instructional method like group work.

55. C: The most effective way for Ms. Wilson to convey her high expectations to her students would be to work with them to create a contract that includes both her and the students' goals for themselves, as well as specific steps that she and the students will take to reach those goals. This

method not only conveys Ms. Wilson's confidence to the students, but it also allows her and her students to openly commit to specific steps they will take to realize the goal of passing the test. While apprising the students' parents of the situation might also be helpful, this method doesn't involve the students themselves, and wouldn't be as effective for conveying high expectations and realizing results.

56. C: Students in low-income schools may have poor perceptions of their academic ability, but extensive research shows that this disadvantage can be overcome with effective instruction and high expectations. While additional resources (D) may be helpful in providing more effective instruction, they are neither necessary for nor a guarantee of academic improvement.

57. B: The most important quality of a middle school classroom discipline plan is clarity of rules and consequences. This allows a teacher to enforce the discipline plan consistently, which in turn makes all students feel safe and respected. This will reduce discipline problems in the class.

58. C: The first step Mr. Mencia should take to correct this problem is to find a way to take attendance that is more engaging for the students. Students are more likely to misbehave if they are not engaged in the classroom proceedings. Mr. Mencia might consider adopting a more efficient system for taking attendance, or find a way to incorporate the procedure into classroom instruction.

59. D: While all of these causes may contribute to the class' behavior, the most important reason for it is that middle school students, especially sixth-graders, tend to be anxious about completing transitions. Since students at this level are not used to changing classes, doing so within the allotted time makes them anxious and they want to be as prepared as possible by packing up their belongings. Mrs. Brown could effectively combat this behavior by assuring students that they will have plenty of time to get to their next class, and allowing a few minutes at the end of the class for the students to prepare for the transition.

60. C: Before punishing the students or assuming that they don't understand the material, Mr. Tollison should ensure that all of the students know what the homework assignment is and correctly record it before leaving the classroom. Students may not complete the assignment correctly if they fail to write it down, especially if the assigned problems are shouted out hastily at the end of class.

61. B: Ms. Kincaid should call the parents who have not responded to notify them directly about the conferences. When one strategy (sending notes) does not appear to be effective, the teacher should shift her strategy accordingly. Answer D is inappropriate because it is unfair to place the responsibility of getting parents to attend conferences on fourth grade students. Asking students directly (A) would also be inappropriate because it would not necessarily yield reliable information and it could also make students feel uncomfortable or "singled-out" on the basis of their parents' behavior.

62. D: Mr. Ivanov should find someone to help him write a note to the parents in Spanish explaining that he will help them find a volunteer translator if they do not have a friend or family member who could translate for them. Since parent-teacher communication is very important to students' development, Mr. Ivanov should make every reasonable effort to ensure that the parents can participate in conferences. Simply telling the parents or his principal to find a translator would create an unnecessary barrier to the parents' participation in the conferences. Asking fifth-graders to serve as translators for their own parent-teacher conferences would be inappropriate since

students of this age are not usually present during these conferences, and their presence could prevent a frank discussion between the teacher and the parents from occurring.

63. B: Since fourth graders are in the concrete operational stage of development, they grasp concepts best through hands-on, concrete explanations. Showing that multiplying two fractions together produces a fraction of a fraction and demonstrating this using manipulatives would be more effective than verbal explanations. While answer A might also be effective, this exercise simply convinces students of the truth of the assertion, rather than showing them why it is true.

64. C: The most effective way to evaluate the effectiveness of the new textbook would be to compare current students' improvement on a criterion-referenced test over the course of a year to previous students' improvement on that same test. This method would help to eliminate intervening variables (standardized test difficulty and changing focus, as well as variations in students' initial level of academic achievement) that would make the other measures suggested problematic.

65. B: The major educational benefit of using class discussion is that it allows students to explore the subtleties of learning objectives by considering them in various contexts and from various social, cultural and historical perspectives. This is an important aspect of the development of higher-order thinking skills.

66. C: By dividing her fourth grade students into ability groups and spending at least one hour each week working with each group in a way that meets the members' unique needs (A), Ms. Morse is targeting various ability levels, but she is not necessarily targeting different learning styles or teaching the same lesson to the various groups. Differentiated instruction involves presenting a single lesson in a variety of ways that allow students of varying ability levels and learning styles to comprehend it.

67. B: The first step that Mr. Copeland should take is to try to create a tutoring program in which older students and literate parents volunteer to provide homework support after school or during lunch. While guiding parents to community resources that can help them improve their reading skills would also be helpful (A), it would still take a significant amount of time for these parents to develop their skills to the level at which they could comfortably help their students with reading homework.

68. C: Ms. Holloway should first contact the student's social services caseworker about the problem so that he or she can inform each of the students' successive foster parents of the importance of helping the student with math. While contacting the parents (B) would normally be the first step if the student were at home or with a permanent foster family, contacting the student's caseworker is more effective in a situation where a student is frequently shifted between different families. The caseworker can ensure that each successive family is aware of the student's academic status, and perhaps arrange ongoing math tutoring for him.

69. B: While parental involvement does not guarantee academic success, students whose parents are involved in their schooling typically perform better than students whose families are less involved. While many factors contribute to this outcome, one important factor is that by being involved, parents convey to their children their belief that education is valuable.

70. D: Mr. Mailer should explain to the parents that the decision is ultimately theirs, but also provide them with educational resources about reading disabilities and emphasize that delaying

receipt of special education services can exacerbate the problems associated with reading disabilities. Teachers cannot have students formally tested for learning disabilities without their parents' permission, but it is Mr. Mailer's professional responsibility to advocate for his student and explain to Thomas' parents the possible consequences of their decision to delay testing.

71. B: Mr. Ainsley should respond to the principal's suggestion by using available professional development resources on assessment to develop a plan to improve his use of assessment in the classroom and present it to the principal for review. This approach will provide the most immediate and effective way to resolve the flaw in his instructional approach, and it will also allow him to get feedback from the principal so that he knows that he has correctly understood and responded to the principal's suggestion.

72. B: In order to begin resolving the problem, Ms. Mattingly should first confer with her principal and other fourth grade teachers to determine whether her grade level expectations for academic achievement align with those of the district as a whole. Since she was previously unaware of the fact that her students were falling behind, the most logical explanation for this situation is that her academic expectations for her students are not as high as those used by school administrators in constructing the test. She should definitely not ignore the standardized test results (A) or ask the students' parents to resolve the problem themselves (D). She may not need to change her instructional methods either (C), if the problem is simply that her expectations are too low.

73. D: A sudden decline in academic performance could be caused by any of the factors listed. Certain eating disorders can cause declines in academic performance because of physical symptoms like lethargy and the students' attendant lack of motivation. Drug use can also cause lethargy, inattentiveness, and/or hyperactivity that can affect schoolwork. Parental divorce can cause mild depression and inability to focus, which can also contribute to a decline in academic achievement. However, it is important to remember that these problems do not always cause declines in academic achievement.

74. C: Providing learning options is very useful in the middle grades because students are developing a sense of autonomy, and this allows them to exercise it. While the choices students make may reflect their self-concept or choice of peer group in some way, this is not the main area of development that such an exercise fosters. This exercise also reflects the fact that students have different learning styles, but this is not a developmental characteristic unique to middle school students.

75. C: Preparing to argue both sides of the debate develops higher-order thinking skills by promoting students' awareness of competing viewpoints. While organizational skills (D), self-confidence (B), and autonomy all grow during the middle school years, this exercise is most useful for fostering students' growing awareness of multiple viewpoints.

76. A: By asking the teachers to make the learning objectives they have set for their students explicit, and comparing these objectives to the stated district objectives, they can determine whether their learning objectives align with district learning goals for students. This will ensure that all students throughout the district are learning the same basic skills and are progressing at similar paces.

77. B: Reading about life in a different country would be the best example of an activity that prompt students to explore educational content from varied and integrated perspectives. Other examples of

such activities are those that encourage students to explore different viewpoints, learn through thematic units and work in study teams.

78. D: Middle school is a critical time during which students develop a tolerance of diversity, make the decision to continue with school, and tolerance for those who are different. Middle school students also develop higher-order thinking skills, but this represents cognitive development, rather than value development.

79. A: Mr. Reid can appeal to the students' growing sense of autonomy by providing them with several different options for completing the project. While middle school students enjoy autonomy, they also tend to enjoy social interaction, so allowing them to complete the project individually would be unlikely to increase most students' interest in the project.

80. A: The most important skills that students develop through problem solving activities are inquiry and critical thinking skills. While time management and social skills may be secondary benefits of such activities if they are conducted in groups, the ability to think critically is the primary benefit.

81. D: Asking students to act out a scene from a play that they are reading in class is a kinesthetic learning activity because it involves them physically in the material that they're learning. Answer A, sorting candies, is also a kinesthetic activity, but it would not be age-appropriate for middle school students. Answer B, having students recite a pneumonic device aloud, would be helpful for auditory learners and students with high levels of musical intelligence. Although writing (C) is also a physical activity to some extent, writing activities are not typically considered kinesthetic because they are largely stationary and the physical act of writing is secondary to the intellectual processes that are occurring. In kinesthetic activities, the activity directly facilitates the learning process.

82. A: Publicly posting students' names and test grades would violate students' right to privacy under the Federal Educational Right to Privacy Act (FERPA). The other answers listed are within teachers' rights and would not violate students' rights unless school rules specifically prohibit them.

83. C: The best option would be to refer the students to the school's peer mediation program. Peer mediation can be effective for resolving disputes among students, and would be preferable to separating the students because it would teach them to work through problems with peers. Answer A is incorrect because there is no indication that the conflict is racial in nature, and D would not be effective because fighting between students is not something that cannot typically be accommodated through rule changes.

84. A: Allowing students to discuss the questions in pairs gives students the opportunity to try out their answers in a "safe" environment before stating them in front of the class. This will make students more comfortable participating in the discussion, thus making it more effective.

85. A: Of the four options, asking the students to write down the instructions would be least effective. Having students write down the directions as she explains them does not provide Ms. Fry with any way of knowing whether the students have comprehended the directions or have recorded them correctly. Also, writing is challenging for some students and can distract them from the content of what is being explained.

86. D: The most effective way for Mrs. Alito to meet the student's needs without making him feel uncomfortable or disrupting the rest of her class would be to keep an eye on the student and provide him with a nonverbal signal that he can use if he wants to go to the resource room. This would prevent him from disrupting the class and drawing attention to himself by asking to leave (B) or doing relaxation exercises (C). Answer A (checking in on the student every few hours) would not be effective because it would not be sufficiently responsive to the student's needs.

87. A: Microsoft Excel would be useful because it would allow students to create spreadsheets of their monthly expenses and calculate the totals using mathematical functions. Outlook is an email program which would not be useful for this task, and Adobe Pagemaker would not be useful either, because it is a page layout program.

88. C: Copying the assigned homework questions from a textbook for a student who was home sick for a few days is unlikely to violate fair use standards for copyrighted material because it is a temporary, spontaneous use of a small portion of a copyrighted work. Generally, copying and using whole chapters or books (even e-books) is prohibited because it deprives the work's creators of income, and the same is true of copying and repeatedly using a DVD movie in class.

89. A: Copying a sentence verbatim from a website and citing the website in your bibliography is a good start, but any sentence that is copied verbatim from a source must also be cited within the text and enclosed in quotation marks. Otherwise, copying a sentence verbatim (even if it is cited in your bibliography) constitutes plagiarism. Paraphrased sentences do not need quotation marks, but they should be cited within the text and included in your bibliography.

90. B: The most important thing the teacher needs to determine is when the website was last updated. This will indicate whether the information is up-to-date, since this is a major concern with rapidly changing scientific information. Many websites may "look ok," but actually have not been updated for many years. Whether the information is available in book form (A) and where the professor is employed (C) are both irrelevant, and while it maybe useful to know if the information is copyrighted, this use of the information would probably not violate copyright law since it is spontaneous, temporary, and does not involves copying large chunks of the text or using it without attribution.

91. B: Conducting a teleconference with the parent while they're on their lunch break would probably not be effective because it would require students to gather around one speakerphone or each have their own phones. A videoconference could be arranged so all of the students can easily see the parent and the parent can see the students and respond to their questions, and Powerpoint or videotaping would also be effective at conveying the information if videoconferencing technology was not available.

92. D: Adobe Pagemaker would be most appropriate for students to produce a school newspaper. Microsoft Word could also work, but it would produce only a rudimentary design because it is intended for use in simpler personal, educational and business documents. Adobe Flash is for creating computer animation, and Access is a database creation program.

93. A: A primary goal of acceptable use policies regarding school computers is to deter students and school employees from accessing inappropriate information or engaging in illegal activities using school computers. Such policies are not educational, and do not teach students about copyright law or plagiarism (C). They cannot prevent computer users from accidentally stumbling upon inappropriate material while using the Internet (B). Transferring documents created on school

computers to home computers (D) is not generally a violation of acceptable use policies, since it typically involves creating a document for a school assignment, saving it on a disc or flash drive, and saving it on the student's home computer.

94. B: Students should be fairly competent in the use of basic document functions, word processing and keyboarding prior to sixth grade, and should have mastered these skills by eighth grade. However, the relevance of technology to future job prospects and daily life requires higher-order thinking skills that are developed in middle school, and so it is not introduced until around sixth grade. It should also be mastered by eighth grade.

95. C: Incorporating self-assessment into the classroom is important because it prepares students for the future when they will need to evaluate their own work in the absence of an instructor.

96. C: By giving students detailed feedback on their performance and providing opportunities to incorporate the feedback and demonstrate improvement, a teacher can give students a sense of control over their learning. For example, a teacher might provide students with detailed feedback on an essay, and then give them a chance to rewrite and improve it to achieve a higher grade.

97. C: Rubrics are effective assessment tools because they provide students with more specific feedback. They do this by including evaluations of two or more specific learning objectives or performance categories within a single assignment, as opposed to providing one undifferentiated grade for a complex activity. Rubrics should include at least two categories (for example, content/organization and spelling/grammar for an essay), and there is no limit to the number of categories that a rubric can have. Since even the simplest assignment, such as completing a math problem, is composed of several components (applying the correct formula, calculating the answer correctly, and writing the problem neatly, for example), rubrics can be used for grading many different types of class work.

98. A: student-led conferences encourage middle school students to take ownership of their learning by evaluating their strengths and weaknesses. In a student-led conference, students meet with parents and teachers to discuss a portfolio of their work. The parents direct questions mainly to the student, so this increases the student's accountability for and ownership of his or her learning.

99. D: teachers should provide parents with the option of meeting privately with the teacher, participating in a student-led conference or adopting a hybrid model. Parent-teacher conferences should be held for all students if possible, regardless of their academic performance and behavior, and student-led conferences are an appropriate format for all students. However, it is important for teachers to provide parents with options so that they can speak privately with the teacher if necessary.

Secret Key #1 - Time is Your Greatest Enemy

Pace Yourself

Wear a watch. At the beginning of the test, check the time (or start a chronometer on your watch to count the minutes), and check the time after every few questions to make sure you are "on schedule."

If you are forced to speed up, do it efficiently. Usually one or more answer choices can be eliminated without too much difficulty. Above all, don't panic. Don't speed up and just begin guessing at random choices. By pacing yourself, and continually monitoring your progress against your watch, you will always know exactly how far ahead or behind you are with your available time. If you find that you are one minute behind on the test, don't skip one question without spending any time on it, just to catch back up. Take 15 fewer seconds on the next four questions, and after four questions you'll have caught back up. Once you catch back up, you can continue working each problem at your normal pace.

Furthermore, don't dwell on the problems that you were rushed on. If a problem was taking up too much time and you made a hurried guess, it must be difficult. The difficult questions are the ones you are most likely to miss anyway, so it isn't a big loss. It is better to end with more time than you need than to run out of time.

Lastly, sometimes it is beneficial to slow down if you are constantly getting ahead of time. You are always more likely to catch a careless mistake by working more slowly than quickly, and among very high-scoring test takers (those who are likely to have lots of time left over), careless errors affect the score more than mastery of material.

Secret Key #2 - Guessing is not Guesswork

You probably know that guessing is a good idea. Unlike other standardized tests, there is no penalty for getting a wrong answer. Even if you have no idea about a question, you still have a 20-25% chance of getting it right.

Most test takers do not understand the impact that proper guessing can have on their score. Unless you score extremely high, guessing will significantly contribute to your final score.

Monkeys Take the Test

What most test takers don't realize is that to insure that 20-25% chance, you have to guess randomly. If you put 20 monkeys in a room to take this test, assuming they answered once per question and behaved themselves, on average they would get 20-25% of the questions correct. Put 20 test takers in the room, and the average will be much lower among guessed questions. Why?

1. The test writers intentionally write deceptive answer choices that "look" right. A test taker has no idea about a question, so he picks the "best looking" answer, which is often wrong. The monkey has no idea what looks good and what doesn't, so it will consistently be right about 20-25% of the time.
2. Test takers will eliminate answer choices from the guessing pool based on a hunch or intuition. Simple but correct answers often get excluded, leaving a 0% chance of being correct. The monkey has no clue, and often gets lucky with the best choice.

This is why the process of elimination endorsed by most test courses is flawed and detrimental to your performance. Test takers don't guess; they make an ignorant stab in the dark that is usually worse than random.

$5 Challenge

Let me introduce one of the most valuable ideas of this course—the $5 challenge:
- *You only mark your "best guess" if you are willing to bet $5 on it.*
- *You only eliminate choices from guessing if you are willing to bet $5 on it.*

Why $5? Five dollars is an amount of money that is small yet not insignificant, and can really add up fast (20 questions could cost you $100). Likewise, each answer choice on one question of the test will have a small impact on your overall score, but it can really add up to a lot of points in the end.

The process of elimination IS valuable. The following shows your chance of guessing it right:

If you eliminate wrong answer choices until only this many remain:	Chance of getting it correct:
1	100%
2	50%
3	33%

However, if you accidentally eliminate the right answer or go on a hunch for an incorrect answer, your chances drop dramatically—to 0%. By guessing among all the answer choices, you are GUARANTEED to have a shot at the right answer.

That's why the $5 test is so valuable. If you give up the advantage and safety of a pure guess, it had better be worth the risk.

What we still haven't covered is how to be sure that whatever guess you make is truly random. Here's the easiest way:
- *Always pick the first answer choice among those remaining.*

Such a technique means that you have decided, **before you see a single test question**, exactly how you are going to guess, and since the order of choices tells you nothing about which one is correct, this guessing technique is perfectly random.

This section is not meant to scare you away from making educated guesses or eliminating choices; you just need to define when a choice is worth eliminating. The $5 test, along with a pre-defined random guessing strategy, is the best way to make sure you reap all of the benefits of guessing.

Secret Key #3 - Practice Smarter, Not Harder

Many test takers delay the test preparation process because they dread the awful amounts of practice time they think necessary to succeed on the test. We have refined an effective method that will take you only a fraction of the time.

There are a number of "obstacles" in the path to success. Among these are answering questions, finishing in time, and mastering test-taking strategies. All must be executed on the day of the test at peak performance, or your score will suffer. The test is a mental marathon that has a large impact on your future.

Just like a marathon runner, it is important to work your way up to the full challenge. So first you just worry about questions, and then time, and finally strategy:

Success Strategy

1. Find a good source for practice tests.
2. If you are willing to make a larger time investment, consider using more than one study guide. Often the different approaches of multiple authors will help you "get" difficult concepts.
3. Take a practice test with no time constraints, with all study helps, "open book." Take your time with questions and focus on applying strategies.
4. Take a practice test with time constraints, with all guides, "open book."
5. Take a final practice test without open material and with time limits.

If you have time to take more practice tests, just repeat step 5. By gradually exposing yourself to the full rigors of the test environment, you will condition your mind to the stress of test day and maximize your success.

Secret Key #4 - Prepare, Don't Procrastinate

Let me state an obvious fact: if you take the test three times, you will probably get three different scores. This is due to the way you feel on test day, the level of preparedness you have, and the version of the test you see. Despite the test writers' claims to the contrary, some versions of the test WILL be easier for you than others.

Since your future depends so much on your score, you should maximize your chances of success. In order to maximize the likelihood of success, you've got to prepare in advance. This means taking practice tests and spending time learning the information and test taking strategies you will need to succeed.

Never go take the actual test as a "practice" test, expecting that you can just take it again if you need to. Take all the practice tests you can on your own, but when you go to take the official test, be prepared, be focused, and do your best the first time!

Secret Key #5 - Test Yourself

Everyone knows that time is money. There is no need to spend too much of your time or too little of your time preparing for the test. You should only spend as much of your precious time preparing as is necessary for you to get the score you need.

Once you have taken a practice test under real conditions of time constraints, then you will know if you are ready for the test or not.

If you have scored extremely high the first time that you take the practice test, then there is not much point in spending countless hours studying. You are already there.

Benchmark your abilities by retaking practice tests and seeing how much you have improved. Once you consistently score high enough to guarantee success, then you are ready.

If you have scored well below where you need, then knuckle down and begin studying in earnest. Check your improvement regularly through the use of practice tests under real conditions. Above all, don't worry, panic, or give up. The key is perseverance!

Then, when you go to take the test, remain confident and remember how well you did on the practice tests. If you can score high enough on a practice test, then you can do the same on the real thing.

General Strategies

The most important thing you can do is to ignore your fears and jump into the test immediately. Do not be overwhelmed by any strange-sounding terms. You have to jump into the test like jumping into a pool—all at once is the easiest way.

Make Predictions

As you read and understand the question, try to guess what the answer will be. Remember that several of the answer choices are wrong, and once you begin reading them, your mind will immediately become cluttered with answer choices designed to throw you off. Your mind is typically the most focused immediately after you have read the question and digested its contents. If you can, try to predict what the correct answer will be. You may be surprised at what you can predict.

Quickly scan the choices and see if your prediction is in the listed answer choices. If it is, then you can be quite confident that you have the right answer. It still won't hurt to check the other answer choices, but most of the time, you've got it!

Answer the Question

It may seem obvious to only pick answer choices that answer the question, but the test writers can create some excellent answer choices that are wrong. Don't pick an answer just because it sounds right, or you believe it to be true. It MUST answer the question. Once you've made your selection, always go back and check it against the question and make sure that you didn't misread the question and that the answer choice does answer the question posed.

Benchmark

After you read the first answer choice, decide if you think it sounds correct or not. If it doesn't, move on to the next answer choice. If it does, mentally mark that answer choice. This doesn't mean that you've definitely selected it as your answer choice, it just means that it's the best you've seen thus far. Go ahead and read the next choice. If the next choice is worse than the one you've already selected, keep going to the next answer choice. If the next choice is better than the choice you've already selected, mentally mark the new answer choice as your best guess.

The first answer choice that you select becomes your standard. Every other answer choice must be benchmarked against that standard. That choice is correct until proven otherwise by another answer choice beating it out. Once you've decided that no other answer choice seems as good, do one final check to ensure that your answer choice answers the question posed.

Valid Information

Don't discount any of the information provided in the question. Every piece of information may be necessary to determine the correct answer. None of the information in the question is there to throw you off (while the answer choices will certainly have information to throw you off). If two seemingly unrelated topics are discussed, don't ignore either. You can be confident there is a relationship, or it wouldn't be included in the question, and you are probably going to have to determine what is that relationship to find the answer.

Avoid "Fact Traps"

Don't get distracted by a choice that is factually true. Your search is for the answer that answers the question. Stay focused and don't fall for an answer that is true but irrelevant. Always go back to the question and make sure you're choosing an answer that actually answers the question and is not just a true statement. An answer can be factually correct, but it MUST answer the question asked. Additionally, two answers can both be seemingly correct, so be sure to read all of the answer choices, and make sure that you get the one that BEST answers the question.

Milk the Question

Some of the questions may throw you completely off. They might deal with a subject you have not been exposed to, or one that you haven't reviewed in years. While your lack of knowledge about the subject will be a hindrance, the question itself can give you many clues that will help you find the correct answer. Read the question carefully and look for clues. Watch particularly for adjectives and nouns describing difficult terms or words that you don't recognize. Regardless of whether you completely understand a word or not, replacing it with a synonym, either provided or one you more familiar with, may help you to understand what the questions are asking. Rather than wracking your mind about specific detailed information concerning a difficult term or word, try to use mental substitutes that are easier to understand.

The Trap of Familiarity

Don't just choose a word because you recognize it. On difficult questions, you may not recognize a number of words in the answer choices. The test writers don't put "make-believe" words on the test, so don't think that just because you only recognize all the words in one answer choice that that answer choice must be correct. If you only recognize words in one answer choice, then focus on that one. Is it correct? Try your best to determine if it is correct. If it is, that's great. If not, eliminate it. Each word and answer choice you eliminate increases your chances of getting the question correct, even if you then have to guess among the unfamiliar choices.

Eliminate Answers

Eliminate choices as soon as you realize they are wrong. But be careful! Make sure you consider all of the possible answer choices. Just because one appears right, doesn't mean that the next one won't be even better! The test writers will usually put more than one good answer choice for every question, so read all of them. Don't worry if you are stuck between two that seem right. By getting down to just two remaining possible choices, your odds are now 50/50. Rather than wasting too much time, play the odds. You are guessing, but guessing wisely because you've been able to knock out some of the answer choices that you know are wrong. If you are eliminating choices and realize that the last answer choice you are left with is also obviously wrong, don't panic. Start over and consider each choice again. There may easily be something that you missed the first time and will realize on the second pass.

Tough Questions

If you are stumped on a problem or it appears too hard or too difficult, don't waste time. Move on! Remember though, if you can quickly check for obviously incorrect answer choices, your chances of guessing correctly are greatly improved. Before you completely give up, at least try to knock out a couple of possible answers. Eliminate what you can and then guess at the remaining answer choices before moving on.

Brainstorm

If you get stuck on a difficult question, spend a few seconds quickly brainstorming. Run through the complete list of possible answer choices. Look at each choice and ask yourself, "Could this answer the question satisfactorily?" Go through each answer choice and consider it independently of the others. By systematically going through all possibilities, you may find something that you would otherwise overlook. Remember though that when you get stuck, it's important to try to keep moving.

Read Carefully

Understand the problem. Read the question and answer choices carefully. Don't miss the question because you misread the terms. You have plenty of time to read each question thoroughly and make sure you understand what is being asked. Yet a happy medium must be attained, so don't waste too much time. You must read carefully, but efficiently.

Face Value

When in doubt, use common sense. Always accept the situation in the problem at face value. Don't read too much into it. These problems will not require you to make huge leaps of logic. The test writers aren't trying to throw you off with a cheap trick. If you have to go beyond creativity and make a leap of logic in order to have an answer choice answer the question, then you should look at the other answer choices. Don't overcomplicate the problem by creating theoretical relationships or explanations that will warp time or space. These are normal problems rooted in reality. It's just that the applicable relationship or explanation may not be readily apparent and you have to figure things out. Use your common sense to interpret anything that isn't clear.

Prefixes

If you're having trouble with a word in the question or answer choices, try dissecting it. Take advantage of every clue that the word might include. Prefixes and suffixes can be a huge help. Usually they allow you to determine a basic meaning. Pre- means before, post- means after, pro - is positive, de- is negative. From these prefixes and suffixes, you can get an idea of the general meaning of the word and try to put it into context. Beware though of any traps. Just because con- is the opposite of pro-, doesn't necessarily mean congress is the opposite of progress!

Hedge Phrases

Watch out for critical hedge phrases, led off with words such as "likely," "may," "can," "sometimes," "often," "almost," "mostly," "usually," "generally," "rarely," and "sometimes." Question writers insert these hedge phrases to cover every possibility. Often an answer choice will be wrong simply because it leaves no room for exception. Unless the situation calls for them, avoid answer choices that have definitive words like "exactly," and "always."

Switchback Words

Stay alert for "switchbacks." These are the words and phrases frequently used to alert you to shifts in thought. The most common switchback word is "but." Others include "although," "however," "nevertheless," "on the other hand," "even though," "while," "in spite of," "despite," and "regardless of."

New Information

Correct answer choices will rarely have completely new information included. Answer choices typically are straightforward reflections of the material asked about and will directly relate to the question. If a new piece of information is included in an answer choice that doesn't even seem to relate to the topic being asked about, then that answer choice is likely incorrect. All of the information needed to answer the question is usually provided for you in the question. You should not have to make guesses that are unsupported or choose answer choices that require unknown information that cannot be reasoned from what is given.

Time Management

On technical questions, don't get lost on the technical terms. Don't spend too much time on any one question. If you don't know what a term means, then odds are you aren't going to get much further since you don't have a dictionary. You should be able to immediately recognize whether or not you know a term. If you don't, work with the other clues that you have—the other answer choices and terms provided—but don't waste too much time trying to figure out a difficult term that you don't know.

Contextual Clues

Look for contextual clues. An answer can be right but not the correct answer. The contextual clues will help you find the answer that is most right and is correct. Understand the context in which a phrase or statement is made. This will help you make important distinctions.

Don't Panic

Panicking will not answer any questions for you; therefore, it isn't helpful. When you first see the question, if your mind goes blank, take a deep breath. Force yourself to mechanically go through the steps of solving the problem using the strategies you've learned.

Pace Yourself

Don't get clock fever. It's easy to be overwhelmed when you're looking at a page full of questions, your mind is full of random thoughts and feeling confused, and the clock is ticking down faster than you would like. Calm down and maintain the pace that you have set for yourself. As long as you are on track by monitoring your pace, you are guaranteed to have enough time for yourself. When you get to the last few minutes of the test, it may seem like you won't have enough time left, but if you only have as many questions as you should have left at that point, then you're right on track!

Answer Selection

The best way to pick an answer choice is to eliminate all of those that are wrong, until only one is left and confirm that is the correct answer. Sometimes though, an answer choice may immediately look right. Be careful! Take a second to make sure that the other choices are not equally obvious. Don't make a hasty mistake. There are only two times that you should stop before checking other answers. First is when you are positive that the answer choice you have selected is correct. Second is when time is almost out and you have to make a quick guess!

Check Your Work

Since you will probably not know every term listed and the answer to every question, it is important that you get credit for the ones that you do know. Don't miss any questions through careless mistakes. If at all possible, try to take a second to look back over your answer selection and make sure you've selected the correct answer choice and haven't made a costly careless mistake (such as marking an answer choice that you didn't mean to mark). The time it takes for this quick double check should more than pay for itself in caught mistakes.

Beware of Directly Quoted Answers

Sometimes an answer choice will repeat word for word a portion of the question or reference section. However, beware of such exact duplication. It may be a trap! More than likely, the correct choice will paraphrase or summarize a point, rather than being exactly the same wording.

Slang

Scientific sounding answers are better than slang ones. An answer choice that begins "To compare the outcomes..." is much more likely to be correct than one that begins "Because some people insisted..."

Extreme Statements

Avoid wild answers that throw out highly controversial ideas that are proclaimed as established fact. An answer choice that states the "process should used in certain situations, if..." is much more likely to be correct than one that states the "process should be discontinued completely." The first is a calm rational statement and doesn't even make a definitive, uncompromising stance, using a hedge word "if" to provide wiggle room, whereas the second choice is a radical idea and far more extreme.

Answer Choice Families

When you have two or more answer choices that are direct opposites or parallels, one of them is usually the correct answer. For instance, if one answer choice states "x increases" and another answer choice states "x decreases" or "y increases," then those two or three answer choices are very similar in construction and fall into the same family of answer choices. A family of answer choices consists of two or three answer choices, very similar in construction, but often with directly opposite meanings. Usually the correct answer choice will be in that family of answer choices. The "odd man out" or answer choice that doesn't seem to fit the parallel construction of the other answer choices is more likely to be incorrect.

Special Report: How to Overcome Test Anxiety

The very nature of tests caters to some level of anxiety, nervousness, or tension, just as we feel for any important event that occurs in our lives. A little bit of anxiety or nervousness can be a good thing. It helps us with motivation, and makes achievement just that much sweeter. However, too much anxiety can be a problem, especially if it hinders our ability to function and perform.

"Test anxiety," is the term that refers to the emotional reactions that some test-takers experience when faced with a test or exam. Having a fear of testing and exams is based upon a rational fear, since the test-taker's performance can shape the course of an academic career. Nevertheless, experiencing excessive fear of examinations will only interfere with the test-taker's ability to perform and chance to be successful.

There are a large variety of causes that can contribute to the development and sensation of test anxiety. These include, but are not limited to, lack of preparation and worrying about issues surrounding the test.

Lack of Preparation

Lack of preparation can be identified by the following behaviors or situations:
- Not scheduling enough time to study, and therefore cramming the night before the test or exam
- Managing time poorly, to create the sensation that there is not enough time to do everything
- Failing to organize the text information in advance, so that the study material consists of the entire text and not simply the pertinent information
- Poor overall studying habits

Worrying, on the other hand, can be related to both the test taker, or many other factors around him/her that will be affected by the results of the test. These include worrying about:
- Previous performances on similar exams, or exams in general
- How friends and other students are achieving
- The negative consequences that will result from a poor grade or failure

There are three primary elements to test anxiety. Physical components, which involve the same typical bodily reactions as those to acute anxiety (to be discussed below). Emotional factors have to do with fear or panic. Mental or cognitive issues concerning attention spans and memory abilities.

Physical Signals

There are many different symptoms of test anxiety, and these are not limited to mental and emotional strain. Frequently there are a range of physical signals that will let a test taker know that he/she is suffering from test anxiety. These bodily changes can include the following:
- Perspiring
- Sweaty palms
- Wet, trembling hands
- Nausea
- Dry mouth
- A knot in the stomach
- Headache
- Faintness
- Muscle tension
- Aching shoulders, back and neck
- Rapid heart beat
- Feeling too hot/cold

To recognize the sensation of test anxiety, a test-taker should monitor him/herself for the following sensations:
- The physical distress symptoms as listed above
- Emotional sensitivity, expressing emotional feelings such as the need to cry or laugh too much, or a sensation of anger or helplessness
- A decreased ability to think, causing the test-taker to blank out or have racing thoughts that are hard to organize or control.

Though most students will feel some level of anxiety when faced with a test or exam, the majority can cope with that anxiety and maintain it at a manageable level. However, those who cannot are faced with a very real and very serious condition, which can and should be controlled for the immeasurable benefit of this sufferer.

Naturally, these sensations lead to negative results for the testing experience. The most common effects of test anxiety have to do with nervousness and mental blocking.

Nervousness

Nervousness can appear in several different levels:
- The test-taker's difficulty, or even inability to read and understand the questions on the test
- The difficulty or inability to organize thoughts to a coherent form
- The difficulty or inability to recall key words and concepts relating to the testing questions (especially essays)
- The receipt of poor grades on a test, though the test material was well known by the test taker

Conversely, a person may also experience mental blocking, which involves:
- Blanking out on test questions

- Only remembering the correct answers to the questions when the test has already finished.

Fortunately for test anxiety sufferers, beating these feelings, to a large degree, has to do with proper preparation. When a test taker has a feeling of preparedness, then anxiety will be dramatically lessened.

The first step to resolving anxiety issues is to distinguish which of the two types of anxiety are being suffered. If the anxiety is a direct result of a lack of preparation, this should be considered a normal reaction, and the anxiety level (as opposed to the test results) shouldn't be anything to worry about. However, if, when adequately prepared, the test-taker still panics, blanks out, or seems to overreact, this is not a fully rational reaction. While this can be considered normal too, there are many ways to combat and overcome these effects.

Remember that anxiety cannot be entirely eliminated, however, there are ways to minimize it, to make the anxiety easier to manage. Preparation is one of the best ways to minimize test anxiety. Therefore the following techniques are wise in order to best fight off any anxiety that may want to build.

To begin with, try to avoid cramming before a test, whenever it is possible. By trying to memorize an entire term's worth of information in one day, you'll be shocking your system, and not giving yourself a very good chance to absorb the information. This is an easy path to anxiety, so for those who suffer from test anxiety, cramming should not even be considered an option.

Instead of cramming, work throughout the semester to combine all of the material which is presented throughout the semester, and work on it gradually as the course goes by, making sure to master the main concepts first, leaving minor details for a week or so before the test.

To study for the upcoming exam, be sure to pose questions that may be on the examination, to gauge the ability to answer them by integrating the ideas from your texts, notes and lectures, as well as any supplementary readings.

If it is truly impossible to cover all of the information that was covered in that particular term, concentrate on the most important portions, that can be covered very well. Learn these concepts as best as possible, so that when the test comes, a goal can be made to use these concepts as presentations of your knowledge.

In addition to study habits, changes in attitude are critical to beating a struggle with test anxiety. In fact, an improvement of the perspective over the entire test-taking experience can actually help a test taker to enjoy studying and therefore improve the overall experience. Be certain not to overemphasize the significance of the grade - know that the result of the test is neither a reflection of self worth, nor is it a measure of intelligence; one grade will not predict a person's future success.

To improve an overall testing outlook, the following steps should be tried:
- Keeping in mind that the most reasonable expectation for taking a test is to expect to try to demonstrate as much of what you know as you possibly can.
- Reminding ourselves that a test is only one test; this is not the only one, and there will be others.

- The thought of thinking of oneself in an irrational, all-or-nothing term should be avoided at all costs.
- A reward should be designated for after the test, so there's something to look forward to. Whether it be going to a movie, going out to eat, or simply visiting friends, schedule it in advance, and do it no matter what result is expected on the exam.

Test-takers should also keep in mind that the basics are some of the most important things, even beyond anti-anxiety techniques and studying. Never neglect the basic social, emotional and biological needs, in order to try to absorb information. In order to best achieve, these three factors must be held as just as important as the studying itself.

Study Steps

Remember the following important steps for studying:
- Maintain healthy nutrition and exercise habits. Continue both your recreational activities and social pass times. These both contribute to your physical and emotional well being.
- Be certain to get a good amount of sleep, especially the night before the test, because when you're overtired you are not able to perform to the best of your best ability.
- Keep the studying pace to a moderate level by taking breaks when they are needed, and varying the work whenever possible, to keep the mind fresh instead of getting bored.
- When enough studying has been done that all the material that can be learned has been learned, and the test taker is prepared for the test, stop studying and do something relaxing such as listening to music, watching a movie, or taking a warm bubble bath.

There are also many other techniques to minimize the uneasiness or apprehension that is experienced along with test anxiety before, during, or even after the examination. In fact, there are a great deal of things that can be done to stop anxiety from interfering with lifestyle and performance. Again, remember that anxiety will not be eliminated entirely, and it shouldn't be. Otherwise that "up" feeling for exams would not exist, and most of us depend on that sensation to perform better than usual. However, this anxiety has to be at a level that is manageable.

Of course, as we have just discussed, being prepared for the exam is half the battle right away. Attending all classes, finding out what knowledge will be expected on the exam, and knowing the exam schedules are easy steps to lowering anxiety. Keeping up with work will remove the need to cram, and efficient study habits will eliminate wasted time. Studying should be done in an ideal location for concentration, so that it is simple to become interested in the material and give it complete attention. A method such as SQ3R (Survey, Question, Read, Recite, Review) is a wonderful key to follow to make sure that the study habits are as effective as possible, especially in the case of learning from a textbook. Flashcards are great techniques for memorization. Learning to take good notes will mean that notes will be full of useful information, so that less sifting will need to be done to seek out what is pertinent for studying. Reviewing notes after class and then again on occasion will keep the information fresh in the mind. From notes that have been taken summary sheets and outlines can be made for simpler reviewing.

A study group can also be a very motivational and helpful place to study, as there will be a sharing of ideas, all of the minds can work together, to make sure that everyone understands, and the studying will be made more interesting because it will be a social occasion.

Basically, though, as long as the test-taker remains organized and self confident, with efficient study habits, less time will need to be spent studying, and higher grades will be achieved.

To become self confident, there are many useful steps. The first of these is "self talk." It has been shown through extensive research, that self-talk for students who suffer from test anxiety, should be well monitored, in order to make sure that it contributes to self confidence as opposed to sinking the student. Frequently the self talk of test-anxious students is negative or self-defeating, thinking that everyone else is smarter and faster, that they always mess up, and that if they don't do well, they'll fail the entire course. It is important to decreasing anxiety that awareness is made of self talk. Try writing any negative self thoughts and then disputing them with a positive statement instead. Begin self-encouragement as though it was a friend speaking. Repeat positive statements to help reprogram the mind to believing in successes instead of failures.

Helpful Techniques

Other extremely helpful techniques include:
- Self-visualization of doing well and reaching goals
- While aiming for an "A" level of understanding, don't try to "overprotect" by setting your expectations lower. This will only convince the mind to stop studying in order to meet the lower expectations.
- Don't make comparisons with the results or habits of other students. These are individual factors, and different things work for different people, causing different results.
- Strive to become an expert in learning what works well, and what can be done in order to improve. Consider collecting this data in a journal.
- Create rewards for after studying instead of doing things before studying that will only turn into avoidance behaviors.
- Make a practice of relaxing - by using methods such as progressive relaxation, self-hypnosis, guided imagery, etc - in order to make relaxation an automatic sensation.
- Work on creating a state of relaxed concentration so that concentrating will take on the focus of the mind, so that none will be wasted on worrying.
- Take good care of the physical self by eating well and getting enough sleep.
- Plan in time for exercise and stick to this plan.

Beyond these techniques, there are other methods to be used before, during and after the test that will help the test-taker perform well in addition to overcoming anxiety.

Before the exam comes the academic preparation. This involves establishing a study schedule and beginning at least one week before the actual date of the test. By doing this, the anxiety of not having enough time to study for the test will be automatically eliminated. Moreover, this will make the studying a much more effective experience, ensuring that the learning will be an easier process. This relieves much undue pressure on the test-taker.

Summary sheets, note cards, and flash cards with the main concepts and examples of these main concepts should be prepared in advance of the actual studying time. A topic should never be eliminated from this process. By omitting a topic because it isn't expected to be on the test is only setting up the test-taker for anxiety should it actually appear on the exam. Utilize the course syllabus for laying out the topics that should be studied. Carefully go over the notes that were made in class, paying special attention to any of the issues that the professor took special care to emphasize while lecturing in class. In the textbooks, use the chapter review, or if possible, the chapter tests, to begin your review.

It may even be possible to ask the instructor what information will be covered on the exam, or what the format of the exam will be (for example, multiple choice, essay, free form, true-false). Additionally, see if it is possible to find out how many questions will be on the test. If a review sheet or sample test has been offered by the professor, make good use of it, above anything else, for the preparation for the test. Another great resource for getting to know the examination is reviewing tests from previous semesters. Use these tests to review, and aim to achieve a 100% score on each of the possible topics. With a few exceptions, the goal that you set for yourself is the highest one that you will reach.

Take all of the questions that were assigned as homework, and rework them to any other possible course material. The more problems reworked, the more skill and confidence will form as a result. When forming the solution to a problem, write out each of the steps. Don't simply do head work. By doing as many steps on paper as possible, much clarification and therefore confidence will be formed. Do this with as many homework problems as possible, before checking the answers. By checking the answer after each problem, a reinforcement will exist, that will not be on the exam. Study situations should be as exam-like as possible, to prime the test-taker's system for the experience. By waiting to check the answers at the end, a psychological advantage will be formed, to decrease the stress factor.

Another fantastic reason for not cramming is the avoidance of confusion in concepts, especially when it comes to mathematics. 8-10 hours of study will become one hundred percent more effective if it is spread out over a week or at least several days, instead of doing it all in one sitting. Recognize that the human brain requires time in order to assimilate new material, so frequent breaks and a span of study time over several days will be much more beneficial.

Additionally, don't study right up until the point of the exam. Studying should stop a minimum of one hour before the exam begins. This allows the brain to rest and put things in their proper order. This will also provide the time to become as relaxed as possible when going into the examination room. The test-taker will also have time to eat well and eat sensibly. Know that the brain needs food as much as the rest of the body. With enough food and enough sleep, as well as a relaxed attitude, the body and the mind are primed for success.

Avoid any anxious classmates who are talking about the exam. These students only spread anxiety, and are not worth sharing the anxious sentimentalities.

Before the test also involves creating a positive attitude, so mental preparation should also be a point of concentration. There are many keys to creating a positive attitude. Should fears become rushing in, make a visualization of taking the exam, doing well, and seeing an A written on the paper. Write out a list of affirmations that will bring a feeling of confidence, such as "I am doing well in my English class," "I studied well and know my material," "I enjoy this class." Even if the affirmations aren't believed at first, it sends a positive message to the subconscious which will result in an alteration of the overall belief system, which is the system that creates reality.

If a sensation of panic begins, work with the fear and imagine the very worst! Work through the entire scenario of not passing the test, failing the entire course, and dropping out of school, followed by not getting a job, and pushing a shopping cart through the dark alley where you'll live. This will place things into perspective! Then, practice deep breathing and create a visualization of the opposite situation - achieving an "A" on the exam, passing the entire course, receiving the degree at a graduation ceremony.

On the day of the test, there are many things to be done to ensure the best results, as well as the most calm outlook. The following stages are suggested in order to maximize test-taking potential:

- Begin the examination day with a moderate breakfast, and avoid any coffee or beverages with caffeine if the test taker is prone to jitters. Even people who are used to managing caffeine can feel jittery or light-headed when it is taken on a test day.
- Attempt to do something that is relaxing before the examination begins. As last minute cramming clouds the mastering of overall concepts, it is better to use this time to create a calming outlook.
- Be certain to arrive at the test location well in advance, in order to provide time to select a location that is away from doors, windows and other distractions, as well as giving enough time to relax before the test begins.
- Keep away from anxiety generating classmates who will upset the sensation of stability and relaxation that is being attempted before the exam.
- Should the waiting period before the exam begins cause anxiety, create a self-distraction by reading a light magazine or something else that is relaxing and simple.

During the exam itself, read the entire exam from beginning to end, and find out how much time should be allotted to each individual problem. Once writing the exam, should more time be taken for a problem, it should be abandoned, in order to begin another problem. If there is time at the end, the unfinished problem can always be returned to and completed.

Read the instructions very carefully - twice - so that unpleasant surprises won't follow during or after the exam has ended.

When writing the exam, pretend that the situation is actually simply the completion of homework within a library, or at home. This will assist in forming a relaxed atmosphere, and will allow the brain extra focus for the complex thinking function.

Begin the exam with all of the questions with which the most confidence is felt. This will build the confidence level regarding the entire exam and will begin a quality momentum. This will also create encouragement for trying the problems where uncertainty resides.

Going with the "gut instinct" is always the way to go when solving a problem. Second guessing should be avoided at all costs. Have confidence in the ability to do well.

For essay questions, create an outline in advance that will keep the mind organized and make certain that all of the points are remembered. For multiple choice, read every answer, even if the correct one has been spotted - a better one may exist.

Continue at a pace that is reasonable and not rushed, in order to be able to work carefully. Provide enough time to go over the answers at the end, to check for small errors that can be corrected.

Should a feeling of panic begin, breathe deeply, and think of the feeling of the body releasing sand through its pores. Visualize a calm, peaceful place, and include all of the sights, sounds and sensations of this image. Continue the deep breathing, and take a few minutes to continue this with closed eyes. When all is well again, return to the test.

If a "blanking" occurs for a certain question, skip it and move on to the next question. There will be time to return to the other question later. Get everything done that can be done, first, to guarantee all the grades that can be compiled, and to build all of the confidence possible. Then return to the weaker questions to build the marks from there.

Remember, one's own reality can be created, so as long as the belief is there, success will follow. And remember: anxiety can happen later, right now, there's an exam to be written!

After the examination is complete, whether there is a feeling for a good grade or a bad grade, don't dwell on the exam, and be certain to follow through on the reward that was promised...and enjoy it! Don't dwell on any mistakes that have been made, as there is nothing that can be done at this point anyway.

Additionally, don't begin to study for the next test right away. Do something relaxing for a while, and let the mind relax and prepare itself to begin absorbing information again.

From the results of the exam - both the grade and the entire experience, be certain to learn from what has gone on. Perfect studying habits and work some more on confidence in order to make the next examination experience even better than the last one.

Learn to avoid places where openings occurred for laziness, procrastination and day dreaming.

Use the time between this exam and the next one to better learn to relax, even learning to relax on cue, so that any anxiety can be controlled during the next exam. Learn how to relax the body. Slouch in your chair if that helps. Tighten and then relax all of the different muscle groups, one group at a time, beginning with the feet and then working all the way up to the neck and face. This will ultimately relax the muscles more than they were to begin with. Learn how to breathe deeply and comfortably, and focus on this breathing going in and out as a relaxing thought. With every exhale, repeat the word "relax."

As common as test anxiety is, it is very possible to overcome it. Make yourself one of the test-takers who overcome this frustrating hindrance.

Additional Bonus Material

Due to our efforts to try to keep this book to a manageable length, we've created a link that will give you access to all of your additional bonus material.

Please visit http://www.mometrix.com/bonus948/megaprokms to access the information.

Stafford Library
Columbia College
1001 Rogers Street
Columbia, MO 65216